SCHELLING'S TREATISE

ON THE ESSENCE

OF HUMAN FREEDOM

132
et
of
s
in-
itself

...t is the unity
1...ng it—
of
from

128 gathering of
The unruly to its
inner law

126 The un-unfolded
fullness of God's
nature

127 longing as
eternal—contin-
ual consumpt-
ion of itself

107 Definition-ground
& existence

109 ground &
causa sol

William Hamilton

587 / 265

124 Nature of the
ground in God is
longing

see 150
Hegel's
Hegel's
Absolute

115 ground &
existence

119 —

139 deepening of the
ground is the & expan-
sion of existence

Schelling's Treatise on the Essence of Human Freedom

Martin Heidegger

Translated by

Joan Stambaugh

OHIO UNIVERSITY PRESS

ATHENS

Library of Congress Cataloging in Publication Data

Heidegger, Martin, 1889–1976.
Schelling's treatise on the essence of human freedom.

(Series in continental thought ; 8)
Translation of: Schellings Abhandlung über das Wesen der menschlichen Freiheit.
Includes bibliographical references and index.
1. Schelling, Friedrich Wilhelm Joseph von, 1775–1854. Philosophische Untersuchungen über das Wesen der menschlichen Freiheit. 2 Liberty.
I. Title. II. Series
BJ1463.S356H4313   1985   123'.5   83-19472
ISBN 0-8214-0690-6
ISBN 0-8214-0691-4 (pbk.)

© Translation Copyright 1985 by Joan Stambaugh.
Schelling's Abhandlung Über das Wesen der menschlichen Freiheit © 1971 originally published by Max Niemeyer Verlag Tübingen.

99 98 97   7 6 5 4   (paperback edition)

Ohio University Press books are printed
on acid-free paper. ∞

TABLE OF CONTENTS

PREFACE

This study of Friedrich W. Schelling's treatise *On Human Freedom* should come as a welcome investigation of a philosophy less known to English readers than that of the other two major German Idealists, Johann Gottlieb Fichte and George Wilhelm Friedrich Hegel. Schelling's treatise is available in an excellent English translation, *Of Human Freedom* (Chicago: Open Court, 1936), by James Gutmann who also wrote the introduction. The reader can thus study the treatise as a whole and perhaps initiate a kind of dialogue between Martin Heidegger's interpretation and his own understanding of it. In general, the longer passages of Schelling quoted in this book are taken intact from Professor Gutmann's translation. There are some minor discrepancies in my translation of Heidegger's text and Professor Gutmann's terminology. Much of the terminology in the Heidegger text was chosen with an eye to Heidegger's own interpretation rather than Schelling's treatise proper.

This is perhaps the most "straightforward" study of Heidegger's yet to appear in English. At the same time it deals with questions at the borderline of our familiarity with German Idealism. Thus the basic problems at stake here lie at the very heart of the Idealist tradition: the question of the compatibility of the system and of individual human freedom, the question of pantheism and the justification of evil. Schelling is the first thinker in the rationalist-idealist tradition to grapple seriously with the problem of evil. He does not, as did, for instance, Descartes, Spinoza, and Leibniz, simply dismiss evil as contributing to the variety and perfection of the whole or as a simple lack or privation of being having no real existence in its own right. Rather, Schelling goes the way of seeking the origin of evil in the self-assertion of the creature.

These questions are the great questions of the philosophical tradition, inevitably familiar and important to philosophers. However, where these questions lead Schelling, and with him Heidegger, are possibilities which come very close to the boundaries of the Idealist tradition. To take one of the most important examples, Schelling's concept of the "groundless," what reason can no longer ground and explain, points back to Jacob Boehme and indirectly forward to the direction of Heidegger's own inquiry; it would surely not be congenial to a Fichte or a Hegel.

It is hoped that this hitherto unpublished dimension of Heidegger's thinking will prove to be stimulating and provocative to English readers. Schelling is one of the thinkers to whom Heidegger has the most affinity, and this study should be fruitful for an understanding of both.

Joan Stambaugh

EDITOR'S PREFACE

In its main part, this work contains the principle part of a lecture course given at the University of Freiburg in the summer semester of 1936. The manuscript was copied and abbreviated references were made into connected sentences. I am very grateful to Professor Heidegger for his helpful advice in collating this text.

Since this manuscript is based on the outline for a lecture course, it was sometimes necessary in the revision to replace helpful remarks with the insertion of clarifying words. In a few cases, repetitions or short side remarks were omitted when they seemed superfluous. On the whole, the style of speech has been preserved.

The Appendix contains excerpts from the manuscripts of an advanced seminar on Schelling held in the summer semester of 1941. Mr. Fritz Heidegger had already obtained a copy of these manuscripts. In addition, the Appendix contains an extract of seminar notes from 1941 to 1943.

I would like to thank Dr. Hartmut Buchner and Dr. Friedrich W. von Hermann for their painstaking help in reading the galleys. I would also like to thank Dr. Buchner for his references in the notes at the end of this book.

Hildegard Feick

Introductory Remarks of the Lecture Course, Summer Semester, 1936

1. SCHELLING'S WORK AND THE TASK OF THIS INTERPRETATION

Schelling discusses the essence of human freedom in a treatise bearing the title: *Philosophical Inquiries into the Nature of Human Freedom and Matters Connected Therewith*. This treatise appeared for the first time, together with other works by Schelling published earlier, in a volume entitled *F. W. Schelling's Philosophical Writings*, Vol. 1 (Landshut, Philip Krüll, University Bookstore, 1809).[1]

Eighteen hundred and nine: Napoleon ruled, that means here, he oppressed and abused Germany. Ever since 1806 the *Reich* did not even have a nominal existence. That year, sixteen German princes formed the *Rheinbund* under Napoleon's protection. On the first of August they announced their separation from the *Reich* on the *Reichstag* of Regensburg. On August sixth Franz II answered by laying down the German Kaiser crown. On October fourteenth Prussia suffered its worst fall in Jena and Auerstadt. Napoleon wrote to the sultan, "Prussia has disappeared." The king had fled to Memel in the last corner of German soil. Prussia was pushed back to the right bank of the Elbe by the Tilsit peace treaty. Kursachsen joined the *Rheinbund*. "French" was the official language up to the Elbe.

In 1808 Napoleon called a meeting of princes in Erfurt. There Goethe had a conversation with Napoleon. They talked about poetry, particularly about tragedy and the portrayal of fate. Napoleon said tragedies "belonged to a darker period. What do we want with fate now? Politics is fate." "Come to Paris, I demand it of you. There is a larger view of the world there."

Eighteen hundred and nine: Goethe became sixty years old. *Faust*, part one, had just appeared. Five years earlier, in 1804, Kant had died at the age of eighty. Four years before, 1805, Schiller was snatched away before his time. In 1809 Napoleon suffered his first serious defeat in the battle of Aspern. The Tirolean peasants revolted under the leadership of Andreas Hofer.

Meanwhile Prussia had begun to regain its "firm and certain spirit" (Fichte) in the north. Baron von Stein directed the new form of the administration.

1

Scharnhorst created the spirit and form of a new army. Fichte gave his addresses to the German nation at the Berlin academy. Through his sermons at the Trinity Church (*Dreifaltigkeitskirche*) Schleiermacher became the political teacher of Berlin society.

In 1809 Wilhelm von Humboldt became the Prussian minister of culture and worked on the founding of the University of Berlin for which the writings of Fichte and Schleiermacher prepared the way. That same year the royal court returned to Berlin from Königsberg. The following year Queen Luise died. Next year Heinrich von Kleist, the poet who was long driven by the dark plan of getting rid of Napoleon by force, shot himself at Wannsee—Napoleon, whom Goethe admired as a great "phenomenon of nature," whom Hegel called the "world soul" as he saw him ride through the city after the battle of Jena, and about whom the old Blücher said, "Let him do what he wants, he is a stupid fellow." Meanwhile, Hardenberg, the diplomat, became the Prussian chancellor of state. He kept the growing Prussian-German revolt from attacking prematurely.

All these new men, however—quite different from each other and idiosyncratic in their manner—were in agreement as to what they wanted. What they wanted is expressed in that word of exhortation that circulated among them: they called the new Prussian state the "state of intelligence," that is, of the Spirit. The soldier Scharnhorst demanded more and more insistently courage above all in the case of war, but in the case of peace—knowledge, more knowledge, and culture. Culture meant at that time essential knowledge which shaped all of the fundamental positions of historical existence, that knowledge which is the presupposition of every great will.

The profound untruth of those words that Napoleon had spoken to Goethe in Erfurt was soon to come to light: Politics is fate. No, Spirit is fate and fate is Spirit. The essence of Spirit, however, is freedom.

Schelling's treatise on freedom was published in 1809. It is his greatest accomplishment and at the same time was one of the most profound works of German, thus of Western, philosophy.

In 1807, two years before Schelling's treatise on freedom, Hegel's first and greatest work appeared: *The Phenomenology of Spirit*. The preface to this work contains a sharp denial of Schelling and led to a final break between the two who had been friends since their youth. The third in the band of young Swabian friends, Hölderlin, was taken at this same time by his gods into the protection of madness.

Thus the three who had shared the same room as fellow students in the Tübingen Stift were torn apart in their existence and consequently also in their work, but they were not simply dispersed. Each one, according to his own law, shaped the German spirit. The transformation of that spirit into a historical force has not yet come about. It can only come about when we have once again learned to admire and preserve creative work.

When Schelling published his treatise on freedom, he was thirty-four years old. He published his first philosophical work in his last year as a student (1794), *On the Possibility of a Form of Philosophy in General*. A philosophical theme could not possibly be any broader than this. From this work to the treatise on freedom a stormy development of his thinking takes place. Each year of this span of fifteen years brings one or more treatises and in between such decisive works as the *First Sketch of a System of a Philosophy of Nature* (1799) and the *System of Transcendental Idealism* (1800). The former brought Fichte's Idealism into a completely new realm and brought Idealism as a whole onto a new track. The latter became the precursor for Hegel's *Phenomenology of Spirit* and the precondition for Schelling's own later steps. In 1801 *Presentation of My System of Philosophy* appeared.

After the treatise on freedom, Schelling did not publish anything more, apart from a few speeches and the polemical piece against F. H. Jacobi. But this span of forty-five years until his death in 1854 means neither a resting on his previous achievements nor an extinction of the power of thought. If the shaping of his actual work was never completed, this was due to the manner of questioning which Schelling grew into after his treatise on freedom.

Only in this light can the period of silence be understood, or, rather, the other way around. The fact of this silence throws light upon the difficulty and novelty of questioning and on the thinker's clear knowledge of all this. What is usually brought forward to explain this period of Schelling's silence is only of secondary significance and is basically mere gossip. Schelling himself is a bit guilty here in that he was not insensitive enough to it. But the labor of thinking that was going on during this period of silence as an author can be more or less judged by the ninety lectures which we have from the *Nachlass* [posthumous works]: More or less, for between lectures and a finished self-contained work there is not only a difference of degree, but an essential difference. But, if one may say so, Schelling had to get stranded in his work because his manner of questioning didn't allow an inner center in the standpoint of philosophy at that time. The only essential thinker after Schelling, Nietzsche, broke down in the middle of his real work, *The Will to Power*, for the same reason. But this double, great breakdown of great thinkers is not a failure and nothing negative at all—on the contrary. It is the sign of the advent of something completely different, the heat lightning of a new beginning. Whoever really knew the reason for this breakdown and could conquer it intelligently would have to become the founder of the new beginning of Western philosophy.

During the time of his greatest productivity and his deepest solitude, Nietzsche once wrote the following verses in a dedication copy of his book *Dawn of Day* (1881):

>Whoever one day has much to proclaim
>Is silent about much

Whoever must one day kindle the lightning
Must be for a long time—cloud (1883).

Schelling's treatise on freedom is one of those very rare works in which such a cloud begins to form. It still hovers over us. We who come later have only this one thing as our next duty: to point out this cloud. That is to happen by our interpreting the treatise on freedom. The immediate intention of this interpretation is, however, threefold:

1. To comprehend the essence of human freedom and that means at the same time the question of freedom. Thus, the innermost center of philosophy is brought to knowledge—and we place ourselves knowingly *in* it.
2. From this center to bring Schelling's philosophy closer to us as a whole and in its fundamental traits.
3. In this way, we attain an understanding of the philosophy of German Idealism as a whole in terms of its moving forces: for Schelling is the truly creative and boldest thinker of this whole age of Geman philosophy. He is that to *such* an extent that he drives German Idealism from within right past its own fundamental position.

He did not, however, bring his questioning to that metaphysical place into which Hölderlin had to project himself poetically, thus remaining far more alone than anyone. The history of the solitude of these poets and thinkers can never be written; it is also not necessary to write it. It is sufficient if we always keep some of it in mind.

In the next lecture we will start with the interpretation of Schelling's treatise on freedom. The procedure of our interpretation is as follows: We shall follow the path of the treatise step-by-step and develop at certain junctions what is necessary to know historically and that means at the same time thematically. When we gain such an understanding of the treatise, it moves away from us and into the occurrence of the philosophy of German Idealism, revealing the innermost law of this history and thus what we ourselves must have penetrated in order to come out of it. In the history of man, essential things are never overcome by turning one's back and apparently freeing oneself in mere forgetfulness. For what is essential comes back again and again. The only question is whether an age is ready and strong enough for it.

2. SCHELLING'S DATES; EDITIONS OF HIS WORK, AND LITERATURE ON HIM

Two things should precede the interpretation of Schelling's treatise: (1) A short, mostly external, sketch of Schelling's life; (2) A reference to the most necessary and useful tools for our work.

Regarding 1: when a thinker's work, or pieces and traces of his work, are available, the "life" of a philosopher is unimportant for the public. We never get to know what is essential in a philosophical life through biographical descriptions anyhow. If we, nevertheless, make a few general references to Schelling's life, we do so with the intention of making it possible to order the course of his life more clearly in the history familiar to us.

Like many other great Germans, Schelling comes from a Protestant parsonage. He was born January 27, 1775, in the Swabian city of Leonberg—the birthplace of the great astronomer Johannes Kepler. Two years later in 1777, Schelling's father went as a preacher and professor to the theological preparatory school in Bebenhausen near Tübingen. When he was ten years old, the young Schelling went to Latin school in Nürtingen, the town where Hölderlin was spending his boyhood.

In only a year his father had to take the boy out of school again since according to the teacher he had nothing more to learn there. Thus, Schelling was taught together with the older seminar students in Bebenhausen until 1790 when he matriculated as a student at the University of Tübingen at the age of fifteen. The teacher in Bebenhausen recognized in him an *ingenium praecox,* a precocious creative talent. Even before his studies at the university, besides other philosophical school literature which he rejected, Schelling was reading Leibniz's *Monadology.* This work remained decisive for all of his future philosophical thinking. Schelling knew nothing about Kant (yet). But the same year that Schelling went to the University of Tübingen, 1790, was published what became a foundation for the younger generation and the formation of German Idealism, Kant's *Critique of Judgment.*

Schelling studied for five years in Tübingen, two years of philosophy and three years of theology. He took the same course of studies at the same time as did Hölderlin and Hegel both, who five years older than Schelling, left the University earlier. Kant's philosophy, the French Revolution, the Greeks and the argument about pantheism, which was occasioned by Jacobi's essay on Spinoza,[2] determined the spiritual world of Tübingen down to the daily customs.

As was already mentioned, Schelling's first philosophical writing was published in the last year of his studies. It was totally influenced by Fichte's doctrine of science which had just become known.

When in Easter, 1795, Hölderlin, who had heard Fichte in Jena while a house tutor there, visited Schelling in Tübingen, he could assure him that he (Schelling) "was just as far along as Fichte."

Schelling, too, became a house tutor, like his friends, in Leipzig where he eagerly pursued the study of the natural sciences at the same time.

In 1798, when he was twenty-three years old, Schelling was called to Jena as an extraordinary, unpaid professor of philosophy at Fichte's suggestion and under Goethe's influence. The names Weimar and Jena are sufficient to let us know in what a lively and stormy intellectual world Schelling was to develop. In 1801 Hegel, too, came from Frankfurt to Jena to habilitate himself there.

The time in Jena, 1798-1803, was the most fruitful in Schelling's life. He founded his system there, without rigidly remaining within that system. In Jena, for the first time he gave his lectures on the method of academic study which have become famous.[3] Professional and personal reasons led to his departure in 1803. After a short period of teaching in Würzburg, Schelling moved to Munich in 1806 where there was, as yet, no university. He became a member of the Academy of Sciences and the general secretary of the Academy of Arts.

Apart from an interruption by a stay in Erlangen from 1820 until 1827, Schelling remained in Munich until 1841. In 1826, the old Bavarian university, Ingolstadt of Landshut (there ever since 1800), was moved to Munich. The call of Schelling to the university was a matter of course despite many secret intrigues against it.

In 1831, Hegel died—Hegel who had developed a brilliant effectiveness in Berlin ever since 1818 and who ruled over philosophy in Germany. Soon the plan to call Schelling as his successor came to life. But only in 1841, after Friedrich Wilhelm IV took over the government, did this call actually come about. Schelling gave lectures in Berlin until 1846, but he was not able to develop the same brilliant effectiveness as Hegel. This was due not only to the manner of his philosophy at that time; but also to the spirit and the lack of spirit of the whole age. Schelling withdrew from all public activity and lived until his death in 1854 completely for the formation of his planned major work which never got beyond the form of a course of lectures.

When Schelling's name is mentioned, people like to point out that this thinker constantly changed his standpoint, and one often designates this as a lack in character. But the truth is that there was seldom a thinker who fought so passionately ever since his earliest periods for his one and unique standpoint. On the other hand, Hegel, the contemplative thinker, published his first great work when he was thirty-seven years old, and with its publication was immediately settled with regard to his philosophy and his standpoint. Everything that followed was simply a matter of working things out and of application. This, of course, all in a grand style and with a rich certainty.

But Schelling had to give up everything again and again, and again and again bring it back to a new ground. Schelling says once (IX, 217-18), (5, 11-12):*

"He who wishes to place himself in the beginning of a truly free philosophy must abandon even God. Here we say: who wishes to maintain it, he will lose it; and who gives it up, he will find it. Only he has come to the ground of himself and

---

*Quotations from the German text follow volume and page number of the collected works. Volume 7 of the first division of the collected works contains the treatise of freedom from pages 336-416.

has known the whole depth of life who has once abandoned everything and has himself been abandoned by everything. He for whom everything disappeared and who saw himself alone with the infinite: a great step which Plato compared to death."

Schelling took this step several times. For that reason, he usually lacked the peace and continuity of development and, thus, his work often lacked the success of final touches. But all of this has nothing in common with the fatal twisting of a change of point of view.

Through an interpretation of the study on freedom we want to experience what really supported, fulfilled, and snatched this long life again and again to new beginnings. One doesn't need to know anything else other than the picture of the old Schelling to suspect that in this thoughtful life not only a personal destiny was at stake, but also the historical spirit of the Germans as they themselves sought a gestalt.

Regarding 2: the useful tools of our work.

A. The works of Schelling were published soon after his death by his second oldest son, in fourteen volumes in two divisions, 1856-61. The first division encompasses ten volumes. Here, everything which has been published separately and the essays and treatises which had appeared in newspapers, academic speeches, and lecture courses were included, partially supplemented by unpublished writings. In the second division, 1856-58, the later doctrine of the philosopher as it was formed after 1805 was made accessible from the *Nachlass* in the form of lectures (the philosophy of mythology and of revelation).

Schelling's Works. Edited by Manfred Schröter, according to the original edition in the new order offers a *certain substitute* for this collected edition which has become so rare. Up until now, six main volumes have appeared since 1927. They also contain the page numbers of the old edition.[4]

Another useful addition is *Schelling's Works: A Selection in Three Volumes,* 1907, in the Meiner Philosophical Library. There are also separate, individual writings as is the case with our text.

Three volumes, *From Schelling's Life in Letters, 1869-1870,* edited by G. L. Plitt,[5] are indispensable as source material for Schelling's life history, but also for the development of his works.

In addition, Fichte's and Schelling's philosophical correspondence from the *Nachlass* of both thinkers, 1856.[6]

The collection *Letters of the Romantic Writers,* 1907, which was published by Gundolf, gives an immediate self-contained picture of the sources, above all during the time in Jena.

B. Only two of the writings *about* Schelling and his work are worthy of mention.

1. Still the best presentation, as a whole, is by Kuno Fisher, *Schelling's Life, Works, and Doctrine,* first edition, 1872, 1923 in the fourth edition as vol. VII of his *History of Modern Philosophy.* Kuno Fisher's work is excellent as it is modest and yet

draws on a rich knowledge of the whole age. The work on the sources of his life history in its broad description is masterful, even though it is antiquated in details. The treatment of Schelling's work takes place in the form of a simple report, often in useful statements of content which don't do anything philosophically but also don't spoil anything.

2. H. Knittermeyer gives a new shorter presentation under the title: "Schelling and the Romantic School," Munich, 1929, in the collection, *History of Philosophy in Individual Presentation*, Vol. 30-1. Knittermeyer's book is serious, carefully thought out, and freshly written, and brings as a supplement a reliable guide to all the writings on Schelling[7] and Romanticism. But the decisive philosophy of Schelling as it is developed in the treatise on freedom is not appropriately presented in this book. In addition, the author's orientation to today's dialectical theology narrows the scope of the book, especially where the true metaphysical and speculative questions are touched upon.

3. Windelband's *Primer of the History of Philosophy*, in the new edition of Heimsoeth, 1935, is the best source for the historical presentations of the whole age of German Idealism. In it is contained an "overview of the position of philosophical, historical investigation."

For a general penetrating analysis of intellectual history of the whole age, the investigations of W. Dilthey are eminently usable. These works are all mere preparations for a great and profoundly thought history of German spirit. If it is a question of an interpretation of German Idealism which is immediately useful for a creative dialogue, then Dilthey's work is of no help, no less than the general presentations of this time smaller in value and scope. But where it is a matter of making visible the complex way of the spirit, that of the individual as well as that of the people, everything becomes luminous and great even if the somewhat drifting manner of Dilthey's presentation no longer completely accords with our style. Among the collected works, one should especially mention vol. 2, *Weltanschauung (World View), An Analysis of Man Since the Renaissance and the Reformation. Treatises on the History of Philosophy and Religion;* vol. 3, *Studies on the History of German Spirit;* vol 4, *Hegel's Youth History and Other Treatises on the History of German Idealism;* and individually published: *"Experience and Poetry:* Lessing, Goethe, Novalis, Hölderlin."[8] One often forgets the work of the young Dilthey: *Schleiermacher's Life* (vol. I, 1870). Above all, the second and fourth volumes bring fundamental presentations of the intellectual position of Germany between 1795 and 1806. In the chaos of daily new publications and little *tractati*, we must not forget the enduring works of essential Germans about the great Germans. Also, what is most new in science is not always what is best, and it is the death of science when it loses its great tradition. The whole age is unthinkable without the spirit of Kant. Great and noble and even newly confirmed by the creative criticism of it, his work penetrates everything especially by the power of transformation which emanates from it.

3. SCHELLING'S QUESTION ABOUT FREEDOM AS HISTORICAL QUESTIONING OF BEING*

We shall now begin the interpretation of Schelling's treatise and take his own words as the motto of our interpretation of Schelling's treatise on freedom.

"If you want to honor a philosopher, you must catch him where he has not yet gone forth to the consequences, in his fundamental thought; (in the thought) from which he takes his point in departure" (Schelling's Collected Works WW, Section 2, III, 60).

And these other words: "It is a poor objection to a philosopher to say that he is incomprehensible" (X, 163) (5, 233).

Philosophical Inquiries into the nature of Human Freedom and Matters connected therewith.
First of all, we want to give a brief explanation of the title. What does this title indicate? Inquiries—not a presentation and communication of results and assertions or simply the characterization of a standpoint. We are forced to follow and to accompany the path of philosophical questioning. And it appears to be a matter of a single question, that of the nature of freedom, indeed, of *human* freedom. We are familiar with this question under the common expression: "The problem of freedom of the will." One proceeds as if the human will is free or unfree and figures how that could be proven in a way sufficiently convincing. Freedom is supposed to be a property of man. One believes that one already knows what or who man is. It is only still uncertain whether the property of freedom can be attributed to him and his faculty of will or whether it must be denied him.

Schelling's treatise has nothing to do with this question of the freedom of the will, which is ultimately wrongly put and thus not a question at all. For freedom is here, not the property of man, but the other way around: Man is at best the property of freedom. Freedom is the encompassing and penetrating nature, in which man becomes man only when he is anchored there. That means the nature of man is grounded in freedom. But freedom itself is a determination of true Being in general which transcends all human being. Insofar as man *is* as man, he must participate in this determination of Being, and man *is*, insofar as he brings about this participation in freedom. (*Key sentence:* Freedom not the property of man, but rather: man the property of freedom.)

If the inquiry deals with human freedom, this means that it deals with a particular kind of freedom as the nature of true Being in general. The nature of man is in question; that is, one is questioning beyond man to that which is more essential and powerful than he himself: freedom, not as an addition and attribute of the human will, but rather as the nature of true Being, as the nature of the ground for beings as a whole. In their very point of departure and in accordance with that point of departure, these inquiries are driven beyond man, beyond

Seyn—Schelling's spelling of *Sein* retained throughout—TRANS.

freedom to the question of the nature of Being in general. Indeed, they are immediately within the realm of this question about the nature of Being, a question which proves to be the broadest, deepest and, thus, most essential question of all. Schelling hinted at this broader and broadest connection only in a quite external fashion in the title with the supplement: "and matters connected therewith."

If we pay heed to the direction of the treatise, then it is understandable why we don't need to give more detailed reasons why this treatise was chosen. Because it asks about the whole of Being, we cannot find anything outside of it from where we could, in addition, particularly explain why the inquiry deals with freedom. For the sufficient reason for the question of Being as a whole lies in Being itself and there alone. But man cannot withdraw from Being as a whole. For he is what he is, only by standing in the middle of beings as a whole and perduring* this stand. Man cannot withdraw from beings as a whole. He can be mistaken about them, he can take this and that for all there is, he can take parts for the whole, but always only in such a way that he takes something particular for the whole and, thus, always somehow thinks in terms of the whole and in the direction of the whole. Here, the question remains completely open whether the conception of the whole is always just a relative conception or whether it gets at the whole absolutely.

We stated that no further explanation was necessary why we have chosen this treatise—unless in terms of the treatise itself. For it raises a question in which something is expressed which underlies all of man's individual intentions and explanations, the question of philosophy as such. Whoever grasps this question knows immediately that it is meaningless to ask why and to what purpose we philosophize. For philosophy is grounded only in terms of itself—or else not at all, just as art reveals its truth only through itself.

One can never prove that, and why, philosophy is necessary. Every such attempt at proof already misunderstands philosophy. But for the same reason, it is also impossible to show that philosophy is superfluous and that it is about time to get rid of it, or repress it at the outset. Whoever speaks this way proffers the most brilliant proof for the fact that he is in any case completely unable to speak and treat of that which he only puts down; he is completely ignorant of philosophy.

The fact that the necessity of philosophy cannot really be grounded and that philosophy itself can never be attacked is an advantage for its inner nature, but for its external position it is always a disadvantage. Its claim can never get rid of the suspicion of arbitrariness. Never, as long as we encounter philosophy as something which also exists among man's many activities, as long as we just take notice of philosophy and don't allow ourselves to be transformed by it and understand

Innehält—TRANS.

that philosophy is only to be brought about through freedom and that carrying it out is an act of highest freedom.

But if something like a gradual persuasion to philosophy is impossible and its procedure can never be directly explained and made comprehensible, we can still now demand an explanation why precisely Schelling's treatise and why precisely this treatise on human freedom is taken as a foundation. This, too, can only be explained in terms of the treatise itself and only if we succeed in a philosophical interpretation of it. But this success is questionable not only because it depends on the human strength and human rights of us all, but even more so because it depends on presuppositions which we must yet attempt to secure.

Thus far, a philosophy does not exist which would offer us the conditions for an adequate understanding of Schelling's treatise, an understanding which could bring about a creative transformation. Schelling's own philosophy doesn't bring that about either. For every philosophical work, if it is a philosophical work, drives philosophy beyond the standpoint taken in the work. The meaning of a philosophical work lies precisely in opening a new realm, setting new beginnings and impulses by means of which the work's own means and paths are shown to be overcome and insufficient.

The presuppositions and conditions of a work's origin are in principle not sufficient for its interpretation because the work itself posits new criteria of questioning. And since all explanation always refers only to what is already present and known, not only does what is creative and truly historical remain closed to the historical explanation, what is far more fatal, the sole dominance of historical explanation makes it seem as if what is creative is precisely not there, but only a romantic fantasy. But, if one yet wants to save what is inexplicable in history from being dissolved into what can be explained, one usually flees to edifying and enthusiastic speeches instead of going back to the conditions of true knowing. Explanations in terms of what follows and is effected are also not sufficient, especially since having effects is a problem in its own right. They mostly bring about something haphazard and external which is already known (in its way of effecting).

We shall only really enter and truly gauge the realm of Schelling's treatise on freedom if we grasp what takes it beyond itself. Whether we fulfill this condition is tantamount to the question whether we philosophize or only talk about philosophy. We philosophize only when the position of our human being becomes the real need of the question about Being as a whole. Since, however, our human being is historical, it remains so in philosophizing, too. That means the more originally we begin our philosophical question, the more inwardly we grow in the binding force of our history. The more genuine this inwardness, the more clearly our simple relations appear in which we stand in a historicophilosophical way and which we are to master; that is, to shape from the very ground.

Such a simple, essential relation consists for us with regard to what Schelling's treatise has made a question. At first, this is only an assertion and only the expression of a personal conviction. Whether it is more and something else can only be shown by an interpretation of the treatise.

4. SCHELLING AND HEGEL

But in addition to the lack of objective presupposition for an undertaking of the question, there is another reason which has hindered a philosophical assimilation of this work of Schelling's up to now. That is the predominance of Hegelian philosophy. It existed then as a historical fact and later determined the historical portrayal and judgment of both philosophies.

It was already mentioned that there is a break with Schelling in the preface to Hegel's *Phenomenology of Spirit* (1807). This break concerns the concept of the Absolute as the identity and indifference of all opposites which Schelling had made the fundamental principle of philosophy. With regard to this, Hegel says to consider any existence as it is in the *Absolute* consists in nothing else than saying about it that while it is now doubtless spoken of as something specific, yet in the Absolute, in the abstract identity of A = A, there is no such thing at all, for everything is all one there. To pit this single knowledge, that "in the Absolute all is one," against determinate and complete knowledge, or knowledge which aims at and demands completion—or to give out its *Absolute* as the night in which, as one says, all cows are black—that is the naiveté of vacuous knowledge.* Hegel's break is all the more remarkable in that his basic position as it appears in the *Phenomenology* had developed because of close work together with Schelling in the beginning. This position was also publicly evident in their common editorship of the *Critical Journal of Philosophy* at that time (1802-03). Schelling and Hegel had founded this journal in order "to set stop and measure for the unphilosophical horde." In his treatise "The Difference between the Fichtean and Schellingian Systems of Philosophy" (1801), Hegel himself explicitly acknowledged Schelling's new step beyond Fichte. But in the course of their work together, whose reciprocal effect was fruitful for both, their paths separated. Their personal relationship did not yet separate, although their correspondence began to dwindle after Schelling's departure for Jena. At the beginning of the year of publication of the *Phenomenology,* January 11, 1807, Schelling wrote to Hegel: "I am full of eager expectation for your work which is finally coming out. What must come about when *your* maturity still takes time to let its fruits ripen! I wish you further the quiet and leisure to carry out such sterling and, so to speak, timeless works." The letter concludes: "Farewell, and let us not allow the connection between us to be

*G.W.F. Hegel, *Phenomenology of Spirit*. Baillie translation with minor changes—TRANS.

interrupted so long again. Be assured of the most inviolable and close friendship from your Schelling" (Schelling's Life II, 112 ff.).

On the second of November that year, Schelling wrote his last letter to Hegel to confirm that he had received the *Phenomenology of Spirit* which Hegel had sent him with a letter on May first. Hegel especially noted here that his allusion to Schelling had mostly to do with the "mischief" that was made of his (Schelling's) philosophy, and the parrots. Schelling, however, mentions in his answer that he acknowledged this assurance—but could not find that this differentiation was emphasized expressly and fittingly in the preface.

From then on, Schelling harbored a grudge against Hegel, mainly because Hegel's critique didn't fit and Schelling had already been laying a new foundation of his system for several years. Schelling's discontent with Hegel grew deeper and deeper with the years and often erupted in violent outbursts. Only much later when Schelling himself took Hegel's place in Berlin did his judgment become quiet and objective. Hegel, on the contrary, always acknowledged the great accomplishments of his former friend who was younger and had become famous before him. This was not difficult for him, either, for he knew that he was in possession of the absolute system of absolute knowledge and could easily allow those views validity which he thought were subordinate from this standpoint of all standpoints. In his Berlin lectures on the history of philosophy which Hegel was accustomed to trace up to his own time, he treated Schelling's philosophy as the "last interesting true gestalt of philosophy." And he says of the treatise on freedom, "Schelling has made known a single treatise on Freedom. It is of a deep speculative nature, but it stands alone. In philosophy a single piece cannot be developed" (Hegel, *Works*, Freundesausgabe XV, p. 682).

These words of Hegel show his wonderful objectivity, but also the limitation of his judgment. Hegel didn't see that just this single thing, freedom, was not single for Schelling, but was thought and developed as the essential foundation of the whole, as a new foundation for a whole philosophy. This limited understanding of Schelling is evident, but even more so is the fact that the greatest thinkers never understand each other at bottom, just because they want *the same thing* in the form of their unique greatness. If they wanted different things, then an agreement, that is, here letting each other be, would not be so difficult.

Even today, the judgment of Schelling still stands under Hegel's shadow. Schelling himself suffered a great deal under this in his later life. If our interpretation of the treatise gives a different picture of Schelling's philosophy, then this change of the historical judgment of Schelling is only a side intention. What is decisive is the development of the question itself posed in the treatise. It is a matter of awakening its hidden, but disturbing, force and showing the paths leading ahead. After these somewhat external remarks, let us get to the words of the treatise itself.

A. Interpretation of the First Discussions in Schelling's Treatise.

INTRODUCTION TO THE INTRODUCTION (pages 7- 9)*

1. FREEDOM IN THE SCIENTIFIC WORLD VIEW AS A WHOLE

We shall leave the "preliminary remarks" aside for now and begin right away with the treatise proper.

The treatise is composed as a continuous text without the divisions being expressly made recognizable and easily apparent by headings or numbering of sections. Yet the treatise has a very rigorous and clear inner structure which will become more and more apparent in our interpretation.

The introduction covers pages 7 to 32.[9] It has the task of correcting essential concepts from the realm of philosphy which according to Schelling have always been confused, but especially now, and thus, to prepare the discussion of the leading question.

"Philosophical investigations into the nature of human freedom may, in part, concern themselves with the correct conception of the term, for though the feeling of freedom is ingrained in every individual, the fact itself is by no means so near to the surface that merely to express it in words would not require more than common clarity and depth of perception. In part, such investigations may be concerned with the relation of this concept to a whole scientific world view."

With these introductory sentences, Schelling sets himself two tasks for the treatise on the nature of human freedom: (1) the definition of the *concept* of freedom; (2) the placement of this concept in the closed context of the "whole scientific world view."

Regarding (1): to what extent is the definition of the concept of freedom a task at all? Isn't precisely the answer to this question of what freedom and being free mean clear to everybody without further ado? Must it not be clear in advance

---

*For English readers page references, if not in roman numerals of the German edition, refer to *Schelling: Of Human Freedom*, translated by James Gutmann (Chicago: Open Court, 1936).

since freedom, just as a "fact," is always directly accessible to everybody by himself? Schelling points out that the "feeling" of this fact is directly given to everyone. The feeling of the fact of freedom means the direct experience *that* we are *free*. But Schelling also makes us consider that this fact does not lie on the surface to *that* extent so that we could find the appropriate words for it instantly, words which could tell us what this being free really is. What we encounter in ourselves intuitively as the impression of our being free is not sufficient to serve as the foundation for a determination of the concept. Finally, important decisions about the question of freedom are already being made here at the beginning of the first attempt, according to the way we hold onto the feeling of the fact of being free in ourselves and transform it into knowledge. With regard to later issues, we now want to differentiate: (a) the fact of human freedom and the factuality of this fact; (b) the feeling of this fact and the truth of a feeling in general; (c) the interpretation of what is felt in this feeling and the kind of concept of the comprehensive concept here.

That we have a nose, that our heart beats, that we perceive things, that we speak and hear—all of these are facts which we find in and around ourselves. That we are free, is this also this kind of fact or another kind? What do we mean by fact here?

That today is April 21 is also a fact. That there are dogs and cats is a fact, too. In what, then does the factuality of a fact consist? Can the fact of freedom be shown like, for instance, the finding of a stomach ulcer on the X-ray?

The feeling of a fact. Is feeling an adequate source of experience at all or isn't feeling often just a plain feeling, an indeterminate guessing and deceptive supposition? We do speak also of a sure feeling which we rely upon as something ultimate.

In any case, Schelling explicitly emphasizes that an uncommon clarity and depth of perception are needed in order to feel appropriately the fact of freedom and put it in words.

With which sense do we grasp the fact of freedom if we neither see, hear, touch, smell, or taste it? Is it the sense of an attitude, and what kind of attitude? Wherein does the purity and depth of this sense consist by means of which we perceive the fact of freedom in feeling? Is the sure feeling of freedom founded on the proper attitude or the other way around? Or are attitude and feeling also not the last or the first thing which gives truth, and that means disclosure about freedom? One question replaces another, and we are only at the stage of preliminarily gaining an adequate concept of freedom. The usual discussions about freedom of the will and the attempts to prove its existence or nonexistence all fail in the fundamental error of taking the aforementioned preliminary questions too lightly or else not asking them at all. If they were seriously asked, the illusory question about freedom of the will which continually plays havoc in doctrines of morality and law would have long since disappeared, and it would become evident that the real question about freedom is something quite different from what is talked about in the "problem of freedom of the will."

Regarding (2): the second task of the treatise on human freedom includes the incorporation of the concept in the whole of "a scientific world view." This task seems to need no further explanation, for freedom is an *individual* fact. Even when its nature is defined generally, still this general nature of freedom points to other essential determinations in other connections: for example, freedom is a characteristic of man as personality, as spirit; but at the same time, man is body and nature; the determination of freedom must be contrasted with nature; that is, it must be related to nature. Probably there are still other such relations. Thus, it is clear that the determination of this concept must be supplemented by incorporating the concept within a whole. Schelling speaks of the "whole scientific world view." We should check whether we correctly understand Schelling's expression right away. We must avoid giving later and contemporary meanings to this expression "scientific world view."

Today we understand by "scientific world view" that interpretation of the connection of things in nature and history which is founded on the results of scientific research. Schelling's expression does not have this meaning, for both the term "world view" and also the designation "scientific" are intended in a different, more primordial sense.

In the age of German Idealism, science (*Wissenschaft*)* means primarily and truly the same as philosophy, that knowledge which knows the last and first grounds, and in accordance with this fundamental knowledge presents what is essential in everything knowable in a reasoned-out essential connection. In this sense Fichte uses the term "Doctrine of Science" (the science of science—the philosophy of philosophy) for his major work. Hegel speaks of the "System of Science" (First part; *The Phenomenology of Spirit*), of the *Science of Logic*. What is otherwise and today alone called "the sciences" is only science insofar as it is philosophy, that is, as it is grounded in what is real and essential and ordered according to its standards. The less true essential knowledge an era of cognition and an active field of cognition contains, that is, the less philosophy, the more unscientific this knowledge is, so that it can be called "science" only in an approximate sense. If, according to the altered and narrowed concept of science, we must say today that philosophy is *not* science, that does *not* mean that it is abandoned to chance ideas and opinions, but only that philosophy as what is more primordial cannot be determined by the standards of what is derivative. This necessary connection between science in the fundamental sense (philosophy) and science in today's derived sense was, however, not pointed out first by

---

Wissenschaft—As Heidegger explains in the ensuing text, this is German Idealism's term for philosophy—TRANS.

German Idealism, it only went through a special formation there. Essentially, it is as old as the existence of Western knowledge and Western science. True, the sciences in today's narrower sense of the word are never made *by* philosophy and through philosophy, but neither are they explicable *without* philosophy; that is, can they be projected and truly ensured and brought to an ordered course. Of course, philosophy is not just decoration in order to give a profound outward appearance to everything through the industrious use of philosophical terminology. Philosophy is only essential for science as its innermost silent force. Only an obvious fool could think that the sciences can be renewed by getting rid of and outlawing philosophy at the same time. Such a beginning is just as nonsensical as trying to teach swimming by continuously teaching fear of water.

In Schelling's expression "scientific world view," "science" thus means "philosophical" and this means absolute knowledge of beings as a whole founding itself upon last principles and essential insights. The term "world view" means the same as "world perspective" and was often used as such at that time. A clear and founded use of these words depends first of all on whether an adequate concept of world can be created and set up as a standard. But the question about the concept of world has hardly even been understood up to now, let alone really asked. (Compare *Being and Time*, and concerning the history of the concept of world some references in *Vom Wesen des Grundes*, section II. Compare also *Critique of Pure Reason*, A698, B726: "This Idea" (of a highest ground distinct from the world) "is thus quite founded *respective to the world usage* of our reason" (On "rational world consideration").

The coinage of this term "world view" (*Weltanschauung*) comes from Kant, and he uses it in the *Critique of Judgment*. The term has there a still narrower and more definite meaning: it means the immediate experience of what is given to the senses, of appearances. "*The world* is the totality of sense objects (*universum, universitas rerum*). These objects are things in contrast to persons" (Kant Works, Academie Ausgabe XXI, 70). Man is the *Cosmotheoros* (world onlooker) who himself creates the element of world cognition a priori from which as a world inhabitant he fashions world contemplation at the same time in the Idea (ibid; 31). But behind this use of the word "world," lurks an ambiguity which becomes apparent in the question of how many worlds there can be. There can only be One World, if world equals the totality of things. But there is a plurality of worlds if world is always a perspective of totality (ibid, 30).

It is the direction of this second meaning of the concept of world, which we can grasp as the opening of totality, always in a definite direction and thus limited, that Schelling's use of the concepts "world" and "world view" takes. This concept, too, is prefigured in Kant, and especially in Leibniz. In accordance with the new position of his thinking, Schelling then uses the word "world" decisively in his writings on the philosophy of nature at the end of the nineties. In the use of the term "world view" that Leibnizian thought is at work according to which every monad, every self-contained being, plant, animal, man, the whole of the universe, that is, world in the first sense, always views from a definite point of view and thus with limits, world in the second sense, *mundus concentratus*. In this sense Schelling says:

"Just as human reason represents the world only according to a certain type whose visible expression is human organization, so every organization [living being in Schelling's words] is the imprint of a certain schematism of the world view. Just as we realize that our world view is determined by our original limitation without being able to explain why we are limited, *in just this way*, why our world view is precisely this one and no other, thus life, too, and the representing of animals can only be a special, although incomprehensible manner of original limitation and only this *manner* of limitation would differentiate them from us" (Works I, III, p. 182).

A world view is in itself always a definitely directed and comprehended opening and holding open of the world. A world view is in itself always "perspectival," as such looking through in a directed path and thus holding a field of vision open. The world view always develops its schematism. Animal and plant, too, have their world view, better expressed, are a world view, a way in which world opens itself, although only mutedly and darkly. A world view belongs to the constitution of every being to the extent that it is thought monadically.

"World view" is here a metaphysical determining element of every existing being itself in accordance with which it—in various stages of clarity and consciousness of the drive toward itself—relates to beings as a whole, and behaves and acts in terms of this fundamental relation. Hegel moves in this direction of the word's meaning in a caption in the *Phenomenology of Spirit* (II,453) of the "moral world view." In his lectures on aesthetics he says that "ways of viewing the world" constitute "the religion, the substantial spirit of peoples and times" (X 2, 229).

The name "world perspective" means the same thing. "Scientific world perspective" thus means in our text that project of beings as a whole which is determined in its decisive unity and articulation by true knowledge in the sense of philosophy. Science as such doesn't first need a world view, but *is* in itself a world view if it is science. Science is a schematism of world view if we mean "world view" in this sharply defined sense metaphysically.

The term "world view" was incorporated in everyday language very rapidly in the course of the nineteenth century and thus surrendered its original metaphysical definiteness. Now the term just means the way of looking at the world that is possible and convincing to men and groups of men and classes ("ideology," superstructure as opposed to "stuff" and "life"). At the same time it became the main popular philosophical catchword of liberalism. Karl Jaspers characterized well the now customary usage of the term in his *Psychology of World Views* as follows:

" . . . when we speak of world views, we mean the forces or ideas, in any case what is ultimate and total in man, both subjectively as experience, force and attitude as well as objectively as an objectively shaped world." We can say briefly that world view always means in addition and especially life view. And "view" does not mean here mere reflection and opinion, but rather the forces and directions of action and behavior. However, all of what is thus meant is itself without foundation, has no place any more, but occurs because men form their opinions on the whole, grow up in them and grow into them. World view is only the object of "psychology," of *typology*. Just as there are different kinds of plants and animals according to soil and climate, there are different kinds of world views. Here the "world view" of the "pig breeder" is made to be the decisive "type" of world view in general. Even in its decadent form, the word and the concept of world view still betrays its origin from the quite definite metaphysics of Leibniz (Kant) and Schelling. It is *German* metaphysics, and thus the word and concept of world view are always difficult to comprehend beyond the borders of their origin.

The change in meaning of the term is a very clear mirror in which the decline of all founded and certain metaphysical thinking in the nineteenth century is outlined.

These references were necessary to prevent our understanding Schelling's expression "scientific world view" in the pale and foundationless sense of the later nineteenth century. Rather, for what follows we must consider that under this term a decisive *task* of the philosophy of German Idealism is hidden, a task which is best announced by the key word of that philosophy: *the system*.

The philosophical treatise on the nature of human freedom must (1) delineate this nature in an adequate concept and (2) establish the place of this concept in the system as a whole; that is, show how freedom and man's being free go together with beings as a whole and fit into them.

Thus here, as indeed everywhere, these two sides of the investigation coincide, "since any conception cannot be defined in isolation, and depends for its systematic completion on the demonstration of its connections with the whole. This is especially the case in the conception of freedom, for if it has any reality at all, it cannot be a merely subordinate or incidental conception, but must be one of the dominant central points of the system" (p. 7).

Three things are to be noted.

What is being said here? (1): the determination of a concept always and of necessity extends to a further context. To determine a concept by itself is *eo ipso* impossible because the determination relies upon something determinative which is itself again a concept. But this dependence of every conceptual determination upon a further conceptual context is not a sign of its imperfection and limitation, but through going back to a further conceptual context the concept first receives the last scientific, that is, absolutely founded determinateness.

This contains (2): the treatise's tasks of delineating the concept and of fitting it into the scientific world view, previously separated for the time being, are really one. From this, however, essential consequences follow if we now think back to what was said earlier. The concept is attained with an eye to what is to be grasped, the fact that is given in feeling. The concept itself is predetermined by the complete conceptual context which comprehends beings as a whole and thus also every individual fact, the fact of freedom, too. The first experience of the fact of freedom in feeling, too, is already led by conceptual representations, preconceptions or prehensions. There are no pure facts. Immediate feeling already moves within an interpretation. On the other hand, a conceptual context cannot be thought up and invented by itself out of the void, but the project as a whole must be supported and bound by original experiences of the first facts. For this purpose we must decide and sufficiently prove what the *first* facts are with regard to beings as a whole.

How we feel and experience the fact of freedom already depends upon the leading, tacit preconception in whose light the fact is to illuminate itself. And the manner in which the preconception develops depends upon the direction and the profundity of feeling in which the fact meets us. Being philosophical, the philosophical investigation of human freedom can neither take its position with fact and feeling nor with the conceptual context and its foundation nor with an external coupling of both. From the beginning the investigation's position must be such that in it the feeling of the fact and the conceptual project are viable with equal originality and of necessity. Such a position is not self-evident. A special education is necessary in order to take it and inhabit it. Common sense and everyday opinion have the peculiarity of always leaning to the one side, to the side of the fact or to that of the concept. The doer does deeds, and the scholar teaches knowledge. Rolls are to be found at the baker's and sausages at the butcher's. But where it is a matter of first and last things, one cannot think and proceed so simply. This is especially true of the fact and the concept of freedom.

We come now to (3), the third point to be noted which Schelling expresses in the intervening sentence: "This is especially the case in the conception of freedom, for if it has any reality at all it cannot be a merely subordinate or incidental conception but must be one of the dominant central points of the system." It is necessary to determine each concept in terms of the whole. The concept of freedom is not just one concept among others, but the center of Being as a whole. Thus the determination of *this* concept belongs explicitly and expressly to the determination of the whole itself (compare Hegel's judgment, above p.13).

The concept of freedom is not only one concept among others which somehow has its place in the system, too. Rather, if it has any reality at all, it is the dominant central point of the system.

"If it has any reality at all"—What does that mean: a concept has reality? This manner of speaking goes back to Kant. *Realitas* is that which constitutes the *res*, the thing in what it is, the thingness of a thing, its nature. "A concept has reality" means: what is represented and intended in the concept is not just thought up, but is grounded in the nature of the thing itself, it constitutes the latter. What is thought in the concept is the law of what is real itself. The concept of freedom has reality when being free as a manner of Being belongs together with the nature and essential ground of Being. If this is correct, the concept of freedom is no longer an arbitrary one.

Thus the question of freedom becomes essentially fundamental. If freedom is a fundamental determination of Being in general, the project of the scientific world view as a whole in which freedom is to be comprehended has as its true goal and center ultimately nothing else than precisely freedom itself. The system to be constructed does not also contain the concept of freedom among many others, but freedom is rather the central point of the system. The system itself is "the system of freedom." The essential delineation of the fact of freedom founds the system of philosophy on its real ground. And fitting freedom into the system is nothing else than demonstrating the fundamental fact and illuminating its factuality.

The system itself is the system of freedom. Schelling's efforts from 1809 until his death, the silent work of these forty-five years, was dedicated to the foundation, the building of the system of freedom in a formed work.

"A system of freedom—but with just as great lines, with the same simplicity, as a perfect counterpart to Spinoza's system—this would really be the highest achievement" (Munich lectures 1827, X, 36), (5, 106).

We already stated that this work got stranded. It got stranded because of essential inner difficulties which Schelling himself saw so clearly as such that he speaks of the fundamental difficulty right at the beginning of the decisive treatise, our treatise on freedom, and removes the danger of a hasty and easy self-deception from the very beginning. The next sentence names this difficulty of a system of freedom and it thus names the *special object* of the introductory thoughts.

"To be sure, according to an ancient but by no means forgotten tradition, the idea of freedom is said to be entirely inconsistent with the idea of system, and every philosophy which makes claim to unity and completeness is said to end in denying freedom."

The concept of freedom is generally incompatible with the system. Accordingly, when a philosophy is constructed which is philosophy, that is, which lays claim to a grounded unity and totality of essential knowledge and in the development of this knowledge holds fast to such a claim, it must deny freedom. For freedom is a kind of cause and ground for other things. This cause comes purely from itself and cannot in accordance with its meaning and nature be reduced to something else and grounded in it. Freedom excludes the recourse to grounding. The system, however, demands the thoroughgoing connection of grounding. A "system of freedom"—that is like a square circle, in itself it is completely incompatible. In focusing his innermost philosophical effort on this difficulty, Schelling knows how greatly his position goes against, and evidently must go

[margin handwritten note: freedom & System]

against, older views and also views arising again at his time because the question of the "system of freedom" seems impossible from the outset.

The innermost difficulty of the whole intention of the treatise on freedom is discussed in the introduction, thus making the question itself more transparent. That means essential concepts and relations which are discussed in the treatise proper receive their first anticipatory clarification in the introduction.

The introduction itself begins with a *general discussion* of the self-contradictory idea of a "system of freedom" (pp. 7-9). The development of the difficulty related to a special form of the question and its historical instances extends from page 9 to 23.

2. WHAT IS A SYSTEM AND HOW DOES PHILOSOPHY COME TO BUILD SYSTEMS?

Before following this introductory reflection on the impossibility or possibility of a system of freedom, a preliminary reflection is necessary. For the question whether the concept of freedom is compatible with the system or not obviously only has weight and the trenchancy of an essential uneasiness if on the one hand the system itself is a necessity and an absolute requirement for us, and if on the other hand freedom and its actualization are the deepest need and utmost measure of existence. But if neither of these is the case, every possibility of a real tension between system and freedom disappears. The question how such a conflict—not at all experienced and not at all oppressing us—like that between system and freedom can and should be dissolved then becomes the most indifferent matter in the world, not suited to be treated here.

And in fact: system is not a necessity for us today nor is freedom a need. "Today," that does not mean this very day, nor this year nor even this decade, but rather the whole transitional age from the nineteenth to the twentieth century and at the same time this transition in its whole European expansion. In spite of its vast multiplicity of forms, in spite of its opaque and variegated permeation with the past, this today has a very definite stamp of its own and that means a direction and a manner of its historical domination over existence.

All of this is at first easier to understand with regard to that which this today no longer has.

Nietzsche recognized the condition of this today as the "rise of nihilism." For Nietzsche, nihilism means that the highest values lose their value, that the answers to the why and wherefore lose their binding and shaping force. "Ever since Copernicus, man is rolling out of the center into X," into the indefinite (The Will to Power, nr. 1). What one does and where one belongs, what one values, one goes along with all of this in a self-stupefying routine. There is culture and cultural tendencies, there is the church and society. Some individuals might cling to them in personal honesty and remain satisfied, but from all of this as a totality nothing any longer arises, no criteria and creative impulses any longer come from it, everything just continues to be carried on. Inner devastation and lostness increase beyond measure. What belongs underneath rises to the top. What is merely smart invention claims to be creative work. Lack of reflection is taken for power of action, and science gives the appearance of being essential cognition.

(But this interpretation of existence in terms of values shows Nietzsche's inmost imprisonment in the nineteenth century, that tie which every thinker, poet, and doer must take over in some form. But since it is a necessary limitation, it is not a lack from which an essential objection could be immediately derived.)

How Nietzsche founds and develops this great cognition and what kind of countermovement he introduces is not to be set forth here. It is sufficient if we consider that it is not a matter of the mere thoughts of an out-of-the-way brooder, but of the arousal and shaping of a state of knowledge which itself is already forming history, not just accompanying events like an ineffectual mirror. It belongs to the inmost essence of nihilism that it can be overcome only when more and more deeply known, thus never through deciding one day to close one's eyes to it. Therefore, reflection and ever more keen reflection! Knowledge, ever more unswerving knowledge. A knowledge which is not good and bearable for everyone, but is inevitable for those who have essential things to do in all areas of human activity.

The fact that the question of how freedom is related to system, whether a system of freedom is possible or not, the fact that the question of system doesn't appeal to us today at all is not a matter of chance, but is a necessary consequence of dominant nihilism, a consequence of the fact that thinking and the will to comprehend in general appear to us as a hopeless effort in the face of transpiring reality. The express renunciation of the system then supposedly means, however, taking the situation and valuation of knowledge, as it is today, seriously. Taking the situation seriously is only the first step toward the reflection and the honesty of a thinking which rejects all veiling and counterfeiting. But then our indifference to system and complete insensitivity to the question of the system of knowledge, then all of this is for the best and a sign that we are no longer pretending—a first, although only a negative, step toward honesty and thus toward overcoming nihilism. With this indifference to system we would then approach Nietzsche's real will which makes nihilism evident for the sole purpose of overcoming it and beginning to introduce this overcoming.

What does Nietzsche say about system? In one of his last writings, *Twilight of the Idols*, written in the fall of 1888 in Sils-Maria, the first section bears the title "Sayings and Arrows." Number 26 reads: "I distrust all system-makers and avoid them. The will to a system is a lack of uprightness" (VIII, 64). And from a somewhat earlier period, the years of the first version of *The Will to Power* (1884) comes the following remark: "The will to a *system*: for a philosopher morally speaking a finer decadence, a sickness of character;—unmorally speaking his will to appear more stupid than he is—more stupid, that means: stronger, simpler, more imperious, less cultured, more commanding, more tyrannical . . ." (XIV, 353). Nietzsche says of himself that he is not limited enough for a system (XIV, 354, all quotes from the *Grossoktavausgabe*).

With this, the renunciation of system appears to be elevated to a principle. And we can right away spare ourselves the question about the system of freedom and about system in general as being a plenty antiquated and in any case merely suspicious question—and thus spare ourselves having to do with the whole treatise. *If* namely Nietzsche were an infallible and thus well-established authority for us. He is that no more than any other of the great thinkers. Besides and above all Nietzsche's words, which we quoted and which everyone especially likes to quote today, "about," that means here "against" system in philosophy, do not exhaust what he has to say about it, they don't even get at what is decisive.

It could be that a renunciation of system is necessary now, but not because system is in itself something impossible and empty, but on the contrary because it is the highest and essential thing. And this is indeed Nietzsche's innermost conviction. The will to a system is, however, a lack of uprightness, namely, when this will rages *without* and *before* the overcoming of nihilism, because it then only furthers nihilism, an anesthetization within the general spiritual devastation.

Nietzsche's attitude toward system is fundamentally different from that of Kierkegaard who is usually mentioned here together with Nietzsche. Kierkegaard does completely reject the system, but (1) by "system" he means only the Hegelian system and misunderstands it at that; (2) Kierkegaard's rejection of system is *not* a *philosophical* one, with philosophical intention, but a religious one. What Kierkegaard brings against "the system" from the standpoint of a Christian believer is ingenious—for example, when he says "the philosopher of the system is as a man like someone who builds a castle, but *lives* next door in a shed." That is ingenious, but unimportant philosophically because "the system," especially in Hegel's supposed version of it, is dogmatically taken as something self-explanatory in philosophy.

All of this is said by the way in order to show by implication that the combination of Kierkegaard and Nietzsche, which has now become customary, is justified in many ways, but is fundamentally untrue philosophically and is misleading. Kierkegaard's *indirect* significance for philosophy lies in a quite different direction.

In the fall of 1841, Kierkegaard came to Berlin to hear Schelling on the "System of Freedom." He stayed four and a half months there and came back to Copenhagen disappointed.

A legitimate philosophical renunciation of system can only originate from an essential insight into it and from an essential evaluation of system. But then a legitimate renunciation is fundamentally different from mere indifference to system, different from mere helplessness with regard to the question of system.

Of course we find such indifference and helplessness with regard to the idea of a system directly and easily today in ourselves. But if what "we" believe and what *one* thinks can be even less unconditional and unexamined an authority than the words of great thinkers, we may not falsify our helplessness in the question of system without further ado to imply an actual lack of value in the question of a system.

The fact that the question about the possibility of a system of freedom and the question of system in general initially does seem to concern us at all is no evidence against the question, but rather only against us. Evidence against us consists not only in the fact that we no longer know anything intelligent about this question, but also beyond that in the fact that the seriousness and the courage for reflection are threatening to dwindle in us.

Schelling himself emphasizes the following at the end of the reference to the supposed incompatibility of system and the concept of freedom: "It is not easy to dispute general affirmations of this sort; for who knows what restricting notions have already been attached to the word "system" itself, so that the assertion declares something which, to be sure, is very true but also very commonplace."

Thus we ask: (1) What, in general, is a system? (2) How and under what conditions does philosophy come to build a system? (3) Why is "system" precisely in the philosophy of German Idealism a battle call and an inmost requirement? (4) Which questions with regard to the possibility of a system of freedom and system in general does Schelling select in the general discussion of his introduction?

Regarding (1): what, *in general, is a system?* Like many other words which have left their imprint on the realm of our human existence, whether directly or in translation, the word comes from the Greek. When we state this, we are not just naming the original language of the word, but the people, the creative force of that people which in its poets, thinkers, statesmen, and artists brought about the greatest formative attack on the whole of Being which ever occurred in Western history. Essential words are not artificially invented signs and marks which are pasted on things merely to identify them. Essential words are deeds which happen in those moments where the lightning flash of a great enlightenment goes through the universe.

Let us first develop *the meaning of systema* according to its factual possibilities. System comes from the Greek *synistemi*, I put together, and this can mean two things. First, order things in such a way that not only is what is present and occurring distributed and preserved according to an already existent network of places—for example, the way the windowpane is inserted into a completed windowframe—but order in such a way that the order itself is thereby first projected. But this projection, if it is genuine, is not only thrown *over* things, not only dumped on top of them. A genuine projection throws beings apart in such a way that they precisely now become visible in the unity of their inmost jointure—

for example the jointure which determines a living thing, a living being, *systema tou somatos;* we still speak today of the nervous system, of the *systems* of digestion and procreation.

"I place together" can, however, also mean simply I shove—also without a previous network of order—anything together with anything else indiscriminately and endlessly. Accordingly *systema* can also mean mere accumulation and patchwork. *Between* these extreme opposites of meaning—inner jointure and mere manipulation—stands that which gives system its name: a framework, not an inner order, but also not a mere external accumulation.

System can signify several things—on the one hand, an inner jointure giving things their foundation and support, on the other hand, mere external manipulation, and finally in between something like a framework. This fact points out that this inner possibility of wavering between jointure and manipulation and framework always belongs to system, that every genuine system always remains threatened by the decline into what is spurious, that every spurious system can always give the appearance of being genuine. In any case we find in the linguistic usage of the Greeks all the decisive directions of the meaning we discovered: inner jointure, external manipulation, framework.

Thus the *kosmos* is called: *systema ex ouranou kai ges*, a jointure of heaven and earth, certainly not a mere external compilation of both. There is also the phrase *systema tes politeias*, the system of the shaping order of communal nature. *Systema* is understood in another way in the phrase *to tes phalaggos systema*, troop formation in the shape and lining up of the "phalanx." Here the grouping is outer, but not external. It is rather guided by a definite understanding and disposition of the course and order of battle. *Systema* signifies something external when it simply means a pile, a band, or in the case of doctors, accumulation and congestion of the blood and body fluids.

Later the word system is also used in the realm of cognition, of knowledge, and this usage became particularly well known in such phrases as the system of philosophy, the system of sciences. According to what we have said in principle about the word and concept system we can suspect that here, too, system can be intended and used in a genuine and a false sense. Even more than this. Because of the inner possibility of ambiguity which belongs to the nature of the system, the attempt to form a system must itself be ambiguous and in any case not a matter of course. This is the case only where the system of philosophy but, also, that of the sciences are intended in a quite external sense. Thus, we have again and again schoolteachers who have gone wild or retired privy councillors in a provincial court, good people in their profession who get the idea that they have to "make" a system of philosophy or world view. On a foundation of writings read at random to no purpose, large tables and compartments are then projected in which the whole world is stuffed, if possible decked out, with lots of numbers, figures, and arrows. And there are people and places who take this stuff seriously and perpetrate it. But what is fatal is not the fact that such things go on, that is as necessary as the husks in wine pressing. What is fatal is only the fact that people think that such an arbitrarily patched-together network of title compartments represents the sole true form of a "system" and that it is *therefore* suitable not to bother with the question of system at all. To be sure,, the false form of system and the business of constructing systems must be rejected again and again, but only because system in the true sense is one, indeed *the* task of philosophy.

But, again, this does not mean that system is always the pressing and sole task. Still less does it mean that system always has the same form and the same meaning in the manner of external uniformity. There is great philosophy without a system. The whole of Greek philosophy is proof of this. The beginning of Western philosophy was without a system, but yet, or rather especially for that reason, this philosophizing was thoroughly "systematic," that is, directed and supported by a quite definite inner jointure and order of questioning, that questioning which in general created the essential presupposition for all systematics and a possible system. Neither Plato nor Aristotle "have" a "system" of philosophy, neither in the sense of building a finished system nor in the sense of even projecting one. But they did create the presuppositions for the requirement and actualization of building a system, and at first against their wills precisely for an external and false system. Thus, whoever speaks of Plato's system or Aristotle's system is falsifying history and blocking the way to the inner movement of this philosophizing and the understanding of its claim to truth.

The so-called *summas* of medieval theology, too, are not systems, but a form of doctrinaire communication of the content of knowledge. It is true that in contrast to other academic methods of presentation, commentaries, disputations, and questions, the *summas* carry out an order of the material which is independent of the coincidentally treated subject matter and of the necessity at hand of a single teaching lesson and matter of dispute. Still, the *summas* are primarily directed toward teaching. They are handbooks.

The famous *Summa Theologica* of Thomas Aquinas is a handbook, too, a handbook for beginners whose function is to present what is essential in a simple ordered way. One should compare the *Prologue* of the work: "Quia catholicae veritatis doctor non solum provectos debet instruere, sed ad eum pertinet etiam incipientes erudire (secundum illud Apostoli 1 ad Corinth. 3, 1-2: Tamquam parvulis in Christo, lac vobis potum dedi, non escam), propositum nostrae intentionis in hoc opere est, ea, quae ad christianam religionem pertinent, eo modo tractare secundum quod congruit ad eruditionem incipientium." "Since the teacher of Catholic truth not only has to teach those who are advanced (*provecti*), but his duty is also to prepare beginners (*incipientes*) [according to those words of the Apostles I. Cor. 3, 1: In accordance with the small children who you are, I have given myself as drink and not as solid food], because it is thus a matter of preparing beginners, our proposed intention in this work is to treat what concerns Christian Faith in such a way that it corresponds to the knowledge of beginners."

The intention of the *Summa* and thus the whole character of the work could not be more clearly known. But still these *Summas* are often compared with medieval cathedrals. Now, of course, every comparison limps. But this comparison of theological handbooks with medieval cathedrals not only limps and wilts, it is completely impossible. The medieval cathedrals and their towers vault in articulated degrees toward heaven. The counterpart would be that a *Summa* was built up upon a broad foundation to the apex toward heaven; that is, toward God. But the *Summa* starts precisely with the apex and consequently spreads out in practical, moral human life. If the comparison between a school handbook and a building and work of art is already generally questionable, it really becomes impossible when the structural order—which belongs to the comparison—is exactly opposite in both.

But the conceptual confusion increases beyond measure when these *Summas*, as the supposed systems of medieval thought,, are compared with the real systems of Hegel and Schelling, or with the supposed systems of Plato and Aristotle. This kind of intellectual history might be very skillful and effective as an *apologia*, but it has nothing to do with a knowledge of history and, above all, it obstructs the correct *cognition* of the medieval period itself and the manner of *its* shaping of knowledge. But this misinterpretation also prevents what we are most concerned with here, the correct cognition of the nature, and that means also the conditions, of the possibility of a system.

If an affinity to system is present in medieval shaping of knowledge, it is in the manner of subdividing and ordering degrees of the realms of Being. The work of the greatest Western thinker of the Carolinian period, the Irishman, Scotus Eriugena, belongs here: *peri physeos merismou, De divisione naturae*, written around 860. The influence of Neoplatonism is evident here, too, that late Greek philosophy which is already permeated with Judaeo-Christian and Roman thought and which later actually was not without influence on the manner of formation of systems.

"System" is not the mere arrangement of a finished body of doctrine for the purpose of simply teaching beginners in the sciences. In general, a system is not only (and not primarily) an order of completed material of knowledge and values of knowledge for the purpose of correct communication of knowledge, but system is the inner jointure of what is comprehensible itself, its founding development and ordering. Even more, system is the conscious joining of the jointure and coherence of Being itself. If system thus has nothing of the externality and haphazardness of the artificial order of a classification of material under headings and numbers, then the formation of systems stands under quite definite conditions and cannot come about historically at an arbitrary time.

Now we come to (2): how and under what conditions does philosophy come to build a system?

The possibility of the thought of something like a system and the possibility of its starting point and development have their own presuppositions. This concerns nothing less than the interpretation of Being and truth and knowledge in general.

The possibility of systems in the definite historical form in which we know them up to now has only been opened up since the moment when Western history entered what we call the modern period. The possibility of the system of knowledge and the will to system as a manner of rediscovering the human being are essential characteristics of the modern period. To want to find systems in history before this time displays a lack of understanding of the concept system or a misinterpretation in an external sense.

Of course, one can go from the real and unique systems and attempts at systems of the modern period back to the past and show similarities. But this does not prove that the similarity is also a harbinger, the explicit beginning of an early form and the necessity of a will to system. And, insofar as the character of jointure belongs to the essence of Being in general—which, of course, must be shown—there lies in all philosophy as asking about Being the orientation toward jointure and joining, toward system. All philosophy is systematical, but not a system, and not only not a system because it doesn't get "finished." Conversely, what appears to be a system is not always systematic thought, that is, philosophy. From all of this follows that one must know clearly what one means when one says "system."

It would go far beyond the limits of our task if we attempted to present the historical (and that means, at the same time, the factual) conditions for the possibility and development of the idea of system in context. Besides, these conditions are not always present in the same way at the same time; but rather, they develop in the course of modern history in different degrees of clarity and influence, and condition and hinder each other mutually. This means, above all, that the idea of system and the manner of its realization are forced into quite definite paths which come together in the form of the system of German Idealism.

Thus, we now want to name only a few of the main conditions under which the demand of system was able to develop and the first attempts to form a system could come about. However, we may risk this *general* overview only by bearing in mind that in what follows, in following Schelling's treatise, essential points will present themselves to us in a more definite form.

No lengthy proof is necessary to the effect that these conditions for the possibility of forming *a system* are *at the same time* the essential presuppositions for the origin and existence of the *modern sciences*, of what we know today as "science." This modern science is just as different in its factual character from that of the Middle Ages as medieval science is from ancient science. The idea, still extant, of "a" science as it travels through the times by itself and is supposed to be preserved in its eternal value, also has its definite conditions of origin, but it prevents precisely what it wants, the maintenance of the scientific spirit. The latter is maintained only by profoundly renewing itself from time to time just as the falling of a level of achievement can only be prevented by being constantly raised.

The main conditions of the first formation of a system are as follows:

1. In the development of goals of knowledge and in the founding of forms of knowledge, a completely new claim makes itself known. We call that briefly the *predominance of* the *mathematical*. The mathematical is a definitely oriented interpretation of the nature of knowledge in general. Accordingly, there belongs to knowledge the self-originating foundation of what is knowable in terms of and within first principles which need no foundation. Thus, the unity of a foundational context of principles supported *by* first principles and ordered in *accordance* with them is required for the totality of knowledge. The new development of mathematics which helps to determine the beginning of the modern period is not, as one might think, the *reason* for the predominance of the mathematical, but a *consequence* of it. (Compare *What is a Thing,* trans. W. B. Barton, Jr., and Vera Deutsch [Chicago: Henry Regnery Co., 1967], pp. 69ff.)

2. Taken as the criterion for all of knowledge, the mathematical requires of that knowledge an ultimate and absolutely certain foundation. This requirement means to *search* within the total realm of beings for the something knowable which in itself admits of a corresponding foundation of itself. To search for a knowledge which becomes founded by knowing itself and allowing only this as known. Knowledge considers itself founded when it is certain of itself. This certainty and its guarantee become the foundation of all knowledge and, thus, the foundation of the truth of what is knowable. *Now* what is important *above* all is that, in general, something is immediately and unshakably knowable at all times and *only then* is it of *secondary* importance *what* that is in content that is known, that is, appropriated as something manifest, that is, true. This precedence of certainty over truth leads to conceiving truth itself as certainty. Here the precedence of procedure (method) over content is at stake.

3. This mathematical requirement of certainty as the criterion for all knowledge finds a quite definite fulfillment historically. From this, it follows that the *ego cogito* is posited as what is first of all and truly knowable and thus *true*: I think and thus know myself as thinking, I find myself as existing, the being of my ego is absolutely certain. Descartes thus created for the requirement of mathematical certainty the ground and foundation sufficient for *it* and placed knowledge in general upon the self-certainty of the principle: "I think, I—am."

4. The self-certainty of thinking decides what "is," as a principle and thus fundamentally. Thinking and its certainty become the criterion for truth. And only what is *true* can be acknowledged as truly *existent*. The self-certainty of

thinking becomes the court of judgment which decides what can be *and cannot* be, even more, what *Being* means in general.

5. The sole criterion of church doctrine for the whole ordering and forming of truth and knowledge breaks down and yields to the growing predominance of seeking founding itself. The criteria get turned around. The truth of faith and faithful knowledge are now measured in terms of the self-certainty of pure thinking with regard to its correctness.

Thinkers and men like Pascal tried once again to hold fast to pure thinking and pure faith, both in their originality and acumen together and in one. Next to the logic of the understanding comes the "logic of the heart."

But when the ecumenical office loses the sole power as the first and real source of truth, the total realm of beings as it was formed by Christianity does not disappear from view. On the contrary, the order of beings as a whole—God, the creator, the world of creatures, man, belonging to the world and destined for God—these beings as a whole thus experienced now especially *demand* a *new assimilation* on the foundation and with the means of knowledge founding itself.

Here, however, we must take into consideration the fact that through German Protestantism in the Reformation not only Roman dogma was changed, but also the Roman-Oriental form of the Christian experience of Being was transformed. What was already being prepared in the Middle Ages with Master Eckardt, Tauler, and Seuse and in the "German *Theologia*" is brought to bear in a new beginning and in a more comprehensive way by Nicolaus Cusanus, by Luther, Sebastian Frank, Jacob Boehme—and in art by Albrecht Dürer.

6. The shattering of the sole dominance of the church in legislating knowledge and action is understood as a *liberation* of man *to himself*. But what man is as himself, wherein his being a self should consist is determined only in his liberation and by the definitely oriented history of this liberation. Human "thinking," which here means the forming powers of man, becomes the fundamental law of things themselves. The conquest of the world in knowledge and action begins. Not only with regard to its extent, but above all with regard to its style it is quite different from before. Commerce and the economy turn into powers of their own in the most narrow, reciprocal connection with the origin of *technology* which is something different from the previous invention and use of tools. *Art* becomes the decisive manner of self-development of human creativity and at the same time its own way of conquering the world for eye and ear.

Man, freely creating and fulfilling himself in creating; *the genius* becomes the law of being truly human. But the reception of art, too, the manner and extent of its cultivation is primarily decided by human judgment freely standing on its own, by *taste*.

The idea of "sovereignty" brings a new formation of the state and a new kind of political thought and requirement.

In everything recounted just now, an inner context is betrayed, a *change* of European existence in terms of a *ground* which remains in the *dark* for us up until today. Perhaps our century, too, is today still too close to all this—too close especially also in its will to overcome—to be able to appraise what really happened. Perhaps we can never know this "in itself" at all because past history becomes new again and again *as* past through its future.

What does all of this have to do with "system"? Anticipating, we stated in a still undefined indication of the concept: system is the jointure of Being itself, not only an added framework for beings and certainly not an arbitrary concatenation.

What, then, must happen in order that a "system," that is, the exposure and erection of the jointure of Being itself, can come about? Nothing less than the arising of such an interpretation of Being, its determinability and truth and such a position of man with regard to Being which makes the requirement of a "system" possible, even historically necessary. Something like this originated in the beginning, more exactly, occurred *as* the beginning of the modern period.

In a historical moment where man's existence understands itself and brings itself about as being free for an empowering of Being founded upon itself, *as* the most extreme and first goal for *such* human being, the will *must* develop in elevating Being as a whole in a manipulable structure to guiding knowledge. *This will to take charge of Being in its jointure, freely shaping and knowing it* is essentially animated and confirmed by the new experience of man as the genius.

The determination of the *form* of this jointure, however, is at the same time prefigured by the dominance of the *mathematical*. For since this thinking understands itself as the court of judgment over Being, Being itself can only have a mathematical structure. However, since freeing man to himself is a setting free of man in the middle of beings as a whole, that totality (God-world-man) must be understood and ordered in terms of the unity of a jointure and *as* such a unity.

The realm of beings as a whole experienced in a Christian way is *re*-thought and *re*-created according to the lawfulness of thinking determining all Being in the form of a mathematical connection of foundations: *ordo et connexio idearum idem est ac ordo et connexio rerum* (Spinoza, *Ethics,* Part II, Propos. VII). The knowing conquest of Being as jointure, system and the will to system, this is not some discovery of idiosyncratic minds, but it is the innermost law of existence of this whole age. "System," knowledge's will to system, characterizes the changed position of knowledge with regard to the *intellectus* of the Middle Ages in its true ground and extent.

In the concept "system," all of this reverberates at the same time: the mathematical, thinking as the law of Being, the lawgiving of the genius, the freeing of man to freedom in the middle of beings as a whole, the whole itself in its particulars: *omnia ubique.* One understands nothing of what happened to be given the name "baroque" if one has not understood the nature of this formation of system.

The
baroque

For this reason, the formation of system also has its definite stamp. Because Being in general is determined in its essence in terms of the thinkability and lawfulness of thinking, but this thinking is mathematical; the structure of Being, i.e., system, must be mathematical and at the same time a system of thinking, of *ratio*, of reason. The explicit and true formation of the system begins in the West as the will to a *mathematical system of reason*.

3. SKETCH OF MODERN PROJECTS FOR A SYSTEM (SPINOZA, KANT'S WILL TO A SYSTEM, KANT'S SIGNIFICANCE FOR GERMAN IDEALISM)

The *history* of this formation of system is at the same time the true and innermost *history of the origin of modern* science. This history is, however, history, not just the simple unfolding of a program. Countermovements and relapses, deviations, and detours belong to this development of the dominance of reason in the whole of beings. The kind, the breadth, the time of the formation of the system is very different in the various areas of the cognition of nature, the formation of the state, the realization of art and the doctrine of art, in education and in the founding of systematic knowledge, in philosophy. Yes, within philosophy, too, the attempts at a system show different beginnings and variously directed developments. The systems of Descartes, Malebranche, Pascal, Spinoza, Hobbes, Leibniz, Wolff and the Wolffians cannot be stacked in one line and appraised according to the aspect of a continuous development. At times, the will to a system is quite clear, as in the case of Descartes, or peculiarly decided, as in the case of Leibniz, but the development gets stuck in the beginning or else it is absolutely opaque in its manifold beginnings, as in the case of Leibniz. Or else the will to a system is on the border of externalization and the development is broad, lacking nothing, dull.

The sole completed system which is constructed all the way through in its foundational connection is the metaphysics of Spinoza which was published after his death under the title: *Ethica ordine geometrico demonstrata et in quinque partes distincta.* . . . The five parts are I. *De Deo*, II. *De natura et origine mentis*, III. *De origine et natura affectuum*, IV. *De servitute humana seu de affectuum viribus*, and V. *De potentia intellectus seu de libertate humana.*

The title already expresses the dominance of the *mathematical knowledge requirement—ordine geometrico*. The fact that this metaphysics; that is, science of beings as a whole, is called "Ethics" is indicative that man's actions and behavior are of decisive importance for the kind of procedure in knowledge and the foundation of knowledge.

But this system only became possible on the foundation of a *peculiar one-sidedness* which will be discussed. In addition, it became possible because the metaphysical fundamental concepts of medieval scholasticism were simply built into the system with a rare lack of criticalness. The *mathesis universalis*, Descartes's doctrine of method, was taken over for the development of system itself, and the true metaphysical fundamental idea comes from Giordano Bruno in every detail. This system of Spinoza, however, must above all be mentioned here *because* it played a role once again in the eighteenth century in discussions which are linked with the names Lessing, Jacobi, Mendelssohn, Herder, and Goethe, discussions which still cast their last shadows into Schelling's treatise on freedom. The interpretations of Spinoza's system, which are very diverse in their orientation, usually contributed to thinking generally of a "system" of philosophy as something like this very definite and one-sided system. The fact that Schelling's philosophy was interpreted as Spinozism belongs to that remarkable history of the misinterpretations of all philosophies by contemporaries. If Schelling *fundamentally fought against* a system, it is Spinoza's system. However, we cannot present here more exactly the systems of the seventeenth and eighteenth centuries. But gauged by the inexhaustibility of its systematic power, Leibniz's philosophy towers far above all others.

Summarizing, we can say with respect to the main conditions of the first formation of a system in the modern period that the conditions for the possibility of the modern and *first* formation of a system are at the same time the presuppositions for the origin and existence of today's sciences:

1. The predominance of the mathematical as the criterion of knowledge.

2. The self-founding of knowledge in the sense of this requirement as the *precedence* of certainty over truth. Precedence of procedure (method) over content.

3. The founding of certainty as the self-certainty of the "I think."

4. Thinking, *ratio* as the court of judgment for the essential determination of Being.

5. The shattering of the exclusive dominance of church faith in the shaping of knowledge, *at the same time including* the previous Christian experience of Being as a whole in the new questioning. The distinction between knowledge and faith, *intellectus and fides*, is not made here for the first time, but the self-understanding of knowledge and its possibilities and rights does become different.

6. The setting free of man for the creative conquest and rule and new formation of beings in all areas of human existence.

The true ground of this whole change remains obscure. We do not know the whole of its history. And we shall never be able to pick it up from facts anyway.

But we can understand *how* the requirement for a system *emerges* in this change of human existence and in the service of this change.

Where a creative setting free of man in the middle of beings as a whole comes about, all beings themselves must be available beforehand, especially when it is a matter of freely taking over beings.

The will to a freely forming and knowing *control* over beings as a whole projects for itself the structure of Being as this will.

In accordance with the requirements of knowledge and certainty, this structure is itself *mathematical*. In accordance with the self-certainty of thinking (of reason) as the law of Being the structure itself is *rational*.

System is a mathematical system of reason. System is the *law of Being* of modern human existence. System and the character of system make the changed position of knowledge in its own ground and extent.

The historical realization of systems does not show a continuous line either of development or of decline. Between the clarity and depth of the systematic will and its enactment there is a distorted relation.

In the context of our special task we now ask (3): why is "system" precisely in the philosophy of German Idealism a battle call and an inmost requirement?

Regarding (3): because to the determinations of system, that it must be mathematical and a system of reason, the *essential* insight was added that such a system could only be found and formed in accordance with knowledge if knowledge were *absolute* knowledge. In German Idealism "system" was explicitly understood as the requirement of *absolute* knowledge. In addition, system itself became the *absolute requirement* and thus the key term for philosophy as such. This change in the idea of system from the seventeenth and eighteenth centuries to that of German Idealism at the beginning of the nineteenth century accordingly presupposes that philosophy understood itself as absolute, infinite cognition. Herein lies an essentially heightened emphasis on what is creative in human reason, and that means a more primordial knowledge about the nature of reason. Such knowledge could only be gained by a new reflection on reason itself. This reflection is the work of Kant. Although Kant himself never took the fundamental position of German Idealism, as far as German Idealism went beyond Kant, it is certain that this could happen *only* on Kant's foundation and following the lead of the fundamental reflection he accomplished on the nature of human reason. This reflection is basically carried out in the *Critique of Pure Reason*. The critical reflection was supplemented by the *Critique of Practical Reason* and completed in the sense of its own criteria in the *Critique of Judgment*. We do not wish to go into this now either. We simply ask: how does Kant stand with regard to the requirement of a system and how does he determine the *concept* of system and what meaning does his philosophy have for the further continuation of the will to a system?

We indicated the *inner* connection between the conditions of the unfolding of the rule of reason and the will to system. From this the following can easily be drawn: The decisiveness of the will to a system, the assurance in founding system and in the measurement of its dimension, the insight into the ultimate necessity of system—all of this will depend upon the kind and degree of knowledge about the nature of the mathematical and reason. For both of these characterize "system" in its previous form. Defining philosophical cognition as pure cognition of reason as opposed to mathematical cognition is, however, an essential concern of the

Critique of Pure Reason. Thus, it is not a matter of chance that we find in Kant for the first time an explicit, systematic reflection on the nature of system and a determination of his concept in terms of the nature of reason.

Before Kant, what was called *ratio* in the language of the schoolmen and sometimes translated as understanding, sometimes as reason, was ambiguous. Defining *ratio* as opposed to sensuousness remained without a clear principle or a sufficient foundation. Reason was really only understanding: bringing given representations to concepts, separating and comparing concepts. Only through Kant did the understanding become reason. This means the nature of reason was expressly determined, and the understanding was defined in opposition to reason and subordinated to it. This whole procedure of determining the concept of reason takes root in Kant himself, since Kant understands the concept of reason in a broader and a narrower sense. In the broad sense reason means the higher faculty of knowledge; in the narrower sense, reason means the *highest* faculty within the higher faculties of knowledge which Kant distinguishes as understanding, judgment, and reason. In the narrower and, at the same time, essential sense, reason is for Kant the faculty of *Ideas* as principles. Along with the clarification of the concept of reason, the concept of the Ideas is clarified which generally—since Descartes—means *representation*. Ideas are the representations of the unity of the articulated manifold of a realm as a totality. The highest ideas are those in which the essential main realms of beings are represented: the Ideas of God, world, man. According to Kant, on the basis of the insights gained in the *Critique of Pure Reason* these Ideas as representations of reason are not "ostensive." They do not show us the objects themselves in question as given, present, but only in the Idea. Our representation of God is only an Idea. By this, Kant does not want to say that God doesn't exist or is a mere fantasy; God's existence was free of all doubts for Kant. He only wants to say as existing, God can never become certain for us by mere belief in what is thought in the concept of God and by an analysis of these representations. The same is true for the world as a totality. The same is true correspondingly for man as a being determined by freedom (observe the change in the idea of freedom in the *Critique of Judgment).* The Ideas do not bring what is represented—solely by being represented—before us bodily, but only point out the direction in which we must search out the manifold of what is given with regard to its connection, and that means with regard to its possible unity. The Ideas are not "ostensive," but only "heuristic," "regulative," pointing out the search and regulating the finding. The faculty of these Ideas is reason. Thus, reason gives a priori to our intuition and thinking the orientation toward the comprehensive unity and unified articulation of beings as a whole. Thus we have at the same time gained the Kantian concept of *system.*

System is "the unity of manifold knowledge under an Idea" (A832, B860), " . . . what is systematical in knowledge . . . ; i.e., in its connectedness in terms of a principle" (A645, B673). "This unity of reason always presupposes an Idea;

namely, that of the form of a whole of our knowledge, preceding the definite knowledge of its parts, and containing the conditions according to which we are to determine a priori the place of every part and its relation to the rest. Such an Idea accordingly demands the complete unity of the knowledge of our understanding, by which that knowledge becomes not only a mere aggregate but a system, connected according to necessary laws" (ibid.). Reason is what makes all the actions of our understanding "systematical" (A664, B692). Reason makes us "look out" from the very beginning for the unity of a fundamental connection with everything we meet (A655, B683). Reason is the faculty of looking out into a view, the faculty of forming a horizon. Thus, reason itself is nothing other than the faculty of system, and reason's interest is concerned with making evident the greatest possible manifold of knowledge in the highest possible unity. This demand is the essence of reason itself.

Reason is the presupposing faculty, what truly reaches out and encompasses. The presupposition which it posits is that unity on the basis of which knowledge of a realm of objects and a world is at all possible. Kant calls presuppositions which make possible the climbing over (transcendence) of human cognition to a totality of what is knowable *transcendental* concepts of reason.

The "prelude of reason" (*Critique of Judgment*): to *perform* and let play to us that for which there is never an example (*Bei-spiel*) in experience.

According to Kant, reason posits a *focus imaginarius*, a focus in which all the rays of questioning things and of determining objects meet, or, conversely, in terms of which all knowledge has its unity. Reason is the faculty—we can say—of anticipatory gathering—*logos, legein*. Frequently, without expressly knowing it, Kant comes with the certainty of a sleepwalker, better, by dint of the genuine philosophical instinctive relationship, back to the fundamental meaning of the primary philosophical concepts of the Greeks. Reason is in itself systematic, at once the faculty and demand of system. The reflection on the nature of reason, its inner build and its faculty, on the possible paths of its procedure; that is, the doctrine of the method of reason must thus consider and determine reason with respect to the conditions of forming a system as well—as Kant says, in relation to the "*art of systems.*" That is the task of the "architectonic of pure reason."

The term "architectonic" is already used in pre-Kantian philosophy as the term for the presentation of the doctrine of Being: *Prelude to the Architectonic or Theory of What is Simple and Primary in Philosophical and Mathematical Knowledge*, by J. H. Lambert, vols. I and II, 1771.

"Architectonic," herein speaks: tectonic—built, joined and *arche*—according to leading and ruling grounds and principles.

"The architectonic of pure reason" is the transcendental doctrine of method, chapter 3 (A832 ff., B860 ff.). The "systematic unity" is that which makes "ordinary knowledge," that is, a mere aggregation of cognitions, "into science." The systematical is what is scientific in a science. But the systematical is, according to all that has been said, not the external element of an arbitrary arrangement into boxes and paragraphs, but the anticipatory selection of the inner stringent essential unity of respective areas and at the same time the prefiguration of the articulation of the connection in which the manifold appearances of the area stand. Thus, architectonics is "the doctrine of what is scientific in our knowledge in general," that is, the doctrine of what constitutes the scientific element in it.

Kant discovered—and that also always means in philosophy shaped—the inner character of the system of reason as a law of spirit for the first time. He understands the concept of philosophy in general in accordance with this. Since philosophy looks toward those concepts and representations by which all knowing of beings is guided and back to which it is deduced, it treats such things in which the totality of what is knowable comes to its comprehensive end which is at the same time a beginning. Such an end is in Greek, *telos*. The knowing explication of this most extreme and highest focus of all the rays of knowledge through knowledge, this *logos* itself, is the *logos* of *telos*, teleology. Thus, Kant defines the essence of philosophy briefly in the expression: philosophy is *teleologia rationis humanae* (A839, B867). No one knew as clearly as Kant that this rational knowing of reason and its realm is always human reason. This is expressed simply and clearly in the conceptual determination of philosophy quoted. However, it is Kant's conviction that the Ideas of pure reason are "given us as a task by the nature of our reason" and that "this highest court of judgment of all the rights and claims of our speculation cannot itself possibly contain original deceptions and delusions." "Thus, presumably, they (the Ideas) will have their good and purposive determination in the natural disposition of our reason" (A669, B697).

This trust in the truth of the basic fact of human reason is the fundamental presupposition of Kant's philosophy. The fact that the kind of thinking and use of concepts, the performance of the use of reason, its hindrance and furtherance and change of direction stands under the conditions of, for example, the functioning of sex glands neither proves something *for* nor *against* the truth of what is revealed in thinking. The conditions of finding truth are not automatically also the laws of the subsistence of truth, but neither is limitation. And *as long as the essence of truth is as veiled as it is, the laws of the subsistence of truth will really remain in the dark*. If any thinker has shown that reason itself is always *human* reason, it was Kant. To note today that Kant did not yet know anything about possible historical transformations of the use of reason is not difficult after a century and a half of historical, anthropological, and psychological research; it is simply tiresome and unfruitful. However, it is difficult to raise our task and work up to the level of Kant's thinking again.

Kant's philosophy, its essential determination of reason and the system, is, however, the presupposition and at the same time, the motive, for "system" becoming the decisive goal and requirement and field of the highest attempts of thinking in German Idealism.

But if, in accordance with the conditions mentioned, a tendency toward system remains everywhere since the beginning of the modern period, yet through Kant and since Kant, with the changed concept of reason something different is added to the will to system. What is different, however, comes completely to light only in the moment when philosophy is urged beyond Kant. What is urgent about going beyond Kant is nothing other than the task of system.

The difference of interpretation of system and formation of system between Kant and German Idealism can only be shown in rough outline initially. For the development of the demand of a system urges precisely toward understanding system less and less only as the framework of knowledge of beings and more and more as the jointure of Being itself, and toward shaping it accordingly. The nature and position of system in the philosophy of German Idealism can thus only be understood when this philosophy is known in its unified fullness. We are far away from that now. But, still, it is necessary to characterize beforehand the direction of building system if we want to arrive at such knowledge.

We shall attempt this by contrasting the fundamental philosophical position of German Idealism with that of Kant. In doing this, we shall ignore the particular inner differences between the leading thinkers, Fichte, Schelling, and Hegel within German Idealism and bear in mind that such a distinguishing contrast can only direct us toward questioning and can never mean the last statement about the situation. We shall attempt this contrast of German Idealism with Kant following the concept of philosophy.

According to Kant, philosophy is *teleologia rationis humanae*, essential knowledge of that toward which man's reason, and that means man in his essence, is oriented. In this conceptual determination of philosophy, human reason is not understood just as the tool with which philosophy cognizes. Rather, reason is the *object* of philosophical science, and indeed the object with respect to what constitutes the leading and comprehensive unity of reason, its system. This system is determined by the highest concepts of unity and goal, God, world, man. These are the archetypes in which the realm is projected, according to representation, where existing things are then placed. This system is *not* derived *from* experience; but, rather, set up *for* it.

Why doesn't Kant arrive at a system? The philosophy of the *logos* of the *ratio humana* (genitivus objectivus and subjectivus) is now explicitly understood as *forming a system*. The *Critique of Judgment* is understood as the battle for *the system*. But why isn't the system simply carried out? Why isn't Kant himself systematically thought through to the end? Why go beyond him? And how does the new point of view look? However, before we can contrast the philosophical concepts with each other, it is necessary to make visible the motivating difficulty in Kant's system. For this purpose, a look at Kant's last thoughts about a system at a time when the first steps of German Idealism were already coming to light might be of help.

At stake is "a system which is all and one, *without increase and improvement*" (XXI, 8), (*Opus postumum*, first half). "The highest principle of the system of pure reason in transcendental philosophy as the opposing relation of the Ideas of God and the world" (ibid. 18). But in what does this "opposing" rest and consist? And, also, "the concept of the subject unifying them which brings (*a priori*) a synthetic unity to these concepts (God and world) in that reason makes that transcendental unity itself" (ibid. 23).

"System of Transcendental/Philosophy in three sections (as title). God, the world, *universum* and I, Myself, man, as a moral being. God, the world and the world inhabitant, man in the world. God, the world and what thinks both in the real relation opposing each other, the subject as a rational world being."

"The *medius terminus* (copula) in the judgment is here the Judging Subject (the thinking world being, man, in the world). Subject, predicate, copula" (ibid. 27).

The mediating unity, human reason, is the crux of the system. God—what is absolutely in itself and stands within itself, World—what is predicated, what becomes in the word, Man—as the copula (all of this reminiscent of Hamann).

We have long since known that Kant was especially fascinated by the task of system up until his last years. Excerpts from this manuscript of the *Nachlass* have been known for a long time but only since a few weeks ago do we have the first part of the *Nachlass* in a complete edition as vol. XXI of the *Akademie-Ausgabe* of Kant's works. Here, one can see how Kant begins a project of system again and again in numerous repetitions, and for the first time that and why he got stuck with his whole will in an indissoluble difficulty, moreover in a difficulty which runs through the whole of modern philosophy from Descartes to Nietzsche (System and Freedom) (Being and human being).

The highest leading concepts—God, world, man—are Ideas and have a merely heuristic character. In these representations, what is represented is not itself presented and presentable as a being. God is only envisioned as the leading concept for the order of knowledge, and thus all Ideas. It is not asserted that God does not exist. It is only maintained on the basis of the *Critique of Pure Reason:* God's existence, the world as a totality, man as a person, cannot be proved theoretically.

But, now, why are these Ideas necessary and why just these Ideas? And how should their own connection be grounded if these Ideas are not drawn from the beings themselves which they mean and from the corresponding immediate comprehension of these beings? For all this, Kant has no answer other than claiming that these Ideas necessarily belong to the nature of human reason. There is still a remainder here of the old doctrine of *ideae innatae* which does, however, have a deeper meaning than one usually gives it.

But the question remains whether the appeal to the natural disposition of human reason and its possession of the Ideas constitutes a systematic foundation of the system, whether a systematic foundation is thus laid for it. Kant himself cannot fend off doubts here. Thus, as we can now see, questions suddenly arise in his sketches like this one: "Is the division *God* and the *world* permissible" (ibid., p. 5)? If this question of division still exists as a question, then system itself is questionable. Kant also did not succeed in sufficiently clarifying and grounding the kind of knowledge of philosophy as *teleologia rationis humanae*. Kant did succeed in a critique, that is, at the same time a positive essential determination of knowledge as experience, but he neglected the foundation of the essence of that knowledge which was carried out as critique. The critique as critique was itself not founded. (How is the procedure of the critique as "transcendental reflection" determinable? Compare *Critique of Pure Reason*, A260 ff. "Reflection" and *teleologia*.) One could think that such a task could lead into endlessness and, thus, into groundlessness so that "critique" in Kant's sense would not be possible at all. We won't go into a discussion of this question. In this form, it rests on a quite external formalistic consideration. We shall only consider that the noncorresponding *foundation* of the bases of the critique itself became a motivating force which went beyond Kant. The demand for laying the foundations, however, is a requirement of system.

Young thinkers had trouble with the questionability of the Kantian system as a system of Ideas which were to have only heuristic, but not ostensive, character. Precisely because the Kantian requirement of a system was very much affirmed, one turned away from the path on which Kant wanted to satisfy this requirement.

On the other hand, the new way only became possible through the new determination which Kant had given to the essence of reason and which he calls the transcendental. In this determination reason—in spite of being limited to the regulative—is namely understood as a *creative faculty*.

We shall briefly summarize once more the *essential* difficulties which Kant's philosophy leaves behind with regard to system. As the faculty of the Ideas, the leading representations for the knowledge of beings as a whole, reason is in itself oriented toward the totality of Being and its connection. According to Kant, reason is in itself systematic. But Kant didn't show the origin of the Ideas, that is, the ground of system. Even more, as long as the Ideas only have the regulative, indicative characacter as Kant teaches, as long and as far as they as re-presentations do not present what is meant in them as itself, the totality of the Ideas, system cannot be founded at all in terms of the matter itself, beings as a whole. The ground of system cannot be shown. (Ideas are only directions for finding, but themselves are not found!)

The ground of system is obscure; the way to system is not guaranteed. The truth of system is quite questionable. And on the other hand, the demand for system is inevitable. System alone guarantees the inner unity of knowledge, its scientific character and truth. Therefore, in the intention for truth and knowledge, system must first, and above all, again and again itself be questioned, grounded in its essence, and developed in its concept. In this way, it is to be understood that *system* becomes the leading summons for German Idealism and that it means nothing other than the true self-grounding of the totality of essential knowledge, of *the* absolute science, philosophy.

Fichte's first decisive publication is the "doctrine of science," that is, the science of science in the sense of essential knowledge. The doctrine of science is the grounding of the system in its systematic character. Schelling's first writings treat "of the possibility of a form of philosophy"; "On the I as the principle of philosophy." ("Form" of philosophy does not mean the external framework, but explicitly the inner order of its content, more precisely that both belong together here and are the same system. The "principle" of philosophy is the determining ground of the unity of the possible foundation of its context of knowledge, of the system.) Hegel's first larger treatise concerns the "difference between Fichte's and Schelling's systems."[10]

This stormy will to system is inflamed with genuine youthful spirit. But it nevertheless does not merely youthfully jump over the difficulties and merely prematurely wish to erect a scaffold of knowledge for itself. The will to the system is consciously supported and guided by a dispute with Kant's work and above all with his *last* work, the *Critique of Judgment* (and that means: by a unique admiration for Kant).

Although the criticism is harsh on many points, the awareness grows increasingly in these thinkers that only Kant really placed them where they stand. Behind the vehemence of dispute stands the passion of a determination and the knowledge that with them and through them something essential is happening, something which in its time will again and again have the power to create and transform the future.

4. THE STEP BEYOND KANT (INTELLECTUAL INTUITION AND ABSOLUTE KNOWLEDGE IN SCHELLING)

The question still remains now: how does the work of German Idealism look regarding a true realization of Kant's demand for system? We will experience an essential part of this work going through Schelling's treatise; moreover, a part in which the idealistic shaping of system already becomes questionable on its own terms, and transcends itself.

Nevertheless, we now want to try to characterize the kind of work on system which goes beyond Kant, in a way which corresponds to the presentation of Kant's idea of system. This presentation was summarized in Kant's conceptual determination of philosophy as *teleologia rationis humanae*. What is different about the way German Idealism understands philosophy? The fundamental interpretation of these thinkers can be expressed in an adequate correspondence as follows: *philosophy is the intellectual intuition of the Absolute.* By explaining this statement we will know in what way the question of system in German Idealism changed in contradistinction to Kant.

According to Kant, the basic representations of reason are the Ideas of God, world, and man. But these are, according to Kant, only guiding concepts, not objective representations which give the intended object itself. But now—we can briefly present the considerations of German Idealism thusly—*something* is thought in these Ideas; and *what* is thought, God, world, man, is taken to be so essentially determinative that *knowledge* is possible only on the basis of what is thought here. Thus, what is represented in the Ideas cannot be freely invented, it must itself be known in a knowing. This knowing of the whole must be true knowledge of the first order because it supports and determines all other knowing. But as Kant himself rediscovered, knowing is at bottom *intuition*, immediate representation of what is meant in its existing self-presence. Thus, the intuition which constitutes first and true knowing must pursue the totality of Being, God, world, the nature of man (freedom).

In accordance with its nature, this totality can no longer be determined by *relations, in terms of* relations *to something else*—otherwise it wouldn't be the totality. This totality of Being lacks a relation to other things, is not relative, and is in this sense absolutely *absolved* from everything else, released from all relations because it doesn't admit of any such thing at all. This absolute *relationlessness* to anything else, this absolutely absolved is called the *Ab-solute.*

The word is misleading if one takes it literally and according to the manner of common sense as an absolute thing. For with respect to this idea, it must be said what is absolved from others is then *still* related to *others* if only in the *manner* of being *absolved* FROM it, and is on the basis of this relatedness, this *relation, relative* and not absolute.

Indeed, as long as we always think what is thought in our thinking only as a thing, the Absolute cannot be thought because there is no absolute thing and the Absolute cannot be a thing. In the course of the interpretation of our treatise, we shall have ample opportunity to free ourselves from the exclusive rule of common sense and to practice philosophic thinking. It would, of course, only be nonsense in reverse if we wanted to practice and know as practice philosophical thinking in daily considerations and calculations of things. Philosophical thinking cannot be *applied* to customary thinking. But the latter can be turned into the former.

If it is to be knowledge, knowledge of the totality must be intuition. This intuition of the Absolute, however, pursues something which we don't perceive with the senses. Thus, this intuition cannot be sensuous. But unsensuous knowledge was called at that time knowledge through the *intellectus*, intellectual knowledge. Unsensuous intuition is intellectual intuition. True knowing of beings as a whole—philosophy—is intellectual intuition of the Absolute. From here, the concept of reason changes. The word "reason" gets back, we can say, to its original meaning: perceiving, immediately grasping. Intellectual intuition is intuition of reason.

Repeating, we summarize: Schelling is aiming at "the system of freedom." To clarify this intention, we asked four intermediate questions:

1. What, in general, is system?
2. How and under what conditions does philosophy come to build a system?
3. Why is "system" precisely in the philosophy of German Idealism a battle call and an inmost requirement? We shall turn to the fourth question later.

In its first form during the seventeenth and eighteenth centuries, system is the *system of mathematical reason*. Through his new reflection on the nature of reason, Kant showed that and how reason is, in itself, "systematic."

If philosophy is nothing other than *teleologia rationis humanae*, then this means that its inmost and true task is system.

Kant's philosophical effort in the last decade was dedicated exclusively to founding the system of reason. This effort failed, not because of external hindrances, but because of internal reasons. The unity of system and, thus, system itself, could not be grounded. "Is the division God and the world permissible?"

According to Kant's interpretation, the Ideas themselves, God, world, man, do not admit being founded in terms of what they represent. The Ideas are not *ostensive*. They do not themselves present what they mean immediately, but are only a "prelude to reason" which is, however, necessary by nature *(Critique of Judgment)*.

The ground of the Ideas and their unity; that is, the ground of the system, is obscure. The way to system is not guaranteed. The truth of system is questionable. And yet, the demand of system is inevitable.

On the one hand, Kant showed the necessity of system in terms of the nature of reason. On the other hand, that same Kant left system in essential difficulties.

Thus, everything depends on the question of system. The first philosophical publications of Fichte, Schelling, and Hegel thus circle around the question of system.

In which direction do the attempts at system go in German Idealism?

We shall show this by the changed fundamental position of its philosophy, following its concept of philosophy as contrasted with Kant's. Philosophy is now the intellectual intuition of the Absolute.

According to Kant, and especially also according to his demand, philosophy aims at system, the inner unity of the Ideas of God, world, man; that is, at beings as a whole.

Man stands in beings as a whole. He knows about this whole. How far and clearly, how certainly and how richly, we see and know this differs and changes quite a bit. But always and in each case we know about beings as a whole. We know. They are.

We stand constantly in this knowing of Being. Thus, we want to clarify and ground this knowledge in spite of, yes, because of, the critical barrier which Kant erected. For his critique is negatively placed under the presuppositon that beings as a whole must be knowable in the sense of experience or else not at all, and that these beings as a whole must consequently be objects.

Both presuppositions are unfounded. Knowledge does not need sensuous experience, and what is known need not be an object; but is rather precisely a knowing of what is nonobjective, the Absolute. And, since every knowing is intuition, and since the Absolute, however, cannot be sensuously intuited, this intuition of the Absolute must be nonsensuous, must be "intellectual."

But for Kant, there is no knowledge without sensuous intuition. Only those objects are knowable which are given to us through the senses. But German Idealism soon pointed out rightly that Kant lets space and time be given us in intuitions which are by no means sensuous, not sensations, but—as Kant himself says—"pure," that is, nonsensuous intuitions.

Kant did show in his *Critique of Pure Reason* that in order to know objects they must somehow be given to man. But since the *suprasensuous objects*, God, world-totality, and man's freedom, cannot be given by the senses, they are not cog-nitively knowable. Granted that Kant's proof is all right, who, then, however, says that God, world-totality, and freedom are "objects," "things," at all? Kant has only shown that what is meant by the Ideas is not knowable *if* it is an object and can only be made certain of as an object in the experience of things of nature. Kant has not shown that what is represented and meant in the Ideas, is an "object." He also did not show that all intuition has to be objective *in*-tuition. *
Kant only showed that what is meant by the Ideas is not knowable—under the presupposition of the silent demand that it must and could be really knowable only in a sensuous intuition.

But if the Ideas posited by Kant (God. world, man) are not to be pure imaginary fantasies, how else can their truth be evidenced than by a knowledge which, however, must know that it is not supposed to know objects, but, rather, to know what is nonobjective, but still not nothing at all.

This nonobjective knowledge of beings as a whole now knows itself as the true and absolute knowledge. What it wants to know is nothing other than the structure of Being which now no longer stands as an object somewhere over against knowledge, but which itself becomes in knowledge, and this *becoming to itself* is *absolute Being*. As the first presupposition for bringing about intellectual intuition, Schelling especially emphasized again and again and demanded that we free ourselves from the attitude and procedure of the everyday knowledge of things.

"The rage to explain everything, to be able to accept nothing the way it is in its

An-schauung, with the emphasis on looking *at* something (objective)—TRANS.

it only to understand it taken apart into cause and effect, is what above
... .ten tears us away from the indifference of thinking and intuiting. This
indifference is the true character of the philosopher" (*Further Presentations from the
System of Philosophy,* 1802, I, IV, p. 344).

By indifference, nondifferentiation, intellectual intuition, Schelling means that
comprehension in which thinking intuits and intuiting thinks. The indifference is
that in which everything differentiated comes together (Compare Goethe's
"Urphänomen").

"Intellectual intuition is the faculty in general of seeing the universal in the
particular, the infinite in the finite, both unified in a living unity . . . to see the
plant in the plant, the organ in the organ and, in a word, the concept or the
indifference in the difference is possible only through intellectual intuition"
(ibid., p. 362).

It is not a matter of chance that this knowledge tries to explain itself in terms of
its correspondence to mathematical knowledge. In mathematical knowledge,
thinking (the concept thought) is adequate to Being (object). Here one cannot ask
whether what is correct in "thinking" is also correct in "Being." Accordingly,
there is also an absolute unity of thinking and Being in intellectual intuition. This
unity, the shining forth of Being in thinking and what is thought in Being, "now to
see this same evidence, or the unity of thinking and Being not in this or that
respect, but absolutely in and for itself; thus, as the evidence in all evidence, the
truth in all truth, what is purely known in all that is known means to raise oneself
to the intuition of absolute unity and thus to intellectual intuition in general"
(ibid., p. 364).

"We are not different from dogmatism by asserting an absolute unity of
thinking and Being in the Absolute, but rather in *knowledge,* and thus assert a
Being of the Absolute in knowledge and of knowledge in the Absolute" (ibid., p.
365).

But with the demand for knowledge in the sense of intellectual intuition,
German Idealism seems to fall back to the condition of philosophy *before* Kant.
Kant called this philosophy before him "dogmatism" in contradistinction to his
own to which he gave the name of "criticalism," the philosophy which traversed
the *Critique of Pure Reason* and was founded upon such a critique. Thus, German
Idealism must have been interested in preventing its philosophy from being
thrown together with pre-Kantian philosophy.

It is characteristic of "dogmatism" that it simply accepts and asserts the
knowability of the Absolute as a matter of course; it lives in terms of this assertion
or *dogma.* More exactly, in this assertion of the self-evident knowability of the
Absolute lies an untested prejudice about the Absolute itself.

What absolutely is, is what-is-for-itself and what-is-of-itself (substance). But
according to Descartes, true substance is subject, that is, "I think." The Being of

God is pure thinking, *cogitare,* and must therefore also be comprehensible through thinking.

After Kant, this dogmatism is no longer possible. But after Kant, on the other hand, it is not necessary to exclude the Absolute from human knowledge either. Rather, it is a question of making up for Kant's negligence and determining the nature of the knowledge of the Absolute. Thus, Schelling says "We are not different from dogmatism by asserting an absolute unity of thinking and Being in the Absolute; but, rather, in *knowledge,* and thus assert a Being of the Absolute in knowledge and of knowledge in the Absolute" (ibid., p 365).

The Absolute *is* in such knowing of the kind of intellectual intuition, and such knowing is *in* the Absolute.

The knower neither has the Absolute outside of himself as object, nor *within* himself as a thought in the "subject." Rather, absolute knowing is knowing "of" the Absolute in the double sense that the Absolute is the knower and the known, neither only the one nor only the other, but both the one and the other in an original unity.

The philosopher as the knower is neither related to things, objects, nor to "himself," the "subject," but, in knowing, he knows what *plays around* and *plays through* existing things and *existing* man and what *prevails through* all this as a whole *in existing.* (The subject-object and the object-subject.)

"The knowledge that the having-outside-itself of the Absolute (and of course the mere having-for-itself immediately related to this, thus the thought-being of the latter) is itself only an illusion and belongs to illusion is the first decisive step against all dogmatism, the first step toward true Idealism and to the philosophy which is in the Absolute" (ibid., p. 356).

Schelling wrote this in 1802, five years *before* Hegel's *Phenomenology of Spirit!* Whoever knows this work of Hegel's will easily understand that Hegel's *Phenomenology* is only a great, self-contained sequence of variations on this theme. This philosophy of German Idealism, intellectual intuition, is no figment of the imagination, but the real *labor* of the Spirit on itself. It is no coincidence that "labor" is favorite word of Hegel's.

The mathematical system of reason in which beings as a whole (God, world, man) are to be comprehended arrives at the true presupposition of the possibility of itself only when the knowledge of Being—en route through Kant's philosophy—understands itself as absolute knowledge. The interpretation of true knowing as "intellectual" intuition is thus not some arbitrary and, as people think, romantic, escalation of Kantian philosophy, but it makes evident the innermost presupposition, until now hidden, which is placed at the beginning of system in the sense of the mathematical system of reason. For only from that moment on when this idea of system as the absolute system of reason knows itself in absolute knowledge is system absolutely founded in terms of itself, that is, really mathe-

matically certain of itself, founded on absolute self-consciousness and comprehending all realms of beings. And where system knows itself in this way as
unconditioned necessity, the requirement of system is not only no longer something external, but what is inmost and primary and ultimate. Only from this
standpoint of absolute knowing does it become possible, but necessary, too, to
understand the previous stages of the formation of system in their conditioned
and conditioning role. Now the idea of a system according to preliminary forms
and transitional forms, all oriented towards the absolute system, is searched for in
the whole history of Western philosophy. Only now does an inner articulation and
a characteristic of its central age with regard to its systematic character enter the
history of philosophy itself. Until then, the history of Spirit, more or less crudely
formulated, was a sequence of expressions of opinion of individual thinkers. Now,
the history of thinking and knowing is known in its own law of movement and
understood as what is innermost in history itself. And the thinkers of German
Idealism are aware of themselves as necessary epochs in the history of absolute
Spirit.

Only since the philosophy of German Idealism is there a *history* of philosophy
in such a way that history itself is a path of absolute knowing on the way to itself.
History is now no longer what is past, what one is finished with and has dis-
carded, but it is the constant form of becoming of Spirit itself. In German
Idealism, history is understood metaphysically for the first time. Until then, it
was something inevitable and incomprehensible, a burden or a miracle, an error
or a purposeful arrangement, a witches' dance or a teacher of "life," but always
only something which was put together right out of daily experience and its
intentions.

5. IS A SYSTEM OF FREEDOM POSSIBLE? (ONTO-THEO-LOGY. PRINCIPLES OF KNOWLEDGE).

For the thinkers of German Idealism, "system" is not a framework for the stuff
of knowledge; it is also not a "literary task"; it is not the property and product of
an individual; it is also not just a "heuristic" makeshift—system is the totality of
Being in the totality of its truth and the history of the truth. From here, we can
more or less get an idea of what an upheaval attended the attempts at system
when the question of the system of freedom was raised, when the question was
asked whether freedom, which is in a way groundless and breaks out of every
connection, must not be the center of system in general and how it could be this.
Who does not see that this question intrinsically already moves toward a denial of
system? Who does not see that, if system is nevertheless retained, above all,
further steps must be defined as to whether and how something like the "system of
freedom" has a meaning at all, is internally possible? We now want to examine how
Schelling tests this inner possibility of the system of freedom in the introduction to

his treatise and we want first to follow what he says in the general introduction of this introduction with regard to system.

With this we have arrived at our fourth preparatory question and at the same time at the train of thought of the treatise itself again (pp. 7-9).

Regarding (4): what was treated in the previous three points can make the understanding of what follows easier for us and, above all, make the direction of Schelling's questioning clearer.

The previous train of thought was that human freedom is a fact. The conceptual determination of this fact is dependent upon the foundation of the concept in terms of system. Both definition of the concept and systematic determination are one, especially when freedom is "one of the ruling centers of the system." But precisely here difficulties arise. A system of freedom appears to be impossible from both sides. There are two fundamental difficulties: (1) either system is retained, then freedom must be relinquished; or (2) freedom is retained, which means renunciation of system. The first difficulty, insisting on system in opposition to freedom, is first distanced by Schelling by saying that as long as it isn't decided what "freedom" is supposed to mean, the objection is without foundation. The discussion of the second difficulty begins:

> Or, if the opinion be advanced that the concept of freedom contradicts the concept of system altogether and inherently, then it is extraordinary that some sort of system must be present and coexist with freedom at least in the divine understanding. For individual freedom in some manner or other has a place in the universe, it matters not whether this be thought of realistically or idealistically. (Pp. 7-8)

The "either" to which this "or" corresponds is not mentioned explicitly, but it is in fact intended when the first difficulty is stated.

The second difficulty conversely departs from the concept of freedom. If the latter is retained, system would have to be given up. Schelling discusses this objection more in detail. Why? Because it is based on the fact of freedom. For it might appear that we could under some circumstances let go of the requirement of the system and give up system, but not freedom and its factuality. Thus, if freedom is retained, cannot and must not system be denied, and indeed "in general and in itself"? System cannot be denied since it itself is necessarily posited with the positing of the fact of human freedom. How so? If the freedom of the individual really exists, this means that it exists in some way together with the totality of the world. And just this existential coexistence, *systasis*, is what the concept and the word system itself mean.

Insofar as any individual being exists, there must be a system. For an individual existing for itself is something whch sets itself off from something else and thereby posits the others *along with* itself. We can turn the thought into something fundamental—some system *must* exist if there is anything existing for itself at all. System "in general and in itself" cannot be denied insofar as beings are posited at all. Where there are beings, there is jointure and joining.

We can already see here the sameness of Being and jointure shining through. Insofar as we understand "Being" at all, we mean something like jointure and joining. The oldest saying of Western philosophy handed down to us, that of Anaximander, already speaks of *dike* and *adikia*, of the jointure and disjointure* of Being. Here we must keep at a distance all moral and legal and even Christian ideas about justice and injustice.

But if system is not to be denied as such because it belongs to the nature of beings themselves, then it must at least be present, because it is there first of all, in the ground of all Being, in the "primal being," in God.

In the last hour we returned once more to the course of the treatise again.

We wanted to characterize the interim question about "system," its origins and development, up to German Idealism. That occurred by contrasting concepts of philosophy in Kant and in German Idealism. What German Idealism understands as philosophy is just Kant's concept thought through to the end in one direction. "To think through to the end" does *not* mean merely to add on what is lacking, but to know and grasp a prefigured whole in its prefiguration from the very basis and more primordially.

The knowing "of" the Absolute is ambiguous.

The absolute is neither "object" nor "subject."

Absolute knowing in which Being comes to itself is true knowing.

History itself becomes a path of absolute knowing to itself.

For the first time, history is here conceived metaphysically.

The double difficulty in the system of freedom was hinted at. Schelling attempts to show its possible solution by saying that "some kind of system must be present, at least in the divine understanding, with which freedom is consistent."

With this, however, a "theological" turn seems to enter the idea of system. But after what we have said about the origin of system in the modern period, we shall not be surprised at this. God is the leading idea of system in general. But when we speak here of "theological" and "theology" we must remember that the word and concept "theology" did not first grow in the framework and service of an ecclesiastical system of faith, but within philosophy. There is relatively late evidence of the word *theologia,* for the first time in Plato: *mythologia;*[11] this word does not occur at all in the New Testament.

Every philosophy is theology in the primordial and essential sense that comprehension *(logos)* of beings as a whole asks about the ground of Being, and this ground is called *theos,* God. Nietzsche's philosophy, too, for example, in which an essential sentence states "God is dead" is in accordance with this sentence

**Fug and *Unfug*—TRANS.*

"theology." But one should never appraise the theology in philosophy according to some dogmatic ecclesiastical theology; that is, one must especially not think that philosophical theology is only the rational, Enlightenment form of ecclesiastical theology. The assertion often heard of late that modern philosophy is simply a secularization of Christian theology is only true very conditionally and also true only in being restricted to adopting the realms of Being. Rather, the reverse is true that Christian theology is the Christianization of an extra-Christian philosophy and that only for this reason could this Christian theology also be made secular again. All theology of faith is possible only on the basis of philosophy, even when it rejects philosophy as the work of the devil. Moreover, little is said with such fad sentences like "philosophy is secular theology" and "theology is applied philosophy." In order to say something true, so many restrictions are needed that it is better not to make such statements.

At this point in the treatise where the concept of the "divine understanding" turns up for the first time and is called the primal being, it was advisable to refer to the concept of theology primordially belonging to philosophy—all the more advisable since the treatise on freedom essentially moves within the realm of this primordial theo-logy of Being. To repeat, theo-logy means here questioning beings as a whole. This question of beings as a whole, the theological question, cannot be asked without the question about beings as such, about the essence of Being in general. That is the question about the *on he on,* "ontology."

Philosophy's questioning is always and in itself both onto-logical and theological in the very broad sense. Philosophy is *Ontotheology.* The more originally it is both in one, the more truly it is philosophy. And Schelling's treatise is thus one of the most profound works of philosophy because it is in a unique sense ontological and theological *at the same time.*

on

he

beings as such   beings as a whole

on   theion

logos

We shall return to our train of thought. If the freedom of man, and that means of every individual man, exists, then with this existence something is posited in which and in opposition to which the individual individualizes itself, with which it exists together in the totality of Being: a system in general. System must at least lie in the primal being and ground of Being quite apart from the manner in which this ground of Being is related to beings as a whole. But when the inevitability of system is barely guaranteed, new difficulties appear. Schelling names and discusses *two* of them: (1) one can admit system in the primal being, but then state that it is inaccessible for human knowledge. This amounts to saying *there is* "for us" no system; (2) in an abbreviated procedure, one can simply deny "system" in the will and understanding of the primal being, too. What does Schelling say regarding (1)?

> The general statement that this system can never be revealed to human insight again means nothing at all. For it may be true or false according to how it is interpreted, depending on the definition of the principle by virtue of which man can in any wise attain knowledge. The assumption that such knowledge is possible may be characterized in the words of Sextus about Empedocles: the literally minded and the uninformed may imagine that the claim to have this knowledge arises from boastfulness and a sense of superiority towards others, qualities which should be foreign to anyone who has had even a slight training in philosophy. But whoever takes the theory of physics as his point of departure and knows that the doctrine "like is recognized by like" is a very ancient one (supposed to come from Pythagoras but found in Plato and declared long before by Empedocles)—such a one will understand that the philosopher maintains the existence of this (divine) knowledge, because he alone comprehends the god outside himself through the god within himself by keeping his mind pure and unclouded by evil. But, alas, those who are unsympathetic toward science, traditionally regard it as a kind of knowledge which is quite external and lifeless like conventional geometry. (P. 8).

Just as the assertion that system as such excludes freedom doesn't say anything if it is not decided what "system" means, the assertion that system in God is inaccessible to human "insight" remains a vain and empty assertion as long as we do not clarify what "insight" and "knowledge" are to mean. But according to Schelling, the question of the nature of human knowledge can *only* be answered by way of determining "the principle" "with which man knows in general." What does that mean?

How can and why must human knowledge have a principle? How can this principle be determined? Knowing is a way in which truth is developed and acquired. We call the preservation of truth knowledge. But not all knowledge arises from cognition, and all cognition is certainly not scientific cognition. Cognition is *one* way. Truth is the manifestness of beings themselves. In keeping with the context we shall restrict ourselves to the acquisition of truth in the sense of cognition. The definition of truth as the overtness of beings, however, implies that truth, and thus the appropriation of truth, too, varies with the type of being, according to that being's Being. But the *kind* of truth (manifestness of beings) does not only depend on the currently revealed being itself. We cannot go into this now. The unfolding of the manifestness of beings is only possible at all if man stands in a relation to beings. And this relation of man to beings which he himself is *not* must again be different according to the type of Being of that being. On the other hand, this relation of man to beings must constitute something essential for man's own being provided that the development of truth and its preservation do not represent anything arbitrary for him, if indeed cognition and knowing belong to the nature of human being. The relation of man to beings is not the consequence of his cognitions, but, rather conversely, it is the determining ground of the possibility of any cognition at all. This ground is really that in which cognition is grounded, from which it grows, where it "begins," the principle, the determining ground.

The way man has cognition and the decision about what he takes cognition to be and the order of rank of different kinds of cognition, all of this is only determined by the way in which the determining ground of knowledge, the principle, is itself determined, the way in which the relation of man to beings is conceived in advance. How man as existent stands in relation to beings as a whole, is contained in this fundamental relation, how difference and agreement, how the strife and the harmony of the being which he is not and of the being which *he himself* is are determined. Schelling says, "It is a matter of the determination of the principle by which man knows in general." According to our interpretation, this means it is a matter of the determination of the relation of man to beings, a matter of naming this relation in general, of accepting it *as* the ground of the possibility of knowledge and of *expressly* taking it over. With this version of the principle of cognition, knowing and truth in general, and with the version accordingly oriented of the task of a determination of the principle of knowledge in particular, we are, however, already going beyond Schelling and the whole previous treatment of this task as far as the form goes. (The grounding of Da-*sein*.) The principle of knowledge means in general the determining ground for the possibility and manner of the relation of man to beings contained in knowing. The determining ground, the principle, can only be something which supports and guides this relation from the very ground.

Schelling himself does not develop the question about the principle of knowledge as a question at all in this passage. But he does in the central part of the treatise, although here again not explicitly, but still in a way that we are able to connect internally what is said there with the statement touched upon now of the principle of human knowledge. In the central part of the treatise on *human* freedom, Schelling must deal namely with the question of *what* man *is* in relation to beings as a whole, what this relation is and what this relation of *one* of the beings (man) in the whole means for beings. Let us now just point ahead to a later passage of the treatise. Schelling says, "In man there exists the whole power of the principle of darkness and, in him too, the whole force of light. In him there are both centers—the deepest pit and the highest heaven. Man's will is the seed—concealed in eternal longing—of God, present as yet only in the depths—the divine light of life locked in the depths which God divined when he determined to will nature" (p. 38).

To understand this passage means to comprehend the whole treatise. But this comprehension means to encounter the incomprehensible. The incomprehensible, however, is not to be understood as a confused twilight and flowing chaos, but as a clear limit and veil. Only *he* really has the inexplicable who stands completely in what is clear; but not the muddleheaded nor he who makes a principle and a refuge out of the "irrational" before he has understood the rational and has been driven by it to the borderline.

In the sense of the preparatory presentations of the introduction, Schelling is content simply to name this principle of knowledge instead of developing the question of that principle. And he names it, calling upon "a quite ancient doctrine" *(archaion holos to dogma).* It reads briefly: *tois homoiois ta homoia gignoskesthai,* like is known by like. Here Schelling quotes a passage from Sextus (Empiricus) (ca. A.D. 150). He belongs to the philosophical orientation of later skepticism, and dealt with the earlier dogmatic philosophers in this sense, quoting many passages from their writings. Since these writings, especially those of the oldest Greek philosophers, are lost to us, the essentially later critical writings of Sextus are a valuable mine and source of the history of tradition. But, intrinsically, the writings, too, are important and not acknowledged nearly as much as they deserve.

Among these writings there is one with the title, *Pros mathematikous,* Against the mathematicians. The word still has here the original meaning: *mathema,* what is teachable and learnable.

Mathematicians are those who teach the fundamental doctrines, the foundations of all cognition and knowing: the grammarians; rhetoricians; teachers of geometry, arithmetic, astronomy, and music, of everything that was still also known in the Middle Ages as the *septem artes liberales,* the seven liberal arts. Art, *ars, techne* has nothing to do with our concept of "art," but means cognition and knowing, that which is initially necessary to know and find one's way in things at all. Mathematicians are the teachers of the fundamental school. They all tend to treat just what they are teaching as what is solely and primarily essential. They are dogmaticians from the very beginning. They claim to be able to do everything and thus, also, efface the borders between everything. One needs *skepsis* with regard to them—to check, to look at the borders. (Skeptics are for us like the doubters who doubt for the sake of doubting. But they are really those who test.) In the skeptic's writing, "Against the Mathematicians," we find among others a treatise "Against the Grammarians." Schelling quotes the passage from this treatise *Pros grammatikous* (ed. Fabricius) and gives a literal translation in his text.

We cannot go into this passage of Sextus and its context any further (compare *Pros Logikous* lib. VII p. 338-89, ed. Fabricius 1718); in addition, it would not help to clarify our question. The train of thought in Sextus shows that the grammarian is not *pansophos,* that he could not have a corresponding factual knowledge of everything. True, the grammarian's object, the word and precisely words, is related to *all* beings in that all beings are expressed in words. But these *beings as a whole* which language refers to are not exclusively knowable through language and as language in the grammatical sense.

Thus, the grammarian cannot be taken for a philosopher because he is incapable of thinking the totality of beings, that is, incapable of conceiving, let alone replacing, the *principle* of all knowledge in general with his grammatical criteria of knowledge. The highest principle of knowledge is *tois homoiois ta homoia gignoskesthai*. Like is known (only) by like. Now if the object of knowledge in philosophy is beings as a whole, and thus *the ground* of beings, *to theion*, the philosopher as he who knows must stand in what is similar to that which he knows: *to en heautō theō ton ektos katalambanein*, "to comprehend the god outside himself with the god within himself." Knowledge with such a "principle," in short, "such knowledge," viewed from the perspective of the grammarian and measured with the criteria of the *idiotes*, the unknowing, is "boasting and arrogance."

Like everyone who becomes rigid in his own field, the grammarian is blind in a double sense. First of all, he is completely unable to understand the general principle of knowledge (like by like) with his criteria. Second, and in consequence, he is also unable to understand why another kind of knowledge than his can, yes, must, have a transformed principle. Physicists often carelessly say something like "What art historians do is a nice game, but not 'science.' " Conversely, he who has to do with poetic works and the writings of peoples thinks "What physicists and chemists do is really only the production of airplanes and hydrogen bombs, but not essential knowledge." Neither understands the other because neither is capable of coming to *one* original foundation with the other where they understand the manner and necessity of the transformation of *their* own principle in terms of the *fundamental principle*. Neither understands the other in terms of his principle because neither is in any way capable of knowing what a principle is. Schelling does not pursue the history of the principle further and only quotes what Sexus says. The latter, too, refers finally to Empedocles from whom he quotes the following verse (Diels Frg. 109):

> *gaiei men gar gaian opopamen, hudati d'hudor,*
> *aitheri d'aithera dion, atar puri pur aidelon,*
> *storgen de storgei, neikos de te neikei lugroi.*

> For by earth we see earth, but by water water,
> By air, however, divine air, by fire finally destructive fire,
> But love by love, strife, however, by miserable strife.

Here one remembers at the same time the Platonic-Plotinian: *Ou gar an popote eiden ophthalmos helion, helioeides me gegenemenos*. "For the eye could not see the sun if if were not itself 'sun-like!' " In the introduction to his *Farbenlehre* (1810), Goethe reminds us explicitly of the old principle of knowledge and puts it into the familiar verse:

> "If the eye were not sun-like
> How could we look at light?

If God's own power didn't live in us
How could we be delighted by the god-like?"

We return to Schelling's train of thought. System is not to be denied. But it can probably be said that it is only in the divine understanding. An objection occurs to this that it is inaccessible to human knowledge. But to say this means to say nothing as long as it is not established which knowledge is meant and according to what principle it is to be determined. However, Schelling evidently wants something more in rejecting this objection. He wants to name explicitly the principle which is to play a part in his philosophcial treatise: the god outside of us is known through the god within us. We shall see to what extent Schelling grounds this principle explicitly for philosophy and, above all, to what extent he explains and is able to explain the more general and fundamental principle "like is known only by like."

In contrast to Kant's concept of philosophy, the philosophical kind of knowledge in the sense of German Idealism was called "the intellectual intuition of the Absolute" according to its own terminology. We can now connect this version of philosophical knowledge with the *principle* of philosophical knowledge by saying we know only what we intuit. We intuit only what we are; we are only that to which we belong. (But this belonging *is* only by our bearing witness to it. This bearing witness, however, only occurs as Da-*sein*, human *being*.) If one views philosophical knowledge from the perspective of everyday familiarity and calculation, it can be said of philosophy: whoever wants to know in it and in accordance with it must "step back into the god." To merely be exclusively familiar with something is not knowing. "*The* science," that is, philosophy, cannot be measured by some remote and lifeless kind of knowledge, however useful it may be.

"But, alas, those who are unsympathetic towards science traditionally regard it as a kind of knowledge which is quite external and lifeless like conventional geometry."

The mere assertive reliance upon the unknowabililty of the divine primal being cannot shatter the basis of system in God.

However, there is a second way out.

A simpler and more decisive course would be to deny that system exists even in the will or mind of the Primal Being, and to declare that after all there are only individual wills, each being a center for itself and, in Fichte's phrase, each Ego being the absolute substance. However, reason which strives towards unity, as well as the emotional assurance of freedom and personality, is ever denied just by an arbitrary assertion which prevails for a while but at last gives way. Thus Fichte's doctrine was obliged to bear testimony to Unity even if only in the inadequate form of a moral order in the world; but by so doing it immediately fell into contradictions and untenable assertions. (PP. 8-9)

Schelling cites Fichte's doctrine for the denial of system in the divine Primal Being, and thus for system in general. This reference to Fichte is too general and incomplete in this form to exhaust the question of system in Fichte's philosophy, above all in its diverse transformations. Of course, Schelling often argued with Fichte (compare *Treatises on the Explanation of Idealism in the Doctrine of Science. 1796/7*, reprinted in *Philosophische Schriften*, 1809, p. 201-340;[12] *Darlegung des wahren Verhältnisses der Naturphilosophie zu der verbesserten Fichteschen Lehre*, 1806, I, VII, p. 1 ff.). What Schelling wants to point out and may also justifiably point out is that in Fichte, the determination of freedom, as well as the unity of reason, is forced into a definite path by *imperatives*. What one thought one had denied came back in another form, only hidden and unfounded. The infinite action of morality was supposed to raise the Ego as a deed of action *(Tathandlung)* to the highest principle. But at the same time, this exclusion of every other order became again the beginning of the *moral* world order as the order of Being in general. Here we can pass over the relation of Schelling's and Fichte's doctrine all the more since Schelling's treatise on freedom moves on a foundation that is quite foreign to Fichte especially. In another respect, namely for the development of Schelling's beginning system, Fichte is of essential importance, above all as a negative impulse, as something *from which* Schelling recoiled.

6. THE INEVITABILITY OF THE QUESTION ABOUT THE SYSTEM OF FREEDOM

Schelling concludes the introduction to his introduction with three important statements:

1. Certain reasons for the incompatibility of freedom with system can be cited from previous philosophy. But historical references, taken by themselves, don't get any further with the question about the possibility and the essence of the system of freedom. This can only be attained if the question of the compatibility of system and freedom is developed *in terms of the matter itself*, and a foundation is thus gained for its decision. Then the historical recollection, too, gets its driving force and inner justification.

2. The task in question, the founding of the connection of freedom with the world totality, is the primordial impulse to philosophy in general, its hidden ground. The question of the system of freedom is not only an "object" of philosophy, it is also not only the true and comprehensive object, but is in advance and at bottom and finally the *condition* of philosophy, the open contradiction *in* which it stands and which it brings to *stand*, brings about again and again. As a highest willing of the Spirit, philosophy is *intrinsically* a will to self-transcendence, confronting the boundaries of beings which it transcends by questioning beyond beings through the question of Being itself. With the truth of Being, philosophy wants out into the open, and yet remains tied to the necessity of

beings. Philosophy is intrinsically *a strife between necessity and freedom*. And in that it belongs to philosophy as the highest knowledge to know itself, it will produce from itself this strife and thus the question of the system of freedom.

Just as little as the poetry of the poet is the thinking of the thinker merely the course of "experiences" in an individual man in the occurrence of which then certain experiences (works) get isolated. Where they are essential, thinking and writing poetry are a *world occurrence*, and this not only in the sense that something is happening within the world which has significance for the world, but also in the sense in which and through which the world itself arises anew in its actual origins and rules as world. Philosophy can never be justified by taking over and rework-ing a realm of what is knowable, some area or even all areas, and delivering things that are knowable from this, but only by opening more primordially the essence of the *truth* of what is knowable and discoverable in general and giving a *new path* and a *new horizon* to the relation to beings in general. Philosophy arises, *when* it arises, from a fundamental law of Being itself. Schelling wants to say we are not philosophizing *"about"* necessity and freedom, but philosophy is the most alive *"And,"* the unifying strife between necessity and freedom. He doesn't just "say it," *he enacts* this in the treatise.

3. And finally Schelling points out that to renounce truly thinking out the possibility of system amounts to avoiding the matter. Considering the impen-etrability of the essence of freedom, the appeal to what is incomprehensible gives the illusion of *being* the true relation to the matter. But this appeal to the irrational always remains a cowardly flight as long as the shrinking back is not conditioned and demanded by truly not getting any further on the path of the concept. Only on the foundation of the highest exertion of the concept and of questioning does the confession of not knowing receive its justification. Otherwise, the converse appeal that everything is explicable according to one and the same rule without opposition is just as justified as veering off into the irrational. In short, both kinds of behavior and procedure avoid the true task and difficulty. We must first find and guarantee, in general, the right basis on which the strife between necessity and freedom can be conceived, developed, and carried out as a real one.

What was emphasized in these three points in an intensified way is only generally hinted at in Schelling. That is often his style. Only seldom do we find that idiosyncratic element of Hegel's style where everything is driven out to the hardness and dominancy of an idiosyncratic stamp whose ground, of course, is not the obsessive search for the particular, but the inner necessity of one's own way of seeing and knowing. Schelling does not completely lack this, on the contrary—but at the same time, he is striving to present his knowledge in this noncommittal commitment. For this reason, his interpretation must and can often overshoot the mark without running the danger of arbitrary interpretation.

Much as may be adduced from a merely historical consideration of previous systems in support of the contention that freedom and systematic unity are incompatible, we have now here found arguments derived from the nature of reason and knowledge themselves. Hence, it seems that the connection between the concept of freedom and a total world view will always remain the subject of an inevitable problem which, if it is not solved, will leave the concept of freedom ambiguous and philosophy, indeed, totally without value. For this great problem alone constitutes the unconscious and invisible mainspring of all striving for knowledge from the lowest to the highest. Without the contradiction of necessity and freedom, not only philosophy, but every nobler ambition of the spirit would sink to that death which is peculiar to those sciences in which that contradiction serves no function. To withdraw from the conflict by forswearing reason looks more like flight than victory. Another person would have the same right to turn his back on freedom in order to throw himself into the arms of reason and necessity without there being any cause for self-congratulation on either side. (P. 9)

There is an unmistakable proof that Schelling in this transitional passage to the introduction arrives at something decisive.

In our passage, Schelling names the opposition of system and freedom, with whose development and unification he is concerned, in the version of the "contradiction of necessity and freedom." This formulation of opposition is not new as far as it reads, and yet it has a special sound for Schelling, which can be detected in the beginning of the foreword (p. 3) which we have purposely avoided thus far and turn to now.

> Since reason, thought, and knowledge are ordinarily accounted distinctive to the realm of Spirit, the contrast of Nature and Spirit was at first readily taken up in these terms. This way of looking at the matter was adequately justified by the firm belief that reason is found only in man, the conviction that all thought and knowledge are completely subjective and that Nature altogether lacks reason and thought, together with the universally prevalent mechanistic attitude. Even the dynamic factor which Kant revived again passed over into a higher mechanism and was in no sense recognized in its identity with the Spiritual. Now that the root of this old contrast has been dislodged, we may implant a sounder insight that may confidently be entrusted to generally work towards better understanding.
>
> The time has come for the higher distinction, or, rather, for the real contrast to be made manifest, the contrast between Necessity and Freedom in which alone the innermost center of philosophy comes to view. (P. 3).

These few sentences characterize the fundamental movement of the history of the question of freedom in modern philosophy from Descartes to German Idealism. We shall now just point out the main idea. For a long time, freedom has been considered the privilege of Spirit. It has no place in the field of nature. In this respect, freedom bcomes the characteristic of the opposition between nature and Spirit. This opposition is formulated by Descartes as that of mechanical nature, that is, extension, and thinking, *res extensa* and *res cogitans*. There is nothing of Spirit and reason in nature. It is the mere realm of the local motion of mass points. But Spirit itself is the *"I"* as "I think," "subject." Now in that freedom explicitly enters consciousness and becomes a question, as a fact of self-experience it is a determination of Spirit as "*I* think."

According to the opposition set up, as egolike, freedom has what is foreign and other to itself in nature as mechanical nature. Thus, in Kant the question of freedom is still formulated as the opposition of *nature and freedom*. Here one should, however, note that in Leibniz nature is precisely not conceived as the complete lack of reason of what is merely extended (as in Descartes and Spinoza), and the dynamical is also not conceived as something mechanical; but, rather, the reverse. To what extent Leibniz still remains stuck in the opposition of nature and freedom, and Schelling is correct in not naming Leibniz here, will be shown later on.

Schelling now says that it is time "for the higher or rather the true opposition to come forth, that of necessity and freedom." This is at the same time the innermost center of philosophy, that which the whole treatise is aiming for. A "higher opposition"—what does that mean? The opposition is not only different because necessity replaces nature, not only one member of the opposition is different, but the oppositionality itself, that is, freedom especially is different, conceived more primordially. The opposition as a whole is different; it has another basis and another horizon. The root of the earlier opposition "nature and freedom" is "torn up."

This means that nature is not something absolutely spirit-less and, above all, freedom is not something absolutely nature-less, the mere egoity of the "I can." Thus, the members of the earlier distinction "nature and Spirit" become more related, nature becomes spiritlike and Spirit becomes naturelike, and the opposition seems to dissolve in a compensation. True, *this* opposition dissolves;—but *the* opposition in which freedom now stands—becomes at the same time more essential and profound. Now it is no longer a matter of understanding human freedom as distinguished from nature. As long as this is the intention, thought's effort moves in the direction of showing that man's freedom consists in his independence of nature. Beyond that, however, and above all, the much more essential and far more difficult task is to understand man's inner independence of God. With this line of questioning, freedom slips out of the opposition to nature. The opposition into which freedom now comes is generally lifted out of the level of nature (in its previous sense) up to the relational realm of man and God. But, however it may be determined, the ground of beings as a whole is the *unconditioned* and, viewed from the standpoint of beings, the highest necessity. Not nature and freedom, but "the contradiction of necessity and freedom" in the sense discussed is now the real question.

If this is so, then we must create a much broader basis, the broadest there is for the question of freedom, and we must make it clear that the previous distinctions and their foundation are no longer sufficient. But that means at the same time that the question of the place of freedom in the whole of beings, the question of the system, needs completely new principles. Until now, the realm of system was articulated by the distinction of the realms of nature and freedom. And, accordingly, philosophy divided itself, still with Kant, into a metaphysics of nature and a metaphysics of morality (freedom). And the highest systematical task consisted in mediating between both realms as something immovable. Freedom was discussed only in the realm of practical reason and as something theoretically incomprehensible. Now we must show that freedom rules in all realms of beings, but leads to a unique crisis in man and thus demands a new structure of beings as a whole. The realm of system needs a new outline and articulation.

To show the necessity of such a foundation-shattering transformation of the question is the real intention of our introduction beginning now. To this purpose, the question of system must now be formulated more definitely. And the question takes its definiteness from the decided orientation toward the opposition of *necessity and freedom*. Behind this opposition, however, or already *in* this opposition stands the question of man's freedom in opposition to the ground of beings in general, in traditional language: to God. The question of God and the totality of the world, the question of "theism" in the broadest sense, appears.

B. Interpretation of the Introduction to Schelling's Treatise (pages 9–31)

1. THE QUESTION OF THE SYSTEM AND PANTHEISM

We saw previously:

1. The apparent incompatibility of freedom and system cannot be clarified by historical recollections. It must be decided in terms of the matter itself.

2. This strife between freedom as the beginning which needs no ground and system as a closed foundational context is, understood correctly, the inmost motive and law of motion of philosophy itself. Not only the object, but the state of philosophy.

3. The decision about this strife must neither flee the irrational nor rigidify in a boundless rationalism: the matter must prescribe its own kind of procedure. *The matter!* Thus, a more precise indication is necessary, a new formulation of the opposition.

It is important to notice that the previous formulation of the question of "system and freedom" now reads *necessity and freedom*. This is claimed as the more primordial and higher formulation of the question of freedom.

In Schelling's foreword to the treatise on freedom, he refers to what is insufficient in the formulation of the opposition, traditional since Descartes, "nature and Spirit" (*res extensa, res cogitans;* mechanism, I think) which was not yet overcome by Kant either.

Schelling refers to the identity of nature and Spirit. Thus, freedom can no longer be understood as independence of nature, but must be understood as independence in opposition to God. The opposition: necessity and freedom is a higher opposition by means of which the question of the system of freedom gains a new basis, and a new kind of questioning is gained which is to be formulated more definitely.

The real introduction begins: "The same argument has been more pointedly expressed in the sentence, pantheism is the only possible system of reason, but it is inevitably fatalism" (pp. 9–10).

62

The difficulty with regard to the system of freedom is now brought to a definite formulation. The leading statement quoted contains two sentences. (1) The system is intrinsically, as system, pantheism; (2) pantheism is fatalism, the denial of freedom. The two statements can also be stated more clearly: (1) the principle of the formation of system is, in general, a definite interpretation of *theos*, of the ground of beings, a theism in the sense of pantheism; (2) precisely this principle of the formation of system in general, pantheism, demands the inevitability of all occurrence on account of the unconditionality of the ground ruling everything.

If the question of freedom as the question of man's freedom as opposed to the world ground is developed, the system of freedom is completely impossible. For (1): system as system is pantheism; (2) pantheism is fatalism. The crux around which everything turns is "pantheism". The two assertions, the system, as such, is pantheism and pantheism is fatalism, can only be decided as to their truth when we have previously clarified what *pantheism* means.

Now this clarification is actually the external theme of the following introduction. But we must not get caught in the external form of the introduction. We must ask what is in back of this discussion of pantheism. Answer: the fundamental question of the principle, the ground of determination and possibility of system as such. This question is explicated in a series of partial questions which we shall take up in the following order: Is pantheism in general *the* principle of system? And, if so, how? What is the real ground, the ground supporting and determining system in pantheism? Is pantheism as pantheism always also necessarily fatalism? Or is it only a special interpretation of pantheism which excludes freedom? Is that which finally constitutes the real system-forming principle in pantheism at the same time that which does not exclude freedom from the system at all, but even requires it?

For the understanding of the introduction and, thus, the whole treatise in its core, it is, however, of decisive importance to see the question of pantheism through this series of questions. But see through *in what direction?* To gain clarity we shall ask quite simply what does it really mean that Schelling is looking for the principle of the formation of system guided by the question of pantheism? To get an adequate answer, we have to enlarge our scope. That will also serve the purpose of clarifying the direction and claim of our interpretation of Schelling's treatise and placing it in the task of philosophy today.

System is the structure of beings as a whole. This structure knows itself as absolute knowledge. This knowledge itself belongs to system. Knowledge, too, constitutes the inner connectedness of beings. Knowledge is not just an opportunity which sometimes comes to beings, as one might think from the perspective of everyday things. As a developed jointure and a joined connection, Being and the knowledge of Being are the same, they belong together. But how is the jointure of Being determined? What is the law, and what is the fundamental way of the jointure of Being? What is the "principle" of the system? What else besides Being itself? The question of the principle of the formation of system is thus the question in what does the essence of Being consist, in what does Being have its truth? And that is the question in which realm something like Being can become manifest at all and how it preserves this openness for itself and preserves itself in the openness.

We call the "meaning" of Being *the truth* of Being, that which makes Being in its essence open at all and thus comprehensible. And this question is *the* fundamental question of philosophy in general as long as philosophy *is* as the question of what beings are (the fundamental question on whose *foundation* we stand today). The question of the truth of Being is essentially more primordial than the question of Aristotle and later thinkers. Aristotle first made the question explicit which had always been asked by philosophy and forced it into the formulation of what beings as beings are. Herein lies the question of what constitutes Being in beings in general. He was only interested in the question of the Being of beings. And ever since, one has asked again and again about the Being of beings in this sense. That is evident for everyone who can see. But it is just as evident for him who *wants* to see that a *still* more primordial question is necessary—has become a need. We question further back for the truth of Being—not in order to question further at any price, but out of the insight and experience that the question of the Being of beings can never arrive at an adequate answer unless it is previously certain of the *truth* which is at all possible with regard to Being.

But because this question is strange and alienating, it cannot just be set up as a question, but at the same time a complete transformation of the question and point of view is necessary beforehand. And, for this reason, *Being and Time* is a *way* and not a shelter. Whoever cannot walk should not take refuge in it. *A* way, not "the" way, which never exists in philosophy.

True, until now the question of the truth of Being was not taken up and not understood at all. (One should not complain about this. But we want to be cognizant of the situation in order to know always what to do and, above all, what to leave alone). What is remarkable in such a situation is just that there has never been so much talk about "ontology" as today. Among these rather unfruitful discussions only two positions are worthy of notice. The first is that of Nicolai Hartmann, who is searching for the task and possibililty of ontology in an improvement of its previous mistakes. He does not see and does not ask on what basis previous metaphysics with its correct points together with its "mistakes" really rests. The other position is that of Karl Jaspers, who rejects the possibility of ontology in general because he also understands by ontology only what it has previously been taken for and which has remained a mechanical manipulation of rigidified concepts. The former mere revival and the latter mere rejection of previous ontology have the same basis: they fail to recognize the necessity and the kind of fundamental question about the truth of Being. And the reason for this failure lies in the fact that the dominant concept of truth nowhere gets beyond the concept of that truth which can, indeed, remain a foundation for the cognition of beings within certain limits, but never for the knowledge of Being.

Considering this, it is also not astonishing that the historical discussion with the great thinkers and systems stops right *before* the real question and, thus, never becomes a real discussion. Rather, it degenerates into mere rectification and grade-distributing or into a psychological interpretation of philosophy in terms of the philosopher's personality. On the one side, philosophy becomes a kind of specialized science, on the other, a unattached shifting around in concepts as mere signs. Each time the true and unique truth of philosophy is dodged. It is no wonder that philosophy becomes powerless when it, itself, believes that it can live on suicide.

The real question of beings, the primordial ontological question, is that of the essence of Being and the truth of this essence. And now we recognize that to search for the principle of the formation of system means to ask how a jointure is grounded in Being and how a law of jointure belongs to it, and that means to think about the essence of Being. Searching for the principle of the formation of system means nothing other than asking the real ontological question, at least striving toward it.

Now we saw that Schelling is looking for the principle of the formation of system following the lead of the question of pantheism. But the question of pantheism is the question of the ground of beings as a whole, more generally characterized as the theological question. Thus, it is clear—Schelling is driven back from the theological question by that question into the ontological question. To look through the discussions of the question of pantheism means to look into the questioning realm of the fundamental question of philosophy, into the question of the truth of Being. But this question, too, cannot remain by itself, it turns into the question of the Being of truth and of the ground, and this is again the theological question. We use these old terms because they are still most likely to show the primordial questioning realm of philosophy and always keep the tradition present.

$$
\begin{array}{ccc}
 & on & \\
 & he & \\
on & & theion \\
 & logos & \\
\end{array}
$$

But we reject the use of these terms when a commitment to previously customary "ontology" and philosophical theology is intended, whether affirmative or negative. "Ontology" never means for us a system, not a doctrine and a discipline, but only the question of the *truth* and the ground of *Being*, and "theology" means for us the question of the Being of the ground. What is essential is the inner connectedness of both questions. It is better to avoid such terms in general. All the more reason for us to stick to grasping what the matter itself requires. This is to be shown with the help of Schelling's treatise. Since its origin belongs to a past age, we may use older terms like ontology and theology for purposes of abbreviated agreement.

Thus we stated that the inner movement of questioning already starting with the introduction is a continuous playing back and forth between the theological question of the ground of beings as a whole and the ontological question of the essence of beings as such, an onto-theo-logy revolving within itself. Hegel's *Phenomenology of Spirit* is such an onto-theo-logy, only of a different kind; Nietzsche's plan for his main work, *The Will to Power*, is such an ontotheology, again of a different kind.

Only when we bring the text of the treatise together with the movement of this questioning of an ontotheology is there a justification and a necessity to deal with ontotheology. Now we know what the interpretation of the introduction must aim for.

The introduction begins at first in a quite external fashion. Like idealism, realism, criticalism, dogmatism (and), atheism, "pantheism" is a term which almost seems invented for the purpose of hiding the matter and making the position corresponding to the matter look suspicious. Schelling, speaking unmistakably about this, has already had difficulties in this respect and he is to meet up with them again soon after the treatise on freedom is published, in spite of it.

> It cannot be denied that it is a splendid invention to be able to designate entire points of view at once with such general epithets. If one has once discovered the right label for a system, everything else follows of its own accord and one is spared the trouble of investigating its essential characteristics in greater detail. Even an ignorant person can render judgment upon the most carefully thought out ideas as soon as they are presented to him with the help of such labels. But, after all, in an extraordinary assertion of this kind, everything depends upon the closer definition of the concept. (P. 10)

The "extraordinary assertion" is that pantheism as the sole possible form of the system is fatalism. This assertion was stated in a quite definite historical form in Schelling's time by F. H. Jacobi in his piece "On Spinoza's Doctrine in Letters to Mr. Moses Mendelssohn" (1785).[13] Jacobi wants to show here that pantheism is really Spinozism, Spinozism is fatalism, and fatalism is atheism. In this piece, Jacobi wants at the same time to make Lessing into a consistent atheist in this way, and to show in opposition to Mendelssohn, Herder, and Goethe that something like a "purified Spinozism," which they were striving for, was not possible. However, by equating pantheism and Spinozism, Jacobi was indirectly instrumental in newly asking and more sharply defining and answering the question of what pantheism is, and also in bringing the historical interpretation of

Spinoza to other paths. To avoid a misunderstanding here, we must emphasize that Spinoza's philosophy cannot be equated with Jewish philosophy. Alone the familiar fact that Spinoza was evicted from the Jewish community is significant. His philosophy is essentially determined by the spirit of the time, Bruno, Descartes, and medieval scholasticism.

Jacobi himself did not learn anything and did not want to learn anything from the new reflection on pantheism which he had inspired and to which Schelling contributed much that was essential. On the contrary, two years after Schelling's treatise on freedom, Jacobi published a work which unambiguously, but without naming names, repeated the old assertions against Schelling. The work is entitled "On Divine Things and Their Revelation," 1811 (WW III, 245 ff.). Without delay, Schelling answered the next year in a polemical work entitled: "F. W. J. Schelling's Monument to the Work on Divine Things, etc., by Mr. Friedrich Heinrich Jacobi and the Accusation Made in It against Him of an Atheism Purposely Deceiving and Speaking Lies," 1812 (WWI. Abt. VIII, 19 ff.). The title page bears a motto from Spinoza which reads: *Eh, proh dolor! res eo jam pervenit, ut, qui aperte fatentur, se Dei ideam non habere et Deum nullo modo cognoscere, non erubescant, Philosophos Atheismi accusare.* "Oh, what pain! We have now reached the point where those who openly admit that they have *no* idea of God and would not know God in *any* way, that *they* cannot help being stupid enough to accuse the philosophers of atheism." The sly, cunning baselessness of Jacobi's attack is rejected by this passage from Spinoza. One explains in one breath that there is nothing to know about God and that the philosophers are deniers of God. How can one accuse someone of denying God when one oneself explains that one can know nothing about God? Along with Lessing's polemical work, Schelling's polemic against Jacobi belongs to the most brilliant of this species in German literature. It had a corresponding effect. Jacobi was, as one says, "finished"—even with his friends.

At the same time, Schelling's polemic is a supplement to his treatise on freedom in that, as often happens, in the moves and countermoves of the dispute many thoughts become more clear than in the presentation of the matter itself which simply continues on.

But we shall no more go into the particulars of Schelling's controversy with Jacobi than we would go into Jacobi's battle with Mendelssohn, Herder, and Goethe, the controversy which one briefly names the "pantheism controversy." Shortly after Jacobi's work, "On the Doctrine of Spinoza," a statement of Herder's was published under the title "God! Some Conversations" (Gotha 1787). This piece plays a role, for example, in Schiller's correspondence with his friend, Körner. On Goethe's relation to Spinoza, one should compare: Dilthey *Gesammelte Schriften* II, 391 ff.: "From the time of Goethe's studies in Spinoza." This pantheism controversy is itself now easily followed with the aid of "Basic Writings on the pantheism controversy between Jacobi and Mendelssohn," edited with a historical and critical introduction by Heinrich Scholz (Reprints of rare philosophical works, edited by the Kantgesellschaft, Bd. VI. 1916).

2. VARIOUS POSSIBLE INTERPRETATIONS OF PANTHEISM

We are following the question of pantheism now only in the form of Schelling's question, with the intention of seeing what is in back of it as the real philosophical question. In its formal meaning, pantheism means: *pan-theos*, "Everything—God"; everything stands in relation to God; all beings are in relation to the ground of beings. This ground as the One, *hen is as* ground what everything else, *pan*, is in it, in the ground. *Hen kai pan.* The One is also the whole and the whole is also the One. (*Hen kai pan*, this followed Heraclitus's fragment *hen panta einai*, nr. 50, and was according to the spirit of the time the chosen motto of the three young Swabian friends, Schelling, Hegel, and Hölderlin.)

According to its form, pantheism means all beings, all things, are in God. This being—and remaining—within in God is called "immanence." All knowledge about the whole of beings must somehow think the whole in unity with its ground. Thus, every system somehow includes this immanence. Thus, Schelling says, "For it cannot be denied that if pantheism meant nothing but the doctrine of the immanence of all things in God, every rational view would have to adhere to this teaching in some sense or other. But just in what sense is the crucial question here" (p. 10).

With the title "pantheism," something is said only if it is specified in what respect this being-in of beings in God is meant. Accordingly, pantheism allows for various interpretations, among others doubtlessly the fatalistic one, too.

"That the fatalistic point of view can be combined with pantheism is undeniable; but that it is not essentially tied to it is made clear by the fact that many are driven to this pantheistic outlook *precisely because of the liveliest* sense of freedom" (p. 10).

Pantheism *can* be interpreted fatalistically, that is, as excluding freedom, but it does not have to. So little is this necessary that, on the contrary, it is precisely "the liveliest feeling of freedom" which makes us interpret beings pantheistically. With this, Schelling anticipates *in advance* the decisive thought of the introduction. Only the primordial feeling of human freedom allows us to have primordial feeling for the unity of all beings in and in terms of their ground at the same time. Thus we arrive at that connection which we already hinted at in interpreting the first sentence. Having a feeling for the fact of freedom includes a certain anticipation of the whole of beings, and this preliminary feeling for the whole of beings is determined by an anticipation of human freedom. And, for this reason, freedom is "one of the central points of the system."

When Schelling goes into the question of pantheism in detail in the course of his interest in the system of freedom, and in doing so places man's freedom in real opposition to the ground of being as a whole, he is not concerned with discussing the doctrinaire opinion of a world view. The question of the principle of the formation of the system stands behind the question of pantheism.

The question of system is the question of the jointure and joining of Being. What is called ontology today attaches itself to Aristotle's question of the *on he on* and misses the real fundamental question of the truth of Being. Both basic questions—the *on he on* and the *on he theion*—are in themselves quite different in their philosophical orientation. We can characterize their relation to each other by the term "onto-theo-logy."

The term "pantheism" was briefly explained, Schelling's pantheism controversy with F. H. Jacobi was discussed, and the appropriate publications referred to. If pantheism is understood as the immanence of things in God, a fatalistic interpretation is indeed possible, but not necessary, as Schelling emphasizes. For the primordial experience of freedom includes at the same time the experience of the unity of all beings in their ground.

Thus, if gaining a footing in human freedom drives one precisely to posit pantheism, then pantheism as such cannot include the denial of freedom. So if a denial of freedom arises within a pantheistic doctrine, that is not necessarily due to the doctrine being pantheistic, but rather due to the doctrine's misunderstanding of the essence of pantheism. If that is true, we must investigate in what the misunderstanding of the essence of pantheism consists, or expressed positively, in what the true essence of pantheism and its necessity is grounded.

Briefly stated, Schelling's anticipated assertion is that the most primordial, "innermost" feeling of freedom requires precisely pantheism. The fact that pantheism is required by such an experience of freedom already contains a certain interpretation ("explanation") of pantheism. For the time being, Schelling gives a first hint of this explanation of pantheism required by the "innermost feeling of freedom."

> Most people, if they were honest, would have to admit that in terms of their ideas, individual freedom seems to be in contradiction to almost all attributes of a Highest Being; omnipotence, for instance. In maintaining freedom, a power which by its nature is unconditioned is asserted to exist alongside of and outside the divine power, which in terms of their ideas is inconceivable. As the sun outshines all the other celestial lights in the firmament, so, but to a greater degree, infinite power extinguishes all finite power; Absolute causal power in one being leaves nothing but unconditional passivity for all the rest. Thus, there follows the dependence of all earthly creatures upon God, their very persistence being nothing but a constantly renewed creation in which the finite being is produced not as something generic and undetermined, but as this particular individual with such and such thoughts, desires, and actions and no others. To say that God restrains his omnipotence so that men can act, or that he permits freedom, explains nothing; for if God withdrew his power for an instant, man would

cease to be. Since freedom is unthinkable in opposition to omnipotence, is there any other escape from this argument than by placing man and his freedom in the divine being, by saying that man exists not outside God but in God, and that man's activity itself belongs to God's life? From this very point of view, mystics and religious temperaments in all ages have come to believe in the unity of man with God, a belief which seems to appeal to our inmost feelings as much as, or even more than, it does to reason and speculation. Scripture itself finds precisely in the consciousness of freedom the seal and earnest of the faith that we live and have our being in God. How can that very doctrine necessarily be in dispute with freedom which so many have asserted with regard to mankind for the particular purpose of saving freedom?" (Pp. 10–11)

Following this train of thought does not present any special difficulties. Schelling starts out with the idea of freedom which "most people" have. Accordingly, to be free means to be able to initiate an effect by oneself. I am free means I can begin an action of my own accord. As something initiating itself, conditioned only by itself, acting as "I act" is conditioned only by itself, thus *unconditioned* with relation to other things. One get a general feeling from this unconditioned ability as a "fact"; one counts on this ability generally. And, thus, it becomes a fact which also occurs along with other facts and which one also has a feeling of, like, for example, the fact that there is somehow a highest primal being. Some call it "God"; others say "the gods"; others called it "fate" or "predestination." Some are satisfied with this faith in predestination; others demand this faith to be witnessed in a system of faith and clarified in a solid doctrine. Still others keep away from both and salvage themselves in general doubt. But even here the feeling for the world ground becomes evident, for what good would doubt be if what is upsetting about what can be doubted did not constantly erupt? And so "one" has his human freedom, and this general predestination in a general feeling of Being, and appeals now to one or to the other.

"Most people, if they were honest"—that means if they really wanted to consider and think through what they are appealing to there—most people would then have to confess that incompatible elements are brought together in this general feeling of Being. Here man's own prowess, there the omnipotence of the primal being, here something unconditioned, and there something unconditioned. The question now is not only that through freedom—as the beginning which does not need grounding—the connection of grounding is interrupted, that through freedom a gap is placed in the course of events, but that human freedom now stands as something unconditioned in opposition to something else which is unconditioned, and moreover and on the other hand the latter claims to condition everything, including that unconditioned element of freedom. We have only to consider the whole of beings with some honesty in order to experience that we are constantly moving in a contradiction in this general, unclarified feeling of Being or, better yet, are avoiding it with a clouded look. If a highest primal being is posited, the question of master and slave is also decided. "Absolute causality in One Being only leaves unconditioned passivity for everything else." The unconditioned causality of the primal being annihilates our freedom. But this unconditioned causality of the primal being is not limited to the single action of creation, but also concerns the continuance of finite beings, their preservation which has been interpreted as continuous creation, *creatio continua*. It also does not help to take refuge in the piece of information that the primal being withdraws its omnipotence in the moment when man is supposed to act freely. How can man act freely if he *is* not previously as such, and how can he *be* if the primal being stops the preserving power even for a moment?

If man's generally predominant ideas of his own freedom and the existence of a primal being are taken out of fog and innocuousness with some honesty of thought, the following situation ensues. The unconditioned causality of the primal being demands unconditioned unfreedom of man. But in opposition to this demand stands the feeling of our own ability. However, if our freedom persists as something unconditioned, it stands in opposition to the unconditionedness of the primal being. Now if neither the primal being nor the fact of our freedom can be removed, if both thus are in general, the one with the other, and if thus this freedom of ours cannot absolutely be against the unconditionedness of the primal being, what "way out" is left but to realize that man cannot be "next to" (*praeter*), "outside of" (*extra*) God, that he cannot be against God but toward him and that he can only be this if he somehow belongs to the primal being; that is, he is *in* it. This immanence of things in God, that is, pan-theism, is required by the strife honestly experienced; that is, thought through, between human freedom and divine omnipotence.

This opposition becomes a strife only when man's own freedom is experienced and asserted, and the opposition becomes all the more sharp the more stubbornly the opposing members assert their nature. The more inward man's feeling of freedom, the more he feels himself to be existent, the less can he be posited as something nonexistent outside of beings as a whole, the more necessary remaining within these beings is, the more necessary pantheism is. But pantheism cannot mean now that everything nondivine gives itself up and is submerged in a general cloud of steam; rather, man's freedom is to be maintained, but at the same time taken into the Being of the primal being.

As *freedom,* man's freedom is something unconditioned. As *man's* freedom it is something finite. Thus, the question lying in the concept of human freedom is the question of a finite unconditionedness, more explicitly, of a *conditioned unconditionedness,* of a dependent independence ("derived absoluteness"). Where there is freedom, pantheism is required. Conversely, where there is pantheism, there is at least *not necessarily* unfreedom (fatalism); on the contrary, ultimately where pantheism correctly understood is posited, freedom is necessarily required.

This anticipatory explanation of a more primordial pantheism is taken up again only on page 17 and introduced into the real explanation of the treatise. In between (pp. 11–17), Schelling discusses three other explanations of pantheism. In rejecting them, he clears the way for a new interpretation. And since the term "pantheism" is only the theological formula for the question of the ground and jointure of beings as a whole, the question of the system with regard to the system of freedom is further clarified by this critical reflection. The "critique" is, however, as a genuine one at the same time positive; that is, it brings the matter to be treated newly into view and, thus, serves the leading intention of the whole introduction, to set right some "essential concepts."

Schelling then discusses three interpretations of pantheism. "Pantheism" can be defined in the sentence God is everything. The characteristic assertions of the three interpretations of pantheism present three different versions of this sentence. Briefly they are (1) Everything is God, (2) every individual thing is God, (3) all things are nothing.

In his critical discussion of these interpretations of pantheism, Schelling does not, however, so much wish to view certain doctrines according to their historical form, but to point out what is exemplary in this way of thinking. The fact that Spinoza is cited again and again precisely for the discussion of these versions of pantheism is no contradiction to this. We know that ever since the pantheism controversy, Spinoza's pantheism was taken for the classical kind and that wherever Spinozism was the topic, pantheism in general was intended. The fact that Schelling comes to correct the usual interpretations of Spinoza in the course of discussing forms of pantheism is remarkable, but not what is decisive.

The reason Schelling continually speaks of Spinoza and Spinozism is grounded, apart from considerations of his time, in a more far-reaching intention aiming at analyzing the question of freedom and the system of freedom. Schelling wants to show exactly with the example of Spinoza that it is not so much pantheism, nor its theology, but the "ontology" underlying it which entails the danger of fatalism, of the exclusion of freedom and its misunderstanding. From this follows, on the other hand, that this adequate "ontology" decides everything, first and above all, the right experience and feeling of the fact of freedom fundamental to the whole question of freedom. It is decisive for the primordiality of feeling how it is in tune with Being in general and as a whole as the fundamental mood of man's being-there (Da-sein).

We shall briefly follow Schelling's critical discussion of the forms of pantheism guided by the aforementioned "statements of pantheism" as we shall call them.

Regarding (1): *everything is God* (pp. 11–12). ("Another . . . explanation. . . .") What we call (1) Schelling calls "another" because he already relates the previously given interpretation to his kind of pantheism which, instead of excluding freedom, precisely requires it as an inner presupposition. Everything is God, that is, all individual things collected together are promptly equated with God. God is, so to speak, only their sum total; that is, God is really nothing. Schelling explicitly points out that if this is the meaning of the pantheistic doctrine, Spinoza is not a pantheist and cannot be one. For Spinoza especially separated finite things from the infinite ground. They are what they are only as beings in and according to an other, as consequences of the ground. To the contrary, something primordial can never be posited from a collective sum and a synthesizing of what is merely derived—even if its number were endless.

Regarding (2): *every individual thing is God* (p. 12). ("Still more preposterous . . . distinguishes them from God.") Schelling once (I, X, p. 45) calls this interpretation of pantheism the "commonest." Every body, every thing, is "a modified God." In this interpretation of pantheism, it is only a step further to equating it with the grossest fetishism of savages who choose an ostrich feather or a tooth as an object of reverence. In this "insipid" interpretation of pantheism, one fails to understand that already with the determination of a "modified," "derived" God, the god has been denied, and what is meant by this has been put back in the place of the finite thing.

Regarding (3): *all things are nothing* (pp. 15–16). ("Nonetheless . . . evaporate into nothing.) The idea contains the sentence "*God is everything*" which reverses (1) "*everything is God.*" But if all things are nothing, it is at least impossible to mix them up with God and uphold the first interpretation.

All three interpretations share the factor of falsely interpreting pantheism; that is, they leave no possibility for it at all and thus make fools of themselves. The first two interpretations of pantheism dissolve the concept of God so that there is no longer any support left to speak of pantheism in any sense, that is, of theism in general. The third interpretation removes all beings outside of God so that again, but from the reverse side, pantheism is impossible since everything is after all nothing. But the question is whether the sentence "everything is nothing" represents a necessary and the only possible consequence of the sentence "God is everything." In general, this sentence expresses pantheism more adequately than those previously mentioned.

The sentence "God is everything" is not so easily rejected as the sentence "everything is God," *pan-theos*. Pantheism in this latter sense does not capture pantheism in the sense of *theos-pan* which would better be called "theopanism." However, the real difficulties are just beginning. For it is simply not easy to show that if God is posited as the ground of the whole, God is *not* everything, that is, to show how anything which, after all, exists could be excluded from God.

But Schelling is not at all interested here in a factual discussion of these interpretations of pantheism. They get stuck in empty generalities and, what is decisive, they fail to recognize the real question which has to be clarified and answered if anything essential is to be determined about pantheism and the possibility of freedom in it as system.

3. PANTHEISM AND THE ONTOLOGICAL QUESTION (IDENTITY, DIALECTIC OF THE "IS")

The reason that pantheism is immediately misinterpreted in an undifferentiated, insipid, and impossible way in the forms cited and that the real question is not understood lies in the failure to recognize the *ontological* question, in Schelling's words (p. 13), "in the general misunderstanding of the law of identity or of the meaning of the copula in judgment."

Let us repeat the previous train of thought.

The question of pantheism is the question of the principle of the formation of a system. That, however, is the question of the essence of Being.

By an anticipatory reflection, Schelling unsettles the interpretation of pantheism as fatalism current in his time.

He tries to show that pantheism so little necessarily leads to the denial of freedom that, on the contrary, the primordial experience of freedom requires pantheism.

True, the predominant superficiality of thought usually prevents this step.

Superficial thinking is distinguished by the fact that it thinks incompatible things next to each other without looking at them, sometimes appealing to one, sometimes to the other. I am free—I can; freedom is unconditional. The ground of beings as a whole, too, is absolutely unconditional. An opposition prevails. But neither of what is opposed is to be relinquished in favor of the other; both are existent. What other recourse is there than to include freedom in the context of the ground? This is the general, formal concept of pantheism: "immanence." Pantheism is required by freedom.

Human freedom must be understood as something finite and unconditioned. If pantheism leads to fatalism, this cannot be due to the doctrine of immanence as such. But to what then?

Three explanations of pantheism and Schelling's rejection of them were discussed. What is the reason for these insipid and impossible doctrines? Answer: "In the general misunderstanding of the law of identity or of the meaning of the copula in judgment."

But what does the "law of identity" and the "copula in judgment" have to do with pantheism and with the ontological question?

Let us pay heed to the sentences cited in our previous discussion which are supposed to present pantheism in a single connection: everything is God; the individual thing is God; God is everything.

In trying to follow these sentences of pantheism and to recall their context, we first of all quite naturally pay attention to what they discuss: God, the whole, individual things. Similarly, when we hear the sentence "the weather is beautiful," we think of the weather and how it is constituted. *But* we do *not* pay attention to the "is" pronounced in the sentences. This "is"—we take it, so to speak, for granted. We make unquestioned use of it, especially since it has long since been flattened down in its general character. It is taken for a "little connecting word" (Kant), as the copula, band, between subject and predicate. Thus it is in the pantheism sentences, too.

But when we think about it more clearly, then it is evident that it is precisely in the "is" that the heart of the real question is to be sought. For in this "is" nothing less is pronounced than the *band* between God and the whole and individual things, between the *theos* and the *pan*. Since this band characterizes the basic structure of beings as a whole, it determines the kind of articulation of the structure of Being in general, the system. The "is" and what it means—this "is" which we pass right over as something of no importance in saying sentences—is what is decisive. The "is" signifies a manner of stating Being, *on he on*. Thus, if the question of pan*theism* as the question of a system shifts to the question of the "is," that means the theological question necessarily changes to the ontological question.

Barely noticeably, Schelling inserts an interim remark on the law of identity and the copula. What is explained there on the side is an essential foundation for the whole treatise. After what we have said, one can more or less see that the "is" is discussed there. But why does the law of identity get discussed now? Before answering this, we must say something about the manner in which we are dealing with the ontological realm indicated in the context of this interpretation.

We only have now to clarify how Schelling posits and solves the question of the law of identity and the copula, to show how precisely the law of identity and the copula go together, how a fundamental reflection on this context becomes necessary in terms of the question of pantheism. Briefly, we must show that and how Schelling discusses the nature of Being. On what is fundamental to the question of the essence of the copula and the determination of the systematic place where it must be philosophically treated, compare *Being and Time*, section 33. Only this should be explicitly noted now. In the question of the essence of the "is," one cannot budge if one takes the "is" out of the sentence structure like a thing and investigates it like a thing. One also cannot budge if one leaves it in the sentence, but treats "the" sentence, "the" judgment, as something objectively present. These "investigations" are usually geared to the comparison and calculation of different theories which were set up about this "thing." Often the following opinion is prevalent in such cases. The "is" is taken for an expression of Being; thus, the question of Being must be able to be settled by a determination of the nature of the copula. As a band, the "is" belongs to the sentence (judgment). But the judgment is the bearer of truth. Thus, the determination of the nature of truth becomes clear at the same time. The fact that the "is" represents a linguistic expression of the verb "to be" cannot be disputed. But the question remains whether what Being means can be decided in terms of the "is" or, rather, conversely, what the "is" can mean must be decided only in terms of a sufficient essential determination of Being (compare now *Introduction to Metaphysics.*) In any case, as the unseeming expression of Being and as the seeming bearer of the truth of the sentence, this "is" remains something deceptive and this deceptiveness of the "is" has had every possible kind of effect ever since Aristotle, most recently in Nietzsche's immeasurable superficiality with regard to this question.

From the brief references on the manner and direction of the first formation of a system, we know that modern philosophy especially strives to comprehend the essence of Being in terms of the "I think" and the thinking of reason in general. Since the judgment is the basic form of thinking and the basic structure of the judgment, the connection of subject and predicate is formed by the copula. It is not strange that Schelling, too, clarifies and decides the ontological question with reference to the proposition and the copula.

The ontological discussion begins on page 13 with "the reason for such misinterpretations . . ." and continues to page 14 . . . "*explicitum.*" It is taken up again in the introduction, page 18: "For if, at first glance, it seems that. . . ."

Schelling asks the ontological question about the concept of Being with regard to the "is." One takes the latter as a constituent of the proposition. The proposition is the key element in the ontological question. Thus, we already know why the law of identity is mentioned here. Identity means "sameness," stated according to the formula A is A. According to common opinion, this is the "simplest" form of the belonging together of something with something, that something as itself belongs together with itself, is itself. From here, every expression of the Form A is b; C is g, and so forth, can be explained as the expression of a belonging together. Every sentence can be understood as an identity. But if the relation of subject and predicate is that of identity and if this relation is supported by the "is," that means the identity of the predicate with the subject. Schelling, too, accepts this "explanation" of the nature of the proposition as an identity—without further discussion. But he now rightly asks what the meaning of this identity is and what it does not mean, in short, the question what the "is" means and does not mean here. With respect to the latter, Schelling emphasizes that it cannot be seriously questioned that "identity" in any case cannot mean "uniformity." True, "identity" can also mean something like this. Something is all the same as itself. This is true of every something. It is true of every being and even of nothing. Everything is all the same as everything if we take it as a mere something and abstract from every kind of content. In this respect, as something, each thing is as important as the other and we can thus say as the empty sameness of something with itself, identity is the category of pure indifference, that is, of that belonging together which really does not wish to be and cannot be what it is. Identity in this sense of empty sameness is—even though a category of indifference—itself nothing indifferent, but an essential determination of the "something," without which we could never think or act at all. Still, the concept of identity does not exhaust its own complete meaning. Wherever it claims to do this, this idea of identity must be designated as "common" identity.

According to our accepted explanation, identity is expressed in the proposition. One can really already make it clear to a child how identity in the proposition, that is, the belonging together of subject and predicate, is to be understood. For example, "This body is blue." According to the common idea of identity, this sentence means body and blue are the same thing. But body and blue are different things and are also taken as such. If they are both now to be the same according to the proposition as an expression of identity, they can only be such if they are so in a different respect. The same, what is body in *one* respect, is also blue in the *other* respect.

What, then, is meant in the statement of identity? Identity is the belonging together of what is different in one; still more generally expressed, the unity of a unity and an opposition.

Common thinking works in a remarkable way. On the one hand, in the pronouncement and understanding of everyday sentences it is completely secure in what it directly means. The bird sings, the clock chimes, and so forth, singing and birds, clock and chiming, are not taken as the same thing. But on the other hand, when concepts like identity are presented, they are supposedly thought just as securely right away in the current significance of identity as mere sameness and identicalness. As secure as common thinking is in the determination of what it directly means, it is just as insecure and clumsy when it is supposed to comprehend what this seeming immediacy of its opinion really tells it, when it is supposed to think what is thought in the proposition as a unity of what is different.

The sentence, "The bird sings," certainly does not think belonging together (identity) as identicalness. But it is just as certain that "identity" for itself is at first understood as empty sameness. If the usual manner of thinking of common sense is completely transferred to philosophy, that is, if a "higher application" of the usual concept of identity occurs, "identity" is, of course, understood as mere identicalness, and it is completely forgotten that even in everyday thinking "identity" is already meant in a more real sense, although not consciously. Every common statement proves this.

Schelling now gives some examples of the "higher application of the law of identity," that is, philosophical propositions which show the usual interpretation to be a misinterpretation and thus clarify their true meaning at the same time. Even if a proposition about necessity and freedom was not made explicitly among the examples, it would still be easy to see what the whole clarification is aiming at. Let us take the proposition "The perfect is the imperfect!" Subject is predicate; *as* proposition an identity. Commonly understood the sentence says what is perfect and imperfect, good and bad, wise and stupid, are all the same thing. Then the "is" in the sentence would only mean it is all the same. The perfect and the imperfect, both are the same in the sense of empty sameness. But the sentence is not so intended, and the "is" means something different. But what the sentence really means is expressed in the correct intonation: *not* the perfect is *the imperfect*, but the *perfect is* the imperfect. This means what is perfect always takes over the task of being what truly exists in the imperfect. But what is imperfect only takes care of the lack of perfection, what does not exist. The perfect "is," that is, it takes over and makes possible what is imperfect as its own transformation. And thus it is in the statement; the good is the bad. This means evil does not have the power to be of its own accord, but it needs the good above all. And this is what is truly existent *in* evil. What is nonexistent in evil and negative, is not and as such a nonexistent "is" evil itself.

In the "is," we must think more and something quite different from mere "identicalness" in which subject and predicate are thrown together, then appearing to be arbitrarily exchangeable.

Subject is predicate means S grounds the possibility of being of P, is the ground lying at the basis and thus prior. "S is P" means S "grounds," gives P its ground. In this connection, Schelling points out that the old logic was already correct in taking the subject as *antecedens* and the predicate as *consequens* or the subject as *implicitum* and the predicate as *explicitum*. To what extent these references are historically tenable is not the question now. Schelling could have pointed out with much more accuracy and force that S, "subject," means nothing other than what underlies, the underlying foundation. P, predicate, is, of course, taken from a quite different realm of representation, that of saying. The different kinds of origin of S and P perhaps most sharply illuminate the inner questionability of the basic structure of logic, long unquestioned, the *logos* and the *proposition*. But we do not want to treat this further now. It is sufficient to see what Schelling's concern is, namely, to show that the meaning of the "is" and, thus, the nature of Being does not get exhausted in mere sameness. From this follows as the first important, although mostly negative, consequence: A sentence such as "God is everything" must from the beginning not be understood to mean a mere, boundless identicalness of God and all things in the sense of a lawless primeval hodgepodge. If the statement has something philosophically essential to say, it is just the question how the "is" is to be understood here; more exactly, how the higher and truer concept of identity is suited to comprehend what is essential.

From these considerations we summarize the following: (1) the "is" is understood as the identity of S and P; (2) but identity must be understood in a higher sense; (3) the inadequate concept of identity understands identity as mere identicalness; and (4) the correct concept of identity means the primordial belonging together of what is different in the one (This one is at the same time the ground of possibility of what is different).

With respect to this higher concept of identity, Schelling can say later when he once again takes up the question of the law of identity with the same intention that identity is truly not a dead relation of indifferent and sterile identicalness, but "unity" is directly productive, "creative," and progressing toward others. That is so true that precisely in those propositions, too, which seem like pronouncements of an empty identicalness, we always think more and further. For example, "The body is a body" means what we mean by body and is approximately known as such is at bottom what belongs to a body and has its developed nature in it. Externally viewed, the proposition looks as if the predicate simply returned to the subject. But in truth a progression and a bringing forth is contained there.

He who is unable to comprehend identity explicitly in this higher sense and to think and make statements in accordance with this concept remains stuck in "*dialectical adolescence.*" "Dialectical," *dialegein* means here to understand one thing in transition (*dia*) through the other in its essential relation to the other, and not simply to have instant opinions. A dialectical proposition, for example, is the statement: the one is the other. For someone unversed in dialectic, this sentence is simply false and senseless. For him, the one is precisely the one and the other is the other. The names are precisely there in order to say that. And yet, the one *is* the other and the other *is* the one. A single thing *is* what it is, one, only *in contradistinction to* the other. This differentiation from the other and in this respect being itself the other belongs to the one, and therefore the one *is* also and essentially the other and vice versa. "Is" precisely does not mean empty identicalness, for the one is precisely not the same as the other, but different. But in this difference as a relation it belongs together with the other. They are both "identical" in the higher, true sense. The thinking unversed in dialectic, on the other hand, insists upon the following: the one, that is the one, and the other is the other. The thinking unversed in dialectic always thinks in one perspective only: the one, that is the one, and nothing more.

This thinking keeps to only one perspective. It is one-sided thinking which looks in a preoccupied way only in *one* direction, withdrawn and abstract. Thus, Hegel says whoever thinks abstractly, one-sidedly is, however, not a philosopher, but the common man. Only the philosopher thinks truly concretely, that is, thinks things in the unified concrescence of their full nature, concretely. Common sense sees everything only under a single perspective which it happens to fall prey to. It is incapable of even seeing the other side or of thinking both sides together under a higher unity.

The "truth close to life" of the healthy understanding is thus a very questionable thing. Around 1807, Hegel wrote an essay entitled "Who Thinks Abstractly?" (WW XVII, 400 ff.). I like to quote it again as it is in my opinion the best introduction to the philosophy of German Idealism and to philosophy in general with regard to its procedure of thought.

"Thinking? Abstractly?—*Sauve qui peut*! Save yourself, whoever can! I can already hear a traitor call out who has sold out to the enemy, condemning this essay because metaphysics will be talked about here. For *metaphysics* is the word, as is *abstract* and almost *thinking* itself the word before which everyone more or less flees as before someone with the plague." (WW XVII, p. 400)

"Old woman your eggs are rotten," says the shopper to the peddler's wife. "What," retorts the latter, "my eggs rotten? Let them be rotten! She tells me that about my eggs? You! Didn't the lice eat up your father on the country road, didn't your mother run off with the French, and didn't your grandmother die in the hospital—she buys a whole shirt for her honeymoon scarf. It is well known where she got this scarf and her cap. If there were no officers, some people would not be so decked out now and if the honored ladies would look after their household better, many would be sitting in the stocks—let her mend the holes in the stockings." In brief, she leaves nothing uncensured about her. She thinks abstractly and categorizes her according to her scarf, cap, shirts, and so forth, as also according to the fingers and other parts, according to her father and all of the relatives, all of this solely because of her crime in finding the eggs rotten. Everything about her is colored through and through by those rotten eggs. Those officers, however, of whom the peddler's wife spoke—if it were true, which is very doubtful—might have seen quite different things in her." (WW XVII, p. 404)

"Old woman, your eggs are rotten." The old woman doesn't even consider the question whether they are really rotten or not, but only hears the statement "rotten" as a reproach, and now addresses her answer totally to this reproach.

This common sense is everywhere and constantly easily found. "All science is objective, otherwise it would be subjective. I cannot think of a science other than as objective, that is, either everything is objective or subjective, and that is all." But whether perhaps science is *at the same time* objective and *at the same time* subjective, that is, at bottom *neither* the one *nor* the other, that is neither asked nor even comprehended as the possibility of a question.

One wants to say something with that sentence "about science," that means always, to make a philosophical statement, and at the same time one is loath in the same breath to get involved with the basic requirements of philosophical thinking. One has the applause of the masses which exist in science too—but nothing at all has been understood.

In order for us to appropriate fruitfully works of philosophy, we must not cling to titles and opinions, but enter the basic movement of its questioning. This is especially true of the works of German Idealism because on the one hand they are explicitly geared to such a course of thoughtful questioning and on the other hand because a philosophical tradition of 2,000 years is gathered in them. In Schelling's treatise "pantheism" is such a title which can lead us astray to an external treatment of opinions and standpoints, but which means something quite different. The question of Being in general is meant.

We stand in the middle of beings as a whole, we understand Being and orient beings toward a ground.

When Nietzsche, for example, teaches the eternal recurrence of the same, he is very far removed from the suspicion of a dogmatic theology, and yet this doctrine is only a definite interpretation of the ground of beings as a whole.

Let us repeat what is essential in short statements:

Pantheism: God is everything. The "is" is decisive. The jointure between the ground of beings as a whole and the whole of beings.

The "is" as copula in the proposition.

The proposition as *identity.*

Thus copula and "identity" are essential for the discussion of the "is," of Being.

For a long time the "is" has spoken as the unseeming, yet leading, expression of Being. At the same time the "is" as a member of the proposition became the bearer of truth.

Being is understood according to the understanding of the law of identity.

The full and the empty concept of identity as sameness and identicalness was clarified.

Identity as the belonging together of what is different.

This is also meant in the common proposition "The bird sings," and so forth.

Nevertheless, the interpretation according to identity understood in an external sense is still prevalent and also determines the transference to philosophical propositions.

"The perfect is the imperfect."

"The good is the bad."

In such propositions, the "is" must be understood creatively, not as an empty repetition.

Subject and predicate are called *antecedens-consequens* in the old logic.

Schelling demands a knowledge of dialectic in the understanding of the "is."

Hegel clarifies the distinction between abstract and concrete thinking in his essay mentioned earlier. We tried to show the inadequacy of common sense with the example of the question of the objectivity and subjectivity of science.

Schelling rightly says that Greek philosophy already went past dialectical adolescence with its first steps. This is accurate because there is no philosophy at all as long as this adolescence has not been overcome. Overcoming common sense is the first step of philosophy. And philosophy thus remains a constant attack on man's common sense; not with the intention of generally removing the latter or even of putting philosophy in the place of everyday thinking, but in order to make this thinking constantly uneasy so that it might lose its trust in its own self-importance assumed again and again over all thought and knowledge—not, however, in itself in general.

All decisive statements of all philosophy are "dialectical." We understand this expression in the very broad, but essential sense that something, something essential can always only be truly comprehended by going through something else. In this sense Parmenides' saying is "dialectical": *to gar auto noein estin te kai einai* (thinking and Being are the same). Or Heraclitus's saying: *ho theos hemere euphrone, cheimon theros, polemos eirene, koros limos* (the god is day-night, winter-summer, war-peace, satiety-hunger).

"Dialectical" in this sense is Plato's sentence: Nonbeing exists (*to me on - on*). Or Kant's statement: The essence of experience is the essence of the object of experience. Or Fichte's statement: "The I is the non-I." (The I in Fichte must be understood as the living unity of beings and Being. I means what everything "is," what can still become an object for itself, whose own Being can still be existent in the I.) Or Hegel's statement: I am the thing, and the thing is I.

These philosophical statements are "dialectical," that means Being, which is thought in them, must always at the same time be understood as nonbeing. That means the essence of Being is in itself finite. And for this reason where Being is to be absolutely understood as infinite, as is the case in German Idealism, the development of "dialectic" as a special method becomes necessary. Intellectual *intuition* in the sense of German Idealism and the dialectic which it develops do not exclude each other, but require each other reciprocally.

Friedrich Schlegel once said (*Athenäumsfragmente*, 82) that "a definition which is not funny is not worthwhile." This is only the turn of Idealist dialectic to the romantic.

But if this method is separated from the fundamental experiences and fundamental positions of absolute Idealism, "dialectic" becomes the ruin of philosophical cognition instead of the true means. From the fact that the essence of Being in the sense mentioned is "dialectical" it does not directly follow that the method of philosophy always has to be dialectic. When dialectic is only picked up and manipulated externally as a technique of thought, it is an embarrassment and a seduction.

Schelling's interim ontological reflection on the law of identity and the nature of the copula intends to show the higher meaning of philosophical knowledge and the conditions of its acquisition. If the statement "God is everything" is a metaphysico-philosophical one, it can only be discussed at all after the sole possible level of talking about it has been gained, that is, the higher, dialectical understanding of identity and Being, in brief, the realm of ontological questioning. We had to pause longer here with this interim reflection because (1) the main investigation moves in dialectical thinking and because (2) besides, interim ontological reflections, often only in the form of a few sentences, are strewn throughout the treatise again and again and it is important to grasp their intention and scope from the very beginning. (The footnote, pp. 14–15, contains nothing new with regard to content, but it is characteristic of Schelling's manner of dispute. What is important there is Schelling's reference to Leibniz who systematically and comprehensively thought through identity as belonging together for the first time, in the context of a fundamental reflection on the nature of "unity" as the fundamental determination of Being.) (Compare the *hen* in the beginning of Western philosophy.)

4. VARIOUS VERSIONS OF THE CONCEPT OF FREEDOM (THE ONTOLOGICAL QUESTION AS A FUNDAMENTAL QUESTION)

After the interim discussion of three different concepts of pantheism and the ontological reflection inserted there, the course of the treatise steers back to the path anticipated earlier on page 10. It was said with regard to the assertion that pantheism is fatalism that not only does pantheism not exclude freedom, but it is itself required as the sole possible system if freedom is experienced, and that means at the same time comprehended primordially enough. Thus it is of fundamental importance for all further discussion of the treatise on freedom to learn to see more clearly what nonprimordial experience of freedom and what primordial experience of freedom means, wherein the *in*-appropriate concept of freedom corresponding to that experience consists, and how the real concept of freedom arising from a more primoridal experience and creating the interpretation is to be determined.

But we must stay completely in the course of the treatise in order to go straight to the discussion of the distinction between inappropriate and real freedom. For the discussion continues by taking up again the question whether the true character of pantheism lies in the denial of freedom, whether pantheism is essentially fatalism. A short historical discussion which points the way for the correct delineation of the various experiences and concepts of freedom precedes the actual decision.

Schelling says that if the unconditional inference from pantheism to fatalism, and thus the reverse inference from fatalism to pantheism were correct, then pantheism would have to exist everywhere where freedom was not expressly asserted. All of the systems which have not yet penetrated to the true concept of freedom, which do not really posit freedom, would have to be pantheistic. But all systems up to Idealism, that is, up to Kant who forms the transition, did not really posit freedom because they had not yet developed the "real," "formal concept" of freedom, but moved in an inappropriate concept.

How is this distinction between the inappropriate and the appropriate, "formal" concept of freedom to be understood? (Regarding the name "formal": *forma* is what determines, it is essence in general.) Up to now we got to know three concepts of freedom:

1. Freedom as the self-starting of a series of events which needs no foundation, being-able-in-terms-of-oneself.

2. Freedom as being free from something. For example, the patient is free of fever or this drink is tax-free.

3. Freedom as being free *for* something, committing oneself to something. This last concept of freedom leads to the understanding of the "real" concept of freedom (subsumed under 1.).

4. In the inappropriate concept of freedom that interpretation is maintained which sees freedom in the mere dominance of the spirit over sensuousness; of reason over drives, desires, inclinations. This kind of freedom can be evidenced by the "most lively feeling" of such a gaining mastery over . . . as a fact. But with this the "real" concept of freedom has not yet been understood and the essence, the *forma* and the essential ground has not been reached. Only Kant and Idealism succeed in this. According to Idealism, freedom means to stand outside of every causal *nexus* of nature and yet to be a cause and a ground and thus to stand within oneself. But independence does not yet exhaust the essence of freedom either. This only happens when independence is understood as self-determination in the sense that what is free itself gives the law of its own being in terms of itself. But then the explicit determination of the essence of true freedom depends on the actual determination of the essence of man—and the other way around.

5. The formal concept of freedom is independence as standing within one's own essential law. This is what freedom means in the true sense, historically expressed, in the Idealist sense. Kant's philosophy creates and forms the transition from the inappropriate to the appropriate concept of freedom. For him freedom is still mastery over sensuousness, but not this alone, but freedom as independence in one's own ground and self-determination as self-legislation. And yet the determination of the formal essence of human freedom is not yet completed in Kant's concept of freedom. For Kant places this freedom as autonomy exclusively in man's pure reason. This pure reason is not only distinguished from, but at bottom also separated from, sensuousness, from "nature," as something completely other. Man's self is determined solely in terms of the egoity of the "I think." This egoity is only piled on top of sensuousness as man's animality, but it is not really admitted to nature. Nature and what is so designated remains what is negative and only to be overcome. It does not become constitutive for an independent ground of the whole existence of man. But where nature is thus understood, not as what is merely to be overcome, but as what is constitutive, it joins a higher unity with freedom. On the other hand, however, freedom for its part joins with nature, although undeveloped. Only Schelling went beyond Fichte and took the step to this complete, general essential concept of freedom, a step for which Leibniz had shown a general metaphysical direction in another respect. As already mentioned at the beginning of our lecture, at age sixteen Schelling had already read Leibniz's work which is especially relevant here, the *Monadology*. But what appears in Schelling as Leibniz's philosophy is not a piece of Leibniz's system which could somehow be isolated, but is Leibniz creatively transformed on the way through Kant and Fichte. Only in this form may we

understand and inquire into the "dependence" of great thinkers on each other. That all essential thinkers at bottom always say the same thing does not mean that they take over the identical thing from each other, but rather that they transform their own primordial thought which is different back to what is essential and to the origin. And for this reason one can find that what became known only in later ages—after it became known and could thus be seen—was also found in traces in the earlier thinkers without being able to say that the earlier thinkers already thought and knew the same thing in the same way. What was just said must be noted with regard to the concept of freedom, too.

Although the true, that is, "formal" concept of freedom as independence in the development of one's own nature in its metaphysical scope is only comprehended and developed in German Idealism, traces of it can be found earlier. Still, or rather precisely because of this, Schelling can and must say that "in all the more recent systems, in Leibniz's as well as Spinoza's, "the true concept of freedom" is lacking.

Leibniz's system and similar ones, however, may certainly not—this is the interim thought—be thought of as pantheistic, fatalistic systems. A nonpositing of true freedom may be present, and fatalism and pantheism in the fatalistic sense are not necessarily posited along with it. Conversely, pantheism can be posited, and freedom is not necessarily denied. Thus the denial or assertion of freedom must rest on something quite different from pantheism in the sense of the doctrine of the immanence of things in God. Thus, if the compatibility of pantheism and freedom is to be shown, pantheism, that is, system and freedom, must be explained in the direction of this other ground. We already know that the foundation for the question of the compatibility of pantheism and freedom and thus for the question of the possibility of a system of freedom is an ontological one. More precisely, with regard to pantheism and the statements proclaiming it, it is the adequate understanding of Being and the fundamental determination of Being, identity. Thus, we shall recognize as the true metaphysical accomplishment of the treatise on freedom the grounding of a primordial concept of Being— in Schelling's language the more primordial grounding of absolute identity in a more primordial "copula."

Schelling had pointed out a new solution to the whole question by showing that man's most lively feeling of freedom placed him not outside of God and against God, but as belonging to the "life of God." Freedom demands immanence in God, pantheism. Now it must be shown on the other hand that pantheism correctly understood demands freedom. If this evidence is successful, the assertion set up as the key phrase—that pantheism as the sole possible system is necessarily fatalism—is refuted in every respect. Then the way is at least free for the possibility of a system of freedom.

How about the idea that pantheism correctly understood demands the positing of human freedom? What does that mean—pantheism correctly understood? We must now be able to understand this in terms of the historical and fundamental discussion of the statements of pantheism.

The statements of pantheism read: (1) everything is God, (2) individual things are God, (3) God is everything. The first two statements and interpretations of pantheism turned out to be "insipid" because God's nature is annihilated in them and precisely that is lost in relation to which everything and individual things are supposed to be in God. The third statement alone is permissible, but at first as a question. And the question must be geared to the meaning of the "is." We found the identity of S and P stated in a proposition in general and, in this proposition in particular, the identity of God and everything cannot be understood as mere identicalness, but as the belonging together of what is different on the basis of a more primordial unity.

(However, if one takes the inappropriate concept of identity as a base, identity = identicalness, then everything in the sentence "God is everything" is lumped together with God as being the same thing. Everything is not admitted as other, as something different, and thus the possibility of being different, that is, man's standing on his own basis, that is, his freedom, is not admitted either. The ontological foundation, identity, must be properly understood in advance for the demonstration which has now become our task: that pantheism properly understood requires freedom.)

What follows from this for the interpretation of the statement "God is everything"? What is the task of demonstration? We shall characterize it briefly in advance. According to the formal concept emphasized by Schelling again and again, pantheism is the doctrine of the immanence and inclusion of all things in God. All things being contained in God includes in any case some kind of dependence of things on God. With pantheism the dependence of beings on God is posited. Precisely this pantheism must not only allow for freedom, but require it. Thus a dependence must be thought which not only leaves room for the independence of what is dependent but which—note well as dependence— essentially demands of what is dependent that it be free in its being, that is, be independent in virtue of its nature. Schelling gives this demonstration on p. 18. We shall follow the individual steps and watch how the earlier ontological interim reflection comes into play.

For if, at first glance, it seems that freedom, unable to maintain itself in opposition to God, is here submerged in identity, it may be said that this apparent result is merely the consequence of an imperfect and empty conception of the law of identity. This principle does not express a unity which, revolving in the indifferent circle of sameness, would get us nowhere and remain meaningless and lifeless. The unity of this law is of an intrinsically creative kind. In the relation of subject to predicate itself we have already pointed out the relation of ground and consequence; and the law of sufficient reason is therefore just as ultimate as the law of identity. The Eternal as such, must, on this account, also be this ground, without mediation. That for which the Eternal is by its

nature the ground, is, to this extent, dependent and, from the point of view of immanence, is also conceived in the Eternal. But dependence does not determine the nature
of the dependent, it merely declares that the dependent entity, whatever else it may be,
can only be as a consequence of that upon which it is dependent; it does not declare
what this dependent entity is or is not. (P. 18)

The question of pantheism is now directed toward the question of the possibility of human freedom in beings as a whole and above all with relation to their
absolute ground, that is, God. The statement reads: God is everything. With
regard to our question we must venture the statement: *God is* man. From the very
beginning, the "is" does not mean identicalness. Identity is the unity of the
belonging together of what is different. Thus, man is already posited as something different from God. Identity—it was seen more clearly in the relation of
subject to predicate—is the relation of what grounds to what is grounded, the
consequence. God is man, God as ground allows man to be consequence. But
man is then after all something dependent and not at all what is required,
something free and self-contained.

But dependence initially means only that what is dependent is dependent on its
ground in that it is at all, but not in what it is. *That* a son is, for this a father is
necessary. But what is dependent, the son, need not, therefore, be *what* the *ground*
is, a father. What is dependent is at first only dependent on and together with the
ground in the realm of the context in which it comes to Being, that is, in
becoming. Nothing is as yet said about Being itself, finished self-containedness.
On the contrary, if what is dependent were not finally something set free, cut
loose, and placed in itself, dependence without something dependent would be a
consequence without something following. That God *is* man means that God
allows man to be as consequence; that is, man must be self-contained if he is to be
truly a consequence at all.

The necessity of this can be made completely clear right here. If God is the
ground and if God himself is not a mechanism and a mechanical cause, but rather
creative life, then what he has brought about cannot itself be a mere mechanism.
If God as the ground reveals *himself* in what is grounded by him, he can only
reveal *himself* there. What is dependent must itself be a freely acting being, just
because it depends on God.

God looks at things as they are in themselves. To be in itself, however, means to
stand independently in oneself. What God brings before himself, his representations, "can only be independent beings." What rests upon itself, however, is what
is free—is will. What depends on God must be made dependent (*ab-gehängt*)
through him and from him in such a way that it comes to itself to stand as
something independent. What is dependently independent, the "derived absoluteness," is not contradictory. Rather, this concept captures what constitutes the
band between the ground of beings as a whole and beings as a whole. God *is* man;

that is, man as a free being is in God and only something free can be in God at all. Everything unfree and everything insofar as it is unfree is outside of God.

If God is thought as the ground of everything and if the "is" and Being are not misinterpreted, that is, if pantheism is rightly understood, it so little leads to a denial of man's freedom that is precisely requires it. Schelling explicitly emphasizes that this "general deduction" of the possibility of freedom in the whole of beings is still insufficient, and he thinks in advance of that metaphysical derivation of man's origin which is given in the following.

Let us recall essential steps of our previous train of thought:

The question of the possibility of the system of freedom is the key question of Schelling's treatise on freedom. This key question is developed and decided by a critical discussion of the assertion: pantheism—as the sole possible system—is fatalism. Under the title "pantheism," the question of system in general, that is, the question of Being, is expressed.

The various concepts of freedom receive their determination in connection with this question.

A general ontological reflection is inserted here to characterize the foundation on which the reflection and the whole treatise moves and to explain the procedure. (But not only for the sake of this "methodological" intention.)

From this reflection follows: All statements of philosophy are "dialectical"—as statements on Being and the nature of beings. The philosophy of absolute Idealism leads to the development of its own dialectic. As far as their content goes, dialectical statements are foreign to common sense.

The assertion to be rejected equates pantheism with fatalism. A complete refutation must show two things:

1. In terms of freedom: the liveliest feeling of man's freedom requires that man belong to the ground of beings as a whole (requires the positing of pantheism).

2. In terms of system: pantheism correctly understood requires the positing of human freedom.

The five concepts of freedom.

1. Freedom as capability of self-beginning.

2. Freedom as not being bound to anything, freedom *from* (negative freedom).

3. Freedom as binding oneself to, *libertas determinationis,* freedom *for* (positive freedom).

4. Freedom as control over the senses (inappropriate freedom).

5. Freedom as self-determination in terms of one's own essential law (appropriate freedom), formal concept of freedom. *This includes all of the previous determinations.* (Compare below p. 97 and p. 102: the sixth and seventh concept of freedom.)

Regarding the first thesis: the refutation of the assertion that pantheism is fatalism was given earlier.

The second thesis of pantheism correctly understood reads: God *is* man.

"Correctly understood" means that the "is" must be understood as real identity. The creative ground must posit something independently dependent of itself. Dependence concerns the "that." The "what" can be of such a nature that what is dependent is posited as in-de-pendent (*Un-ab-hängiges*). It even has to be posited as such.

The main concern of the introduction is to make clear the fact that not a step can be taken in the whole question of freedom and the system of freedom without an adequate concept of Being and without an adequately primordial basic experience of beings.

Now the stage has been reached in our reflection where the true error of Spinoza can be uncovered. Schelling formulates it precisely and briefly as follows (p. 22): "The error . . . is by no means due to the fact that he posits all things *in God*, but to the fact that they are *things . . .*" and that God "is also a thing for him." That means the error is not a theological one, but more basically and truly an ontological one. In general and as a whole, beings are understood in terms of the being of things, of natural objects, and only thus. Spinozism is not familiar with what is alive and even spiritual as an independent and perhaps more primordial kind of being. The "will," too, is for it a thing ("matter"), and necessity exists solely between things; that is, it is mechanical (compare I, VII, p. 397).

On the other hand, in the previously cited "deduction" of the possibility of freedom in pantheism, God is understood as the creative ground, man as the self-contained free being. Being in general is understood not as the rigid relation of a thinglike cause and another thinglike effect, not as the dead identity of what is all the same, but as progressing, as a band and a binding, which at the same time allows independence to arise and thus binds in a more profound sense, as dependent independence, independent dependence. Being and the primordial band of Being is understood not mechanically, but as having the nature of will, according to the general manner of speaking: as spiritual. But it will become evident that even the Spirit is not the highest: "it is only the Spirit, or the breath of love"—that which Plato already brought to an inner connection with the nature of Being, *eros*. Schelling understands love in the metaphysical sense as the inmost nature of identity as the belonging together of what is different. "This is the mystery of love—that it connects things which would each be for itself and yet is not for itself and cannot be without the other." "Love" understood formally is the nature of the band, the copula, the "is" and Being.

Thus, the perspective of the possibility of a more primordial understanding of Being in general is opened up, the perspective of a "higher kind of thought" as compared with the "mechanical" kind which determined philosophy at the beginning of the modern period, especially in the Western countries. Even so, counter-movements arose here, too—think of Pascal. But it never came about that philosophy as a whole arrived at a new foundation and was built up in terms of a more primordial understanding of Being. Schelling calls it "a striking phenomenon in the history of the development of German Spirit" that the assertion which we already know could be made that the sole possible system is Spinozism. The originator of this "striking" view is Jacobi. Schelling does not fail to point out the hidden, more far-reaching intention of this view. The intention is to warn everyone by way of an inquisition about philosophy in general as something "ruinous." For as fatalism, Spinozism is atheism and every upright person must cross himself when confronted with this.

Fundamentally, Schelling wants to say: it was all right for the "German temper" (*Gemüt*) to defend itself against the dominance of the Western mechanistic way of thinking. However, it is not sufficient, but ruinous in the opposite direction, to appeal to that temper instead of opposing a confused thinking with the hardness and precision of a more primordial and correct thinking. Spirit (*Gemüt*) can and must be the foundation from which thinking and knowing get their motive. But it must not become a place of refuge to be blindly sought, a place which one demands instead of growing with its help into the breadth of what is creative, and that always means what gives measure. Spirit, yes, but the resting place of thinking and knowing—no. Schelling says later (I, X, 199; 5, 269):

"Truly universal philosophy cannot possibly be the property of a single nation. As long as a philosophy does not go beyond the limits of an individual people, one can confidently assume that it is not yet the true philosophy although it may be on its way."

Thus it was also truly German that Jacobi's appeals "to the heart, the inner feelings and faith" did not prevail, but that the "higher light of Idealism", that is, a more strict thinking, came about and gained control in that Idealism which is therefore called German—a higher kind of thinking which received essential inspiration from Leibniz and a first true foundation in Kant.

5. THE NATURE AND BOUNDARIES OF IDEALISM'S POSITION.

That kind of pantheism, that is, that system which, as we have already seen, not only does not deny freedom, but requires it, is founded in the higher kind of thinking of Idealism—it *is* Idealism. Thus, the "system of freedom" has already been secured with Idealism, and Idealism has already been expressed as a system of freedom when it has formed a system. Idealism as a system was founded by Fichte's doctrine of science, substantially complemented by Schelling's philosophy of nature, raised by his system of transcendental Idealism to a higher level, completed by his system of identity and explicitly founded in a self-contained train of thought by Hegel's *Phenomenology of Spirit*. Then why raise the question of the system of freedom again? Schelling says: (p. 24): "However, high as we have been placed in this respect by Idealism, and certain as it is that we owe to it the first formally perfect concept of freedom, Idealism itself is, after all, nothing less than a finished system. And as soon as we seek to enter into the doctrine of freedom in greater detail and exactitude, it nonetheless leaves us helpless."

This means that as far as its plan and inner possibility go, Idealism is indeed the system of freedom. But it is not yet the system of freedom as long as essentially unsolved difficulties still remain in that which gives this system its center and name, as long as essentially unsolved difficulties still remain in the nature of freedom and its determination. Above all, Idealism is not the true System of freedom when it is what prevents us from seeing these unsolved difficulties in the nature of freedom at all and is completely incapable of removing them. And this is actually the case. Idealism did arrive at the formal concept of freedom; it did truly recognize the general nature of freedom as independence and self-determination in the law of one's own being. But it did not understand and has not yet understood the fact of human freedom in its factuality.

Therefore, the question of human freedom must now be explicitly asked in view of the system of freedom. And this question is clearly expressed in the title of the treatise. If in fact freedom determines man's nature, the clarification of the nature of *human* freedom is then the attempt to clarify the nature of man. What good is a system—as the self-knowing jointure of beings as a whole—if man as he who knows is not placed there with the full determination of his essential jointure, if he cannot be an essential point in it?

The "system of freedom," that is, Idealism, totters when the question of the nature of *human* freedom arises. The introduction to the treatise on freedom reaches its goal with the demonstration of the necessity of questioning Idealism itself. The introduction thus gives the treatise its true task and justification. Idealism is to be shattered. That means Schelling himself transfers the foundation of his philosophy to a deeper ground. But in order to understand the necessity of going beyond Idealism in its previous form, we must state more clearly what Schelling means by the term "Idealism." We must state in what sense German Idealism understands itself as Idealism. With this clarification, we shall create the presupposition for the understanding of the pages to follow. However, we can give here neither a history of the concept and the word "Idealism" nor a history of the matter designated by this term. The clarification of the concept "Idealism" must remain within the boundaries of our task.

According to the concept, "Idealism" is that philosophical fundamental point of view in which the *idea* and the actual interpretation of the Idea determines the fundamental question of philosophy. The fundamental question of philosophy is what are beings as such? It is the question about Being. But according to the Greek word *idea*, "Idea" means what is seen in seeing, the outward appearance, the appearance of beings re-presented in being-placed-before-one. We cannot show how the Platonic doctrine of Ideas and the concept of the Idea were transformed in the course of history. (Compare now *Introduction to Metaphysics.*)

Idealism is the interpretation of the essence of Being as "Idea," as the being represented of beings in general.

We shall now reflect upon the situation at the beginning of the modern period. This period was already characterized with regard to the origination of system formations. For Descartes, *idea* means representation, and in a double sense what is represented as such and representing as an action. But all representing is I represent, I think, and all kinds of the ego's behavior, feeling, too, are representation in the broad sense, thinking. We saw that thinking as "I think" becomes the court of judgment over Being: thinking—the *idea*. This doctrine of Being, namely, that Being is definable in its nature in terms of thinking is thus an Idealism.

But in that thinking is understood as "*I think*" and the "I," the *ego sum*, the *subjectum* is taken as the basic reality; Idealism is now that doctrine of Being in which the essence of Being is determined in terms of the "I" (subject). From now on, Idealism is the doctrine of Being in which the "I," as thinking "subject," has priority. The transformation and history of Idealism now becomes dependent upon the concrete interpretation of the "I" (subject), of representing, and that means at the same time of the relation of representing to what it represents, which is now named the object in contradistinction to the subject.

With Leibniz, the thought arises that every being which is somehow self-contained as a being must have the true character of Being which makes itself known after Descartes in man's experience of himself as *ego cogito sum,* that is, as subject, as I think, I represent. Every being, insofar as it is, is intrinsically representing in various stages and degrees from the muted confusion of the lowest living creature up to the absolute luminosity of the divine ego itself and its representing. Representing, *idea* now becomes the essential constituent of every being as such.

Kant, however, realizes on the path from the *Critique of Pure Reason* to the *Critique of Practical Reason* that the real nature of the "I" is not the *I think*, but the "*I act*," I give myself the law from the basis of my being, I am free. In this freedom, the I is truly together with itself, not away from itself, but truly *in* itself. The I as "I represent," the *idea* is now understood in terms of freedom. Idealism as the interpretation of Being now understands the being-in-itself of beings as being free. Idealism is intrinsically the Idealism of freedom. Kant brought philosophy to this point without himself measuring the whole scope of this step.

At this point, Fichte starts out by including earlier ideas in this thought of egoity as freedom and trying to understand the whole of beings in these terms. Through Fichte, the Idealism of freedom becomes a system. Every being which is at all has its being in terms of the I which, however, is originally positing, as I think, deed, and as deed a deed of action (*Tathandlung*), freedom, egoity as freedom is everything. Even the *non*-ego, insofar as it *is*, is non-*ego*, thus egolike. For Kant, on the other hand, nature remained what appears of itself and is opposed to every ego. Not every being is absolutely egolike. But for Fichte, Idealism becomes the doctrine in which the representing I has priority in the interpretation of Being, it becomes absolute Idealism. Nature, too, and especially nature, is only the non-ego; that is, it is also only egoity, namely what is only a boundary for the ego. Intrinsically, it has no being.

But now the countermove on Schelling's part follows against this dissolution of all beings in the egoity of "I think" as "I posit" (with Fichte a "complete deathblow to nature," I, VII, 445). Schelling defends himself against the annihilation of nature in the mere non-ego and shows the independence of nature. Since, however, independent Being means for him, too—following the whole modern basic position—being-a-subject, being-an-ego, he must show that nature also is intrinsically ego-like, not only relative to the absolute ego which posits it, it is only a yet undeveloped "ego." And *there* is the place where Leibniz's doctrine that all beings are representing beings is incorporated, but now in such a way that Kant's insight into the nature of the ego becomes essential at the same time. Egoity is really freedom. Thus, the being of nature in its various realms and stages is a coming-to-itself of freedom. Fichte's statement, "Egoity is everything," must be essentially supplemented by the reversal, "All beings are egoity," and that means freedom. For the nature of the being-in-itself of all beings is freedom.

Schelling finds it (p. 23) especially remarkable that Kant realized in his practical philosophy that the essence of the "ego" is freedom and thus determined the essence of this being in itself in its own being, but then declared on top of this in the *Critique of Pure Reason* that the essence of the thing-in-itself is unknowable. Only one step was necessary, to carry over the insight about man's being-in-itself to the being-in-itself of all beings in general and thus to make freedom into a positive and completely universal determination of the "in-itself" in general.

On this—only roughly sketched out—path, the Idealism of Descartes's "I represent" became the higher Idealism of the "I am free," the Idealism of freedom. Through this development of Idealism, its counterposition realism gained greater clarity through Idealism itself. But what does that mean here, realism? *Res* generally means the matter in the broadest sense, the thing. For Descartes, the I, ego, the *res cogitans*, the subject as well as the object, is also a *res*. But the more the decisive determination of all things moves toward the subject and the more the ego-like quality of the subject is developed and its character as thing disappears, the more the *res* and the real become what stands opposed to the ego as a counterconcept and a limiting concept. Thus, "realism" becomes the term for that interpretation of beings which in its determination of Being ignores the fact that Being is ego-like, representing and free. Beings are as beings "without ego," not representing but only mechanistically effective, not free, but mechanistically compelled.

The opposition of Idealism and Realism is a metaphysical one. It concerns the manner of interpretation of Being in general. (Idealism interprets the Being of beings in an ego-like fashion of freedom; realism interprets it as without ego, compelled, mechanistic.) The traditional term for beings as they are for themselves is "substance." For Idealism, substance is ego-like; that is, subject; for realism, it is without ego, a mere "thing." Because of the unphilosophy of the late nineteenth century with its epistemological errings one is completely misled today and understands the terms "Idealism" and "realism" only and primarily "epistemologically." Idealism is taken as that standpoint which denies the "existence" of the outside world, realism as that which asserts it, yes, even dares the *tour-de-force* of proving this existence of the outside world! With these needy concepts Idealism and realism, nothing can, of course, be understood of what occurred as the history of modern philosophy from Descartes to Hegel as the real history of Idealism. Philosophical realism; that is, realism understood in terms of the question of Being and the interpretation of Being, is that doctrine of Being which understands all beings in a thinglike way and takes the merely stufflike object of nature as the decisive being.

But when all beings are conceived as representing by Giordano Bruno and by Leibniz and when nature is still not evaporated into the mere non-ego in Fichte's sense, then a "higher realism" arises. According to the latter, nature is a constant power for itself, it is not dead, but alive; it is freedom still locked within itself and undeveloped. Schelling's decisive step against Fichte was to include this higher realism in the philosophy of Idealism. What Schelling calls "philosophy of nature," does not merely and not primarily mean the treatment of a special area "nature," but means the understanding of nature in terms of the principle of Idealism, that is, in terms of freedom, but in such a way that nature precisely regains its independence. Yet this independence is not to be thought in Kant's sense as the object of experience either, but as the supporting ground of all beings. Within the whole of philosophy the philosophy of nature is only the "*realistic* part" in contrast to transcendental philosophy, the philosophy of spirit as the "*idealistic.*" Both, however, must be joined in a true unity, that is, in a unity which leaves what is to be unified in its independence and still understands it in terms of a higher ground.

According to what was said, this unity is identity correctly understood. For this reason, Schelling calls the system which comprehends the belonging together of the realistic and the idealistic part the system of identity.

"The expressed intention of his efforts was a mutual interpenetration of realism and idealism" (p. 23) Schelling says about himself and his philosophical work up to the point where the treatise on freedom began to take a new step. But since higher realism is higher only because the *idea,* representation, "I," and freedom were already discovered in nature in certain prefigurations, thus higher only on account of the idealistic concept of Being, the system of identity now attained also remains fundamentally "Idealism."

"The idealistic conception is the true initiation into higher philosophy in our time and especially into a higher realism."

The system of Idealism is a "system of freedom" because the principle of forming the system, the determining ground for the fundamental jointure of Being, "the Idea," is understood as freedom. It is not a matter of chance that the last section of Hegel's *Logic*, on general metaphysics in German Idealism, is entitled *"The Idea."* Idea has now long since ceased to mean the outward appearance of objective beings which we see. Rather, it means the being represented of beings—represented, on the way through Descartes' "I think." That means that this representing of being represented represents itself. Thus, in German Idealism, "Idea" always means beings' appearing to themselves in absolute knowledge. Thus, the absolute Idea is "the most highly intensified apex . . . the *pure personality* which *comprehends* and holds *everything in itself* only through absolute dialectic which is its nature, because it makes itself the most free being—simplicity which is the first immediacy and generality" (Hegel, *Science of Logic*). Absolute Being, the being-in-itself of beings means being free, and being free means self-determination in terms of the law of one's own being. Thus, Being in general means *in* and *for* itself, Being with itself willing oneself, willing as such. Schelling says (p. 24): "In the final and highest instance, there is no other Being than Will. Will is primordial Being."

That means primordial Being is will.

Willing is striving and desiring, not a blind impulse and urge, but guided and determined by the idea of what is willed. What is represented and representing, the *idea,* is thus what truly wills in willing. To understand Being as will means to understand it in terms of the *idea* and thus idealistically.

Leibniz established the position for the idealistic concept of Being. Substance, self-existent beings are what they are as *perceptio* and *appetitus*, representing and striving. This does not mean that substance is first of all something for itself and then after that has two qualities (representing and striving), but that striving is in itself representing and representing is striving. Representing and striving (willing) are the fundamental ways of the Being of beings. On this foundation and accordingly, it is unified within itself, is a being. "Will is primal being." Willing is the primordial essence of Being, says Schelling.

The key to the introduction is the question of pantheism, and this question is the question of the principle of forming a system, and this is the question of the essence of Being, the ontological question. We have now arrived at the answer to the question really raised with the term "pantheism." Being is will. A being is will insofar as it is and according to the order of rank in which it is. On the basis of this concept of Being, the following becomes clear: if pantheism represents the only possible system, it is not fatalism, but Idealism, and as Idealism, it is the Idealism of freedom. Pantheism is the system of freedom, because it is Idealism. Thus Schelling says (pp. 25–56): "Similarly it would be a mistake to believe that pantheism has been put aside and destroyed by idealism; an opinion which could only issue from confusing it with one-sided realism. For it is immaterial to pantheism, as such, whether many individual things are conceived in an absolute substance or many individual wills are conceived in one Primal Will."

The system of freedom is possible as Idealism on the foundation of the Idealistic concept of Being: primal being is will.

But right here the real "*but*" appears. Being is understood as will, as freedom. Thus, the concept of freedom is, after all, expanded to the most general determination of all beings. Thus, in this broad concept of freedom what is lost is precisely that which characterizes the freedom of special and perhaps distinctive beings. In terms of this broad and general concept of freedom, precisely human freedom as human cannot be easily understood. In order to determine human freedom, man's nature must be questioned. On the other hand, freedom as independent self-determination in terms of the law of one's own being only gives the formal concept of freedom, the form, the "how" of being free in general. It is not yet then determined wherein the essence and essential law, the principle of man consists (Compare *Weltalter,* introduction). It has not yet been stated in terms of what and for what purpose man can essentially determine himself and where he remains as a consequence of such a determination. Freedom has not yet been determined as human, as that freedom which is real as human freedom.

What is being free and freedom if it is determined in terms of the factual nature, the reality of man? What is the real and thus alive concept of human freedom? That is the question and it is the question which Idealism did not raise and which it can no longer raise. Idealism meets a boundary here because it itself presupposes for its own possibility the concept of man as the rational ego, the concept which excludes a more primordial fundamental experience of man's nature. But according to the most indigenous requirements of Idealism—to which traditional philosophy also corresponds, as the basic words *nous, logos, idea, idein* show—the nature of man is the determining place for the essential determination of Being in general (see below; compare *Introduction to Metaphysics*). If, then, Idealism must be excluded from a more primordial essential determination of man, it is also denied the possibility of developing the question of Being in general in a sufficiently primordial way. But then Idealism is also no longer capable of establishing and founding the principle of forming a system. Thus, the system is no longer possible as an idealistic one either. Thus, the question of the possibility of the system of freedom is raised anew and with it also the question of whether the system necessarily has to be and can be pantheism; that is, the theological question of the ground of beings as a whole is also raised anew.

6. SCHELLING'S CONCEPT OF FREEDOM: FREEDOM FOR GOOD AND EVIL. THE QUESTION OF EVIL AND ITS GROUND.

The ontological and theological foundation of philosophy, all of ontotheology, becomes questionable. All of this occurs solely because the nature of human freedom and thus the nature of man in general is not experienced and understood in a sufficiently essential way. But what still remains to be experienced? Why is the actuality of human freedom not yet confronted with the most intimate and broad feeling? Why, then, is the nature of human freedom still a question again and again? Why is it necessary to go beyond the stage of philosophy attained up to now, beyond Idealism? Schelling says (p. 26): "For Idealism supplies only the most general conception of freedom and a merely formal one. But the real and vital conception of freedom is that it is a possibility of good and evil. This is the point of profoundest difficulty in the whole doctrine of freedom, which has always been felt and which applies not only to this or that system, but, more or less, to all."

Man's freedom is the capability of good and evil. (Thus, a sixth concept of freedom is added to our list.) Only a brief reminder of the concepts discussed earlier is necessary to see immediately that the experience of being free and the feeling for the fact of freedom now takes another direction and another dimension.

"*Libertas est propensio in bonum,*" said Descartes, and thinkers before him, and again all of modern Idealism after him—freedom is the capability of good. Freedom, says Schelling, is the capability of good and evil. Evil "is added." But it is not simply added as a supplement in order to fill a gap still existing until now in the concept of freedom. Rather, freedom is freedom for good *and* evil. The "and," the possibility of this ambiguity and everything hidden in it is what is decisive. That means that the whole concept of freedom must change.

Evil—that is the key word for the main treatise. The question of the nature of human freedom becomes the question of the possibility and reality of evil. But we must observe here, first, evil makes its appearance just in this essential relation to man's freedom and thus in relation to man's nature even more so. Evil is thus not a special topic by itself. Second, evil is not treated in the sphere of mere morality either, but rather in the broadest sphere of the ontological and theological fundamental question, thus a metaphysics of evil. Evil itself determines the new beginning in metaphysics. The question of the possibility and reality of evil brings about a transformation of the question of Being. The introduction was to pave the way for this.

Now we understand why the introduction to this treatise was interpreted with a certain intricacy. As long as Schelling's treatise on freedom is only cited sporadically to document a special view of Schelling's on evil and freedom, nothing about it has been understood. It now also becomes comprehensible how Hegel's judgment, full of recognition as it is, about this treatise is a mistake: it only treats an isolated question! The treatise which shatters Hegel's *Logic before* it was even published! But if we understand it from the very beginning as always in the light and intention of philosophy's fundamental question of Being, then we understand in looking ahead precisely in terms of it why Schelling had to get stranded with his philosophy in spite of everything; that is, had to get stranded *that* way in which *he* failed. For *every* philosophy fails, that belongs to its concept. Of course, common sense concludes from this that philosophizing is therefore not worthwhile, because only what is palpably profitable has any status for it. Conversely, the philosopher concludes from this that philosophy is an indestructible necessity because he thinks that one day this failure might be overcome and philosophy could be "finished." Philosophy is always completed when its end becomes and remains what its beginning is, the question. For only by truly remaining in questioning does it force what is worthy of question to appear. But by opening up what is most worthy of question, it helps bring about the openness of what overcomes and transcends from the very bottom nothingness and what is naught, helps bring about the openness of Being. Being is what is most worthy because it asserts the highest rank before all beings and in all beings and for all beings. Being is the ether in which man breathes. Without this ether, he would descend to the mere beast and his whole activity to the breeding of beasts.

Because Schelling's treatise on human freedom is at the core a metaphysics of evil; because with it a new, essential impulse enters philosophy's fundamental question of Being; because every development was denied this impulse up to now; and because, however, such a development can only become fruitful in a higher transformation, we shall attempt an interpretation of the treatise on freedom here. That is the truly philosophical reason for this choice.

Schelling shows first of all how the system is split open by the reality of evil. He discusses various possibilities of introducing evil into the system. In the examination of such attempts various versions of the concept of evil are formulated. Thus, in this manner a beginning overall view of the realm of the question is gained at the same time which is to be "evil." The result of this final reflection of the introduction is negative the first time. Previous systems, especially Idealism, are incapable of founding a true system acknowledging the reality of evil. The next time the reflection is affirmative: the determining ground of the system, the essence of Being in general, must be more primordially conceived in order for evil to be comprehensible in its own being and thus introduced into the system, thus making a system of freedom possible.

Since this final reflection no longer presents any particular difficulties if we can presuppose that what was said by way of interpreting the introduction was understood, we can limit ourselves to characterizing the fundamental traits of the final part's train of thought and above all emphasizing what is important for the concept of evil.

In terms of pantheism, the system can be expressed in its fundamental jointure by the sentence: God is everything. We recognized in the "is" the jointure of the ground of beings as a whole and the totality of beings. The relation between ground and totality can be thought in three main forms, which have also been developed historically. The first and most general is the being contained of things in God ("immanence"). The second is God's accompaniment with all things ("*concursus*"). The third is the flowing of things from God ("emanation"). Accordingly, Schelling follows in three paths the various ways out of the difficulty which enters the system with evil.

Let us clarify once more in contour the historical background for Schelling's new kind of questioning. Metaphysically understood with reference to the question of Being, Idealism is the interpretation of Being in terms of thinking. The key terms for this are Being and thinking. Ever since Descartes thinking is *I* think. Idealism means that Being is interpreted in terms of egoity. But after Kant, egoity has its being in freedom. Idealism is the idealism of freedom. All being-in-itself is free being. Egoity is all being and all being is ego-like. Idealism had reached this stage in the historical moment when Schelling embarked on the path of the treatise on freedom. Schelling himself comes to this moment from his own system of identity.

Being is understood as egoity, as freedom. Freedom is will. Thus, Being is originally willing. "*The Will* is primal being."

But at the same time, a limitation becomes apparent here. In that freedom becomes the general determination of all beings, it becomes at the same time unable to grasp what is most appropriate to human freedom in its essence.

Thus, the question arises about *human* freedom. But not as a separate question. For this development of the idealistic fundamental point of view up to Idealism's concept of freedom came about on the foundation of an interpretation of man's nature.

When human freedom now becomes a question anew, the fundamental position of Idealism in general and the higher realism founded by it thus also become questionable. Being is will. Thus, we come to the borderline. At the same time, the transition becomes visible in the question of the nature of will!

Schelling raises the question of human freedom anew, in a direction to which Idealism especially obscures the way at first. Idealism understood freedom as the determination of the pure ego, as self-determination for the law, as self-legislation in good will. Only this will is good.

On the contrary, freedom is understood by Schelling as the capability of good and evil (sixth concept of freedom). Evil is not an addition and a complement; rather, freedom changes through it in its very nature. The question of freedom must be asked as a question.

The question of evil becomes the metaphysics of evil with regard to the system. The task of the main treatise is prepared for in the final part of the introduction. There a first overview of the realm in question is given.

How can the reality of evil be brought into harmony with the system? The previous system has become impossible.

How is the *reality of evil* to be thought?

The preconcept of evil.

In pantheism in its broadest sense, various efforts to unify evil with the system are handed down to us: (1) Immanence, being contained, (2) *concursus*, accompaniment, and (3) system of emanation, the flowing of things from God.

Regarding (1): the possibility of immanence is most fundamentally shattered by the fact of evil. If evil really exists and if, however, God is the ground of beings, then evil would have to be posited in the primal will itself, and God would have to be declared evil. That is impossible. From the standpoint of immanence, the only way out is a denial of the reality of evil, which, however, according to the newer determination amounts to a denial of freedom. Even though the treatment of the first attempt to incorporate evil into the system turns out to be short, the result is of great significance for the form of the whole treatise and thus for the question of the system. Though not explicitly, it is now asserted that the system as the immanence of things in God is impossible, even when this immanence is not understood as identicalness. Therein two blows have already been struck against immanence: (1) immanence is not identicalness, (2) immanence may not be conceived as the immanence of things in God as a thing. And now a further point: no being-in and remaining-within is possible at all (compare below). But since, as we saw, immanence constitutes the form of pantheism in general, pantheism, too, is shattered, at least in its previous form.

Regarding (2): (p. 26–27): "But the difficulty is no slighter . . . this positive [element] also comes from God." The same difficulties make the second way out hopeless. If the ground of beings as a whole is thought only as that which admits evil, this admittance is equivalent to being the cause if beings, in which evil is allowed, are essentially a consequence of the ground in their being. Or else the denial of the reality of evil comes about again, and thus the denial of freedom, and the whole question loses its object.

Both systems, that of immanence and that of *concursus*, are so posited that all positive being is understood as coming from God. But if evil is something positive, then these systems negate themselve since God is always thought as the *ens perfectissimum*, as the highest being excluding every "lack." Thus, one falls prey every time to the escape of conceiving evil as nothing positive in order to save the system.

Regarding (3): (p. 28): "Thus, finally, even if one. . . ." The third way consists in allowing evil to arise only gradually in the course of increasing distance from God and in positing it only at the place of the furthest distance from God, in conceiving it as this complete removal from God. But the hopelessness of this way is easily seen. In the system of things flowing from God (system of emanation) the difficulty of unifying evil with God is not removed, but only postponed. For in order for things to be able to flow from God at all, they have to be somehow in him already. The doctrine of emanation is thrown back upon the doctrine of immanence and again gets caught in its difficulties. Moreover, if the greatest distance from God is to constitute being evil, how is this distance itself to be explained? If its cause does not lie in things themselves, then God is nevertheless the cause of the distance and evil thus understood. Or else things tear themselves away, and just this tearing away is the first guilt and the question remains of where this evil comes from in things.

All three systems do not accomplish what they are supposed to accomplish, the explanation of the possibility of the being of evil existing together with God. That makes us suspect that (1) the ground of beings as a whole has not been adequately conceived, (2) the being of evil has been inappropriately determined and (3) above all, a concept of Being is lacking which would make it possible to conceive the ground of beings in unity with evil as a being.

But is evil then really a being at all? The fact that one falls again and again into the escape of denying the reality of evil indicates, after all, that there must be an occasion for this in the nature of evil itself. Evil is taken for granted as the nongood, as a lack, as something lacking. What is lacking is not there. Nonbeing, nonpresence, we call this nonexistence. It cannot after all be said of something which is in its nature nonexistent that it is a being. Accordingly, the reality of evil is only an illusion. What is actually real can only be what is positive. And what we simply call evil and thus falsify into something positive by this term, this lack is, insofar as it is, always only a different degree of the good—thus taught Spinoza.

The difficulty here lies in the concept of the nonexistent. And we know that Greek philosophy in its beginning was already moved by this question whether the nonexistent is and how it is. Without going into this now, we must hold fast to one thing from our present consideration and transfer it to the following reflections. The question of evil and thus the question of freedom somehow have to do essentially with the question of the being of the nonexistent. Regarded in terms of the principle of the system in general, that is, of the question of Being, that means that the question of the nature of Being is at the same time the question of the nature of the not and nothingness. The reason this is so can only lie in the nature of Being itself.

As a lack, it is true that a lack is a not-being-present. Nevertheless, this absence is not nothing. The blind man who has lost his sight will argue vigorously against the statement that blindness is nothing existent and nothing depressing and nothing burdensome. Thus, nothingness is not nugatory; but, rather, something tremendous, the most tremendous element in the nature of Being. General thoughtlessness, of course, thinks differently: nothingness is just nothing. Every streetcar conductor understands this and for this reason, it is correct.

But even if one thinks and must think that evil as a lack is something existent after all, this determination is still different from that deeper reaching one which we already mentioned *a propos* the first characterization of identity in the statement: the good *is* evil. What is truly existent about the evil is the good. Nevertheless, this does not mean that evil itself is not existent and only a lack. Besides, we must ask here at once: what is this being in the good itself which thus constitutes the being of evil? How is the good to be understood as the ground of evil?

But according to the newly posited concept of human freedom, evil is that for which freedom can also decide. Thus, evil is first posited as such by man's freedom. But then evil and man's freedom thus understood do not signify a difficulty for the system—on the contrary. Since God created man as a being who is free for the good and for the evil, evil first begins with man, on account of his freedom. But the ground of beings as a whole is God. In that God creates man as a free being, he disburdens himself from being the creator of evil and leaves this to man.

But in this oft-cited consideration, there is only one difficulty. What does freedom mean here? If freedom means man's complete indeterminacy, neither for good nor for evil, then freedom is conceived merely negatively, as mere indecisiveness, behind which and before which stands nothing. This in-de-cisiveness thus remains nugatory, a freedom which is anything else but a ground of determination; it is complete indeterminacy which can never get beyond itself. This concept of freedom is again a negative one, only in another respect, familiar in the history of thought as the *libertas indifferentiae*, the seventh concept of freedom in our count.

Freedom as mere indecisiveness is neither freedom for the good nor freedom for evil. It is not freedom for something at all, it is also not freedom from something. Of course, "in-decisiveness" is not nothing; but, rather, something very effective, but not that in terms of which freedom could be determined, on the contrary, rather that which in its turn can only be understood and overcome in terms of freedom.

However, if freedom means the capability for good and evil, we must then ask again how a capability for evil arises from God as pure goodness, how God could posit a free being such as this at all. It is true that we showed earlier the origin of freedom in God, in the general consideration that pantheism correctly under-stood does not exclude the positing of freedom; but, rather, it requires it. But now it becomes clear that that "attempted derivation" actually remains questionable.

"For, if freedom is a power for evil it must have a root independent of God" (p. 28). Thus the only way out is to posit a second power alongside of God, the power of evil which, however, if it is to be independent in itself, must be equipotent with God. Such a dualism of the good and the evil principle is, however, rejected by Schelling because it would lead to a system of the "self-destruction of reason." Reason is namely the capability of unity, of the representing of beings as a whole in terms of one—in the unity of beings, where Being itself means as much as unifiedness, a determination of Being which is very old: *on = hen*.

However, dualism leads to the desperation of reason. This desperation of reason must not come about, that is, reason must be rescued—thus the unspoken, obvious thought goes. More precisely understood, that means that reason must be retained as the court of judgment of all determination of Being. Thus the dualism of two absolutely different and separate principles of the good and the evil is impossible.

But if freedom as the capability of evil must have a root independent of God, and if God, on the other hand, is to remain the one and sole root of beings, then this ground of evil independent of God can only be in God. There must be in God something which God himself "is" not. God must be conceived more primordially.

"God is more of a reality than is a mere moral world-order, and he has in him quite other and more vital activating powers than the barren subtlety that abstract idealists ascribe to him" (p. 31).

Idealism, which elevates God to a pure being of Spirit, precisely in order to save his perfection, turns God's nature into something harmless and unreal. And this for the reason that reality and beings in general are not experienced sufficiently as existing and the concept of Being has remained inadequate. It is true that modern science appears to be exactly a flight from the empty conceptual compartments of medieval scholasticism and to be a conquest of nature. And yet Schelling can say: "The whole of modern European philosophy since its inception (through Descartes) has this common deficiency—that nature does not exist for it and that it lacks a living basis" (p. 30).

Thus primordial experience and sufficient thorough consideration of the fact of evil is intent upon comprehending beings as more existent and asking again the question of the jointure of beings as a whole as the question of the system of freedom. Thus, the introduction's train of thought stops where it was supposed to take us, at the point where the necessity of a new beginning is evident and the step to new questions has become inevitable.

C. Interpretation of the Main Part of Schelling's Treatise. Its Task: Metaphysics of Evil as the Foundation of a System of Freedom (pages 31-98).

The key question of the main investigation is the question of the inner possibility and of the kind of reality of evil. The intention of the investigation is to provide a full and live concept of human freedom. Thus the right center for the plan of the system of freedom is to be gained. And this system wants to answer the fundamental question of philosophy of the essence of Being in a sense which comprehends all impulses to thought.

A *metaphysics of evil* is the foundation of the *question of Being* as the ground of the system which is to be created as a system of freedom. Accordingly, a metaphysics as the foundation of metaphysics is sought for—a circular procedure. Granted, Kant already speaks of the metaphysics of metaphysics. For him, that is the Critique of Pure Reason; for Schelling, the metaphysics of evil. We can measure the distance from Schelling back to Kant and what went on meanwhile in German philosophy.

First of all, we want to get to know roughly the articulation of the main investigation. The titles which we give to characterize the individual sections are only signs of what is treated there. They neither exhaust the content nor do they catch hold of that basic movement of thinking which is started here by Schelling's questions.

    I. The inner *possibility* of evil.
   II. The universal reality of evil as the possibility of individuals.
  III. The process of the individuation of real evil.
  IV. The form of evil appearing in man.
   V. The justification of God's divinity in the face of evil.
  VI. Evil in the system as a whole.
 VII. The highest unity of beings as a whole and human freedom.

I. THE INNER POSSIBILITY OF EVIL.

a) The Question of Evil and the Question of Being.

This first section begins the task immediately, but on the basis of the introduction. Thus everything remains strange and is difficult to follow if we have not mastered the introduction. This means, however, we should not only remember what is noted in the introduction and what the interpretation adds to this, but should also meanwhile have formed a readiness for a unique attitude of seeing and questioning. In this metaphysics of evil, we are to carry out the question of the essence of Being. Being has identity as its essence. Identity is unity as the belonging together of what is different. Yet the separation of what is different is not conceived as a difference, merely thought, empty in the sense of an empty logic that merely intends to make distinctions and which absents itself from everything, but as the occurrence of separating. This separation is always only the farewell to an earlier belonging to each other. The question of the essence of Being as the question of the possibility and reality of evil must follow this motion of increasing separation up to the highest bond. But this following is also not meant as mere "thought" following in imagination, but as a transformation of our real thinking and questioning. This transformation is intrinsically, and not just as a consequence, a returning to primordial fundamental mood. But moods in the essential sense do not come about by one's talking about them, but only in action, here in the action of thinking. Action, too, cannot make the mood, but only summon it. Thus the old difficulty which man can never overcome returns, that only in the process can we gain that which must already be gained for this process. That means the first attempt of following along with the movement of Being demands of itself a repetition. This means that we stay in the motion of questioning. We complain much and loudly about the deadness and unreality of an "abstract" thinking. But we should only complain that we so little and so seldom find our way to the works which are nothing other than the hidden collection of inexhaustible forces with the release of which creative *Dasein* can alone be ignited. *The greatness of a Dasein is first shown by the test whether it is capable of discovering and holding fast to the great resistance of its nature which towers above it.* Why do we make this remark here? In order to point out that essential conditions exist for following the main investigation, that we must at least be prepared for the necessity of an essential returning to a great basic mood. To point that out, however, all of this should not come about for us as "sentimentalities", but only in the hardness and simplicity of the questioning and real thinking which has cut itself loose from the puppet string of common "logic" in order to bind itself to a more primordial and thus stricter logic.

We are asking about the possibility of evil, how it is possible at all. This does not mean in what way it can come from somewhere else, but how it is intrinsically possible, what belongs to it and what belongs together in order for evil to be able to be what it is, thus, inner possibility. But do we not have to know beforehand what evil is in order to decide how it is possible? Yes and no. Yes, we have to know it somehow beforehand; we must have a preconcept of it. This preconcept can take hold only when what is to be conceived has already been experienced. We must have a preconcept or at least he must have one who now wants to unfold the inner possibility of evil. But since the thinker relieves us of this in a forceful way and brings it about, it is at the same time true that we do not immediately need this preconcept. Rather, for us the evidence of the inner possibility of evil is nothing other than the attainment of the concept of evil. It is true that we can anticipate the concept of evil and looking ahead say in a free version: *Evil is the revolt that consists in inverting the ground of the essential will into the reverse of God's.* But so far this is merely an unclear statement, above all lacking the focused perspective from which its meaning is fulfilled. The anticipated delineation of the nature of evil shows at most that we are still very far removed from comprehending. We also cannot decide from this statement which way the revealing of the inner possibility of evil has to go. And it is precisely this way which is important if we want to reach the movement of questioning. Detours are always false ways here.

The first section, which is supposed to treat the inner possibility of evil, contains an essential division (p. 39, at the end of the paragraph, "and this constitutes the possibility of good and evil"). We want to get to know this first part (p. 31, "The philosophy of Nature of our time . . ." up to p. 39). It really contains everything and we may thus not expect to understand it completely at the first try. On the other hand, if our interpretation of the introduction has taken the right direction and has correctly distributed the weight of things, we must already be prepared for what is decisive. The intention of the interpretation was with explicating the ontological question and gathering all questions together with regard to the question of Being. Since this is never explicitly evident in Schelling, our procedure might seem one-sided. But we may reconcile ourselves to this one-sidedness, provided that it is the one-sidedness directed toward the *One* decisive thing. As with every actual interpretation of a work of thought, it is true here that it is not the opinion which a thinker ends up with that is decisive, nor the version in which he gives this opinion. Decisive is rather the movement of questioning that alone lets what is true come into the open.

b.) The Jointure of Being: Schelling's Distinction of Ground and Existence.

The unspoken question, which is nevertheless also a motivating one, is the question of the essence and ground of Being. How does this become evident in the subsequent metaphysics of evil? In the new definition of the nature of human freedom put forth at first as an assertion, as "the faculty for good and evil," evil was explicitly mentioned. Accordingly, evil is a possible resolution of being free, a way of man's *being*-free. But according to the formal concept and within the tradition of the Idealistic interpretation of Being in which Schelling also, in spite of everything, keeps his place, being free is the fundamental determination of the being-in-itself of beings in general. The inner possibility of evil can thus only be elucidated by going back to the question: What belongs to the determination of a self-contained being? (Compare answer to Eschenmayer, I, VII, p. 164 ff.)

Schelling does not ask this question explicitly at first, but, rather, the main investigation starts with an answer:

> The Philosophy of Nature of our time first established the distinction in science between Being insofar as it exists, and Being insofar as it is the mere basis of existence. This distinction is as old as its first scientific presentation. As this very point at which the Philosophy of Nature departs from the path of Spinoza most decisively has been disregarded, it could be maintained in Germany up to the present time that the metaphysical principles of this philosophy were identical with those of Spinoza. And although it is this distinction which at the same time brings about the most definite distinction between nature and God, this did not prevent the accusation that it constituted a confusion of God with nature. As the present investigation is based on the same distinction, the following may be remarked for its explication (P. 31-32).

Briefly, Schelling says that in every "being" its existence and the ground of its existence must be distinguished. What do these terms mean: being, ground, existence?

"Being" (*Wesen*) is not meant here in the sense of the "essence" of a thing, but in the sense in which we speak of a "living being," of "household affairs," of "educational matters." What is meant is the individual, self-contained being as a whole. In every being of this kind, we must distinguish its "ground" and its "existence." This means that beings must be comprehended as existing and as ground-giving.

"Ground" always means for Schelling foundation, substratum, "basis," thus not "ground" in the sense of "ratio," not with the counterconcept "consequence" insofar as the *ratio* says why a statement is true or not true. "Ground" is for Schelling precisely the nonrational. On the other hand, however, we must avoid throwing this ground into the primeval swamp of the so-called irrational.

"Existence" does not really mean the manner of Being; but, rather, beings themselves in a certain regard—as existing; as we speak of a dubious "existence" and mean the existing person himself. Schelling uses the word existence in a sense which is closer to the literal etymological sense than the usual long prevalent meaning of "existing" as objective presence. Ex-sistence, *what emerges from itself* and in *emerging reveals itself.* From this explanation: "ground" as what forms the substratum, "existence" as what reveals itself, it can already be seen that this distinction by no means coincides with a current one in philosophy: that of *essentia* and *existentia*, "essence" and "existence," what-ness and that-ness.

Thus, Schelling also remarks correctly that this distinction, ground and existence, was first discovered and established in his philosophy of nature, in a treatise bearing the title, *Darstellung meines Systems der Philosophie* (1801). This treatise is the first presentation of the system of identity, that step in metaphysics which preserves the independence of nature and the selfhood of spirit to the last degree and yet thinks both together in a higher unity.

A certain indefinite generality and arbitrariness in the usage of leading terms often makes an understanding more difficult, not only of the system of identity, but also of German Idealism in general at this stage. The opposition of nature and Spirit is often understood as that of the real and the ideal. Here ideal means determined by representation in the sense of the explicit *I represent* (intelligence); real—what is thinglike. Or the same opposition in the formulation: *Object-Subject*. And later after *The Ages of the World.*

Object-subject—subject-object.

Being—beings.

But the ontological fundamental principle of the system of identity is: "Everything that is, is only insofar as it expresses absolute identity in a definite form of Being" (I, IV, p. 133). Schelling calls the individual forms and stages of Being "potencies."

Although the distinction cited of the ground and existence of a being can be found in the first presentation of his system, still it is not yet expressly worked out and accordingly planned in its whole scope for the determination of beings. This comes about only in the treatise on freedom. Subsequently, we shall call this "distinction," which according to Schelling constitutes the basic structure of self-contained beings, the *jointure of Being.*

The main investigation begins with an interpretation of this distinction about which it is explicitly noted that "the present investigation is based on it" (p. 32). The difference between ground and existence concerns beings as such in two different respects which, however, belong together. These determinations are thus concerned with the Being of beings in a unified way. We already heard that the primal nature of Being is will. Accordingly, the distinction cited must be contained in the nature of will if it is to provide the essential determination of Being. We must thus meet up with this distinction through a sufficiently primordial analysis of the nature of will. Schelling himself, of course, does not follow this path of essential analysis, neither here nor elsewhere in the treatise. Its task demands another path. In accordance with the main intention of our interpretation, we shall subsequently carry out such an analysis. Schelling, however, begins with an "interpretation"; that is, he shows this difference in beings themselves, not in an arbitrary being, but in *that* being which was always in view in the previous reflections—beings as a whole, regarded according to their basic structure: God and things in the broadest sense of what is dependent, of "what is created" ("creatures"). Of course, this kind of demonstration cannot be similar to pointing out the presence of an insect on grapevines. If we attempt such a demonstration as a criterion for Schelling's method—whether implicitly or explicitly—everything will immediately seem to be arbitrary and lacking conviction. However, we must remember that neither God nor the totality of the world are "things" in the usual sense. We can never bring this being before us like individual "cases" by which we "demonstrate" a sickness or like individual "examples" of birds by which we can empirically illustrate the generic concept "birds." The "interpretation" of the distinction of "ground and existence" with regard to God and creatures must have a different character. Schelling's method is not as arbitrary as it seems at first. He clearly knows about his point of departure and his way. To what extent these are justified and how one can decide about this justification in general is another question.

Schelling begins by showing this distinction of ground and existence in God. Showing means here at the same time illuminating the sense in which it is meant. And this sense points toward the way in which what-is (God) is to be presented to knowledge. Schelling reminds us of a common definition of God's nature as *causa sui*, cause of himself as existing, as ground of his existence. Thus, so it seems—the distinction is shown to be something common. But, says Schelling, ground is meant here only as a concept. Whoever speaks this way does not try at all to determine the factual nature of what they call ground. They completely neglect to say how this ground is ground. We can say that the kind of grounding remains indefinite. Taken in a quite empty sense, ground only means the whence of God's existence and this whence, says the opinion of that definition of the whence, is precisely God himself. Schelling, however, wants to accomplish precisely this: to bring to a conceptual formulation how God comes to himself, how God—not as a concept thought, but as the life of life—comes to himself. Thus a *becoming* God! Correct. If God is the existent being, then the most difficult and greatest becoming must be in Him and this becoming must have the most extreme scope between his whence and his whither. But at the same time, it is true that this whence of God, and also the whither, can again only *be in* God and *as* God himself: *Being!* But the determination of beings in the sense of the presence of something objectively present is no longer adequate at all to conceive this Being. Thus "existence" is understood beforehand as "emergence-from-self" revealing oneself and in becoming revealed to oneself coming to oneself, and because of this occurrence "being" with itself and thus in itself, "being" *itself*. God as existence, that is, the existing god is this god who is *in himself* historical. For Schelling, existence always means a being insofar as it is *aware of itself (bei sich selbst)*. Only that, however, can be aware of itself which has gone out of itself and in a certain way is always outside of itself. Only what has gone out of itself and what takes upon itself being outside of itself and is thus a being aware of itself has, so to speak, "absolved" the inner history of its Being and is accordingly "absolute." God *as the existing one* is the *absolute* God, or God as he himself—in brief: God-*himself*. God considered as the ground of his existence "is" not yet God truly as he himself. But, still, God "is" his ground. It is true that the ground is something distinguished from God, but yet not "outside of" God. The ground in God is that in God which God himself "is" not truly himself, but is rather his ground *for* his selfhood. Schelling calls this ground "nature" in God.

Now the decisive sentence with which Schelling begins may have been clarified: "As there is nothing before or outside of God, he must contain within himself the ground of his existence. All philosophies say this, but they speak of this ground as a mere concept without making it something real and actual. This ground of his existence, which God contains (within himself), is not God viewed as absolute, that is insofar as he exists. For it is only the basis of his existence, it is *nature*—in God, inseparable from him, to be sure, but nevertheless distinguishable from him" (p. 32).

We can already see here how identity now becomes clarified and deepened as belonging together in the sense of the merging of what has separated in a higher unity. Ground and existence are not two constituents out of which the "thing," called God, is put together. Rather, ground and existence are the key terms for the essential laws of becoming of God's becoming in his *Being* as God. Therefore, the common expression for this Being, the "is," must always be understood "dialectically."

For the sake of the importance of this section, let us briefly present the decisive thoughts once more. We began to interpret the first section of the main investigation of the treatise on freedom. It is the *gateway*. If we succeed in going through it, everything else will open up of its own accord.

We understand the main treatise as a metaphysics of evil with a metaphysical intention. The supplement means the question of the nature and reality of evil lays the ground for the question of Being in general. It lays the ground by forcing one to lay the previous ground more deeply. How far Schelling and German Idealism in general had and could have a clear knowledge of this procedure of metaphysics is a subordinate question now.

But the question of evil enters the decisive context of questioning of the treatise on freedom because the nature of human freedom is conceived as the faculty of good and of evil. Evil is a way of man's being free. Schelling wants to understand evil in the system of freedom. He does not, however, want a system of the self-laceration of reason. He thus wants to save the system after all, too, first the system and then the fitting concept of evil which is compatible with it.

But in this way what is distinctive about Schelling's position as a thinker would not be captured. For Schelling does not think "concepts"; he thinks forces and thinks from positions of the will. He thinks from the strife of powers which cannot be made to subside by a technique of concepts. Accordingly, the metaphysical theology carried out here also lies completely outside a formal analysis of the determinations of a dogmatic concept of God.

The first section is supposed to show the inner possibility of evil, that is, those conditions which make evil what it essentially is. The task is clear and the procedure seems simple. Schelling himself gives it an external presentation which gives this appearance. And at first we shall follow this external appearance.

Thus, the course is as follows:

Evil—if it is not absolutely nothing—must be a being. But what belongs to a being? Answer: a ground and an existence. This jointure of Being is to be "elucidated," and then the clarified concept is to be "applied" to the question of the nature of evil.

The reflection actually begins by stating the difference.

Ground: What gives ground, foundation. Thus ground not in the sense of the logical ground which has as its counterconcept the logical consequence.

Existence: The existing, in the meaning of emergence from self, of revealing oneself. In existence and as existence, a being comes to itself. Existing, a being is *itself* what it is. To be a self means in the idealistic interpretation to be "I," I as subject. Thus, Schelling also always means by existence the "subject" of existence. (I,VIII,p.164).

When we consider this, it is easy to see how a complete transformation has taken place since the Greek way of thinking. *Hypokeimenon* is what underlies, the foundation, the ground in Schelling's sense. The Latin translation for this is *subjectum*. But this *subjectum* becomes the I after Descartes so that Schelling now is in the position of opposing the *hypokeimenon* to the *subjectum*.

This distinction, however, is not a simple one, but an "identical" one. Each is in itself related to the other.

This is true of all the leading distinctions which the philosophy of identity incorporated within itself:

nature—Spirit
non-I—I
real—ideal
object—subject
Being—a being
thing—reason
"ground"—"existence"

The interpretation of the distinction:

First consideration: for a long time God has been called *causa sui*. The highest being must take upon himself the most weighty and great becoming, must in himself be the *historical god*.

The ground in God and God himself are separated and, as separated, belong to each other.

The *ground in God* is *that which God as himself is not* and *which still* is *not* outside of him.

The "is" must be understood "dialectically."

Now and in what follows, we have continually the opportunity to understand the "is" in the sense of identity correctly conceived. "It" (the ground) "is" nature in God. "Is" does not simply mean has the quality and the role. Rather, "Is" with a capital letter means that God as the ground takes it upon himself *to presence (wesen)* in the way of nature and to help constitute the Being of God. "It (the ground) is nature in God" and again on the next page, "but God is also prior to the ground."

Schelling says (on the same page): "And nature in general is therefore everything that lies beyond the absolute Being of absolute identity."

"Nature" now does not yet mean what we alone experience immediately as "nature," but signifies a metaphysical determination of beings in general and means what belongs to beings as their foundation, but is that which does not really enter the being of the self. Rather, it always remains what is distinguished from the self.

But when we now follow the instruction that the "is" is always to be thought dialectically, still the difficulties do not disappear in which the first elucidation of the jointure of Being stands. It is accomplished by returning to God. Here something is to be made clear by a reference to something which is obscure and the most obscure of all with regard to its nature and existence. We resist such an elucidation, especially when still another strange thing is connected with the return from the ontological to the theological. That in terms of which the difference (ground and existence) is to be understood as clarified is at the same time to be thought in a way still *strange* to common sense. We are not just required to return to God, we must rather think God still more primordially.

A remarkable interpretation of *elucidation,* yes indeed. And we must therefore first think through the difficulties which turn up in order to get to what really stands behind the appearance of a procedure of elucidation.

c.) The Becoming of God and Creatures. Temporality, Movement, and Being.

The Being of God is a becoming to himself out of himself. Ordinary thinking immediately finds here two seemingly insurmountable difficulties.

(1) A becoming God is no God at all, but something finite and (2) if God becomes out of his ground and first posits this ground itself as such insofar as he has distinguished himself from it, what is produced here is at the same time made into that which is in its turn first produced by what it itself was produced from. That is a "circle" in all possible respects. But for thought a circle is a contradiction, and contradiction is the destruction of all thinkability. Both difficulties have their root in a one-sided thinking which is unable to combine what is different and separated.

According to its formal concept, "becoming" is the transition from not-yet-being to being. Since a *not* occurs here, a lack and thus a finitude can be ascertained in becoming. Formally, without looking at the matter, that is correct (Compare I, VII, p. 403/4). But one forgets to ask whether this "not," that is, the not-yet-existing of the ground, does not ultimately and positively precisely make existence possible, whether the not-yet "is" not for itself just that from which precisely what emerges from itself comes. One forgets to notice that in this becoming what becomes is already in the ground as the ground. Becoming is neither a mere relinquishing of the ground nor an annihilation of it, but on the contrary, what exists first lets the ground be its ground. This becoming is not the mere the precursor of Being which is put aside afterward as, for example, in the case of the becoming of a shoe where the procedure of making it remains outside of the finished product, and the finished product becomes finished by being removed from the realm of procedure. On the contrary, in the case of the non-thing-like becoming of God, becoming as the development of essential fullness is included in Being as its essential constituent.

We are accustomed not only to "measure" every process and all becoming guided by time, but to follow it this way in general. But the becoming of the God as ground to the God himself as existing cannot be represented as "temporal" in the everyday sense. Thus, one is accustomed to attribute eternity to the Being of God. But what does "eternity" mean and how is it to be comprehended in a concept? God's becoming cannot be serialized in individual segments in the succession of ordinary "time." Rather, in this becoming everything "is" "simul-taneous." But simultaneous does not mean here that past and future give up their nature and turn "into" the pure present. On the contrary, original simul-taneity consists in the fact that being past and being present assert themselves and mingle with each other together with being present as the essential fullness of time itself. And this mingling of *true temporality*, this Moment, "is" the essence of eternity, but not the present which has merely stopped and remains that way, the *nunc stans*. Eternity can only be thought truly, that is, poetically, if we understand it as the most primordial temporality, but never in the manner of common sense which says to itself: Eternity, that is the opposite of temporality. Thus, in order to understand eternity, all time must be abstracted in thought. What remains in this procedure is not, however, a concept of eternity, but simply a misunderstood and half-baked concept of an illusory time.

The becoming of the God as the eternal is a contradiction for common sense. That is quite as it should be, for this contradiction characterizes the prevailing of a more primordial Being in which the earlier and the later of clock time has no meaning. What precedes, the ground, does not already have to be what is superior and higher and, conversely, what is superior can very well be what "follows." What is earlier in essence is not necessarily what is superior in essence and what is superior does not become lower by being something later. The "priority" of the one and the "superiority" of the other do not exclude each other here because there is no last and no first here, since everything is at once. But this "at once" is not to be understood as the contraction of the succession of ordinary time into a "now" magnified to giant proportions, but as the sole uniqueness of the inexhaustible fullness of temporality itself. "Ground and existence" are to be conceived *in the unity* of this primordial movement. This unity of their circling is what is primordial. But we must not take the two determinations out of this circle, immobilize them and set what is thus immobilized against each other in a seemingly "logical" thinking. Here a contradiction undeniably appears. But the origin of this contradiction is still more questionable than its appearance.

The ground is in itself what supports what emerges and binds it to itself. But as emergence from itself existence is what grounds itself on its ground and founds it explicitly *as its* ground.

Ground and existence belong together. This belonging together first makes their separation and the discord possible which builds up into a higher unity. Thus two dimensions emerge in the essence of "essence," in the constitution of the Being of beings indicated by ground and existence. First that of the primordial temporality of becoming and then, within this, the necessarily posited dimension of self-increasing, respectively falling beneath, self. These movements belong to the inner flow of the essence of Being if we avoid from the outset making the objective presence or the handiness of things the first and sole criterion of the determination of Being. We are protected from this nearly indestructible inclination only if we question this way of being a thing at the right time and dismiss it in its peculiarity.

But in the perspective of this essential connection of ground and existence, the essential possibility of evil, and thus the outline of its ontological constitution, is to be sought. And only in terms of this constitution does it become intelligible why and how evil is grounded in God, and how God is yet not the "cause" of evil. (Compare I, VII, pp. 375 and 399). Schelling states (p. 33): "God contains himself in an inner basis of his existence, which, to this extent, precedes him as to his existence, but similarly God is prior to the basis, as this basis, as such, could not be if God did not exist in actuality."

In the middle part of this paragraph, Schelling clarifies a correspondence to the determinations ground and existence and their reciprocal relationship.

"By analogy, this relationship can be explicated by referring to the relation of gravitation and light in nature. . . ." "Gravity" corresponds to the ground, "light" to existence. Gravity and light belong to the realm of "nature." But precisely for Schelling gravity and light and their relation to each other are not just an image, but gravity and light "are" in their relation of Being and essence within created nature only a certain expression of the essential jointure in Being itself, the jointure: ground-existence. Gravity is what burdens and pulls, contracts and in this connection what withdraws and flees. But light is always the "clearing," what opens and spreads, what develops. What is light is always the clearing of what is intertwined and entangled, what is veiled and obscure. Thus, what is to be illuminated precedes light as its ground from which it emerges in order to be itself light. When Schelling calls the reference to the relation of gravity and light an "analogical" explanation, this does not mean that it is only a pictorial image. Rather, he means a justified comparison of the one stage of Being with the other, both identical in the essence of Being and different only in potency.

We know that darkness and light, night and day, have always appeared as essential powers in man's reflection on beings, not just as "images." We know especially that "light" as the condition of seeing in our access to things has become determinative for the interpretation of cognition and knowledge in general. The *lumen naturale,* the natural light of reason, is that brightness in which beings stand for man, in keeping with his nature. Finally, we know that in the last decades of the eighteenth century, in the transition to the nineteenth century, the investigation of nature moved to a more primordial ground and new insights were made in which the fundamental appearances of gravity and light played a special role. However, today we no longer have the eyes to reproduce this insight into nature. This questioning of nature is called "romantic philosophy of nature" and is used with the following in mind: all of that is really nonsense. Really, that is, in the light of all the things that contemporary physics and chemistry can do. They can do a great deal and one should avoid minimizing things here. But all the more clearly should the limitations be seen. What today's physics and chemistry, what modern science, cannot do at all, can never do *as such,* is to take the perspective, or even provide it, for deciding the question whether that "romantic philosophy of nature" is nonsense or not. That is itself still a question, but we do not want to go into it now. But let us warn against dismissing the perspectives of the philosophy of nature as impossible viewed from the illusory superiority of technological possibilities of change and against falsifying the essential conditions of things into mere "poetic images." And if everything is supposed to be only "images," then the poetic language of imagery in today's exact science exists no less than before. Rather, it is at best only coarser, more rigid, and more accidental. It would be just as fatal if one wanted to jump head over heels into an earlier philosophy of nature, for which we lack the existential and conceptual basic positions today, or if one wanted to insist upon the present form of science as being something timeless. A transformation, which is necessary, can only occur when what rules us is transformed of its own accord. For this, one must oneself first of all rule what rules us, that is, stand in the middle of it and at the same time beyond it. That is the nature of transition. Ages of transition are the historically decisive ones.

The first elucidation of the distinction of ground and existence in a being, that is, with regard to God's nature, is "supplemented" by a second observation with regard to things.

"A consideration which proceeds from things leads to the same distinction" (p. 33ff.).

But we must consider right away that things as existing are somehow in God, that this being-in-God, however, is determined again and precisely from the nature of the divine Being in that it *is* God who *is* everything. The elucidation of the distinction ground-existence "which proceeds from things" must not be understood as if things could be considered for themselves, and thus show this jointure of Being in them. Rather, to consider things in their being means precisely to question them in their relation to God. For this reason this second "elucidation" steers us back to the same realm; but of course now in such a way that, in keeping with the matter, the "elucidation" of the jointure of Being goes unexpectedly from things over to a presentation of the becoming of things from God, briefly to a metaphysical project of the process of creation.

Here, too, and perhaps here most of all, we are just as inclined to fall prey to thoughts easily oppressing us. And we must not avoid them at all. Rather, everything must be concentrated on one main doubt about Schelling's whole procedure. Before we follow the second elucidation of the jointure of Being, we must gain clarity about this. What is merely "new" is in itself just as open to criticism as what is merely "old."

We would do well to understand again here beforehand the direction of Schelling's thinking. We know from the "introduction" that the question of the relation of things to God goes under the title of "pantheism," and that the formal concept of pan-theism was determined so far by the idea of "immanence." Occasionally, the criticism of Spinoza did show that his error consisted in understanding what was posited as existing in God as a thing, as thinglike. Here thing means beings of the species of dead, material bodies. But we may go on speaking of things' being-in-God if we just do not determine the thingness of the thing exclusively and primarily in terms of those material things.

But even when we understand the thingness of things in the sense of a "higher realism," the doctrine of *immanence* still has the difficulty which leads to what Schelling now undertakes—"to set aside completely the concept of immanence." Why? In the concept of "manence" (*manere*), of remaining, the idea of mere objective presence, of rigid presence, is contained if no other determination is added to transform it. "Immanence" thus leads to the idea of "things being lifelessly contained in God," just as the skirt hangs *in* the closet. Rather, the only concept appropriate to the being of things is that of "becoming." This obviously of necessity results from what was said about God's nature. There we also spoke of a "becoming." If things have their being in God and are in this sense godlike, their being, too, can only be understood as becoming. But the nature of things, which is not identical with God, but different from him, and as different from him, the infinite, is necessarily different in an infinite way—their being cannot consist in that becoming as eternity. Things cannot become in God since God the existing one is purely He himself. They are godlike, and can only become "in" God if they become in that which in God himself is not He himself. And that is the ground in God. This ground in God has now undergone a new determination through this reflection. It is that in which things are, emerging from it.

How is this to be understood? To understand this, we must think God's nature clearly, God, insofar as he is not He himself, that is, God, insofar as he is the ground of himself, God as the truly originating God who is still completely in his ground, the God as he has not yet emerged from himself to himself. This not-yet of the ground does not disappear after God has become the existing one, and it is not cast off as a mere no-longer. Rather, since it is an eternal becoming, the not-yet remains. There *remains* in God the eternal past of himself in his ground. The "afterwards" and "soon" are to be understood here in an eternal sense. The whole boldness of Schelling's thinking comes into play here. But it is not the vacuous play of thoughts of a manic hermit, it is only the continuation of an attitude of thinking which begins with Meister Eckhart and is uniquely developed in Jacob Boehme. But when this historical context is cited, one is immediately ready again with jargon, one speaks of "mysticism" and "theosophy." Certainly, one can call it that, but nothing is said by that with regard to the spiritual occurrence and the true creation of thought, no more than when we quite correctly ascertain about a Greek statue of a god that is a piece of marble—and everything else is what a few people have imagined about it and fabricated as mysteries.

Schelling is no "mystic" in the sense of the word meant in this case, this is, a muddlehead who likes to reel in the obscure and finds his pleasure in veils.

Schelling is also quite clear in the presentation of the originating God in his eternal past about how he must proceed here and can only proceed. We must, says Schelling, bring this being, the ground in God, "humanly closer to us."

But with this, Schelling only expresses what we have probably already had on the tip of our tongue for a long time with regard to the procedure of thought accomplished here: this whole project of divine Being and Being in general is accomplished by man. God is only the elevated form of man. The *morphe* of the *anthropos* is transformed, and what is transformed is asserted to be something else. In scholarly terms, this procedure is called "anthropomorphism." One doesn't need much acumen to find such "anthropomorphism" constantly in Schelling's main treatise. And where there is something like this, and so concrete, the judgment is already a finished one. Such a humanization of the God and of things in general, one says, is after all the opposite of true, "objective" cognition and thus valueless. It leads strict and exact thinking astray in a way perhaps full of feeling, but for that reason all the more dangerous, and it must be rejected. These complaints against "anthropomorphism" look very "critical" and lay claim to the superiority and decisiveness of a purely objective and well-informed judgment. But once a kind of thought is suspected of an uncritical and unobjective anthropomorphism, it is often difficult to take it seriously in its full weight. It cannot surprise us that such a suspicion was immediately placed upon Schelling's treatise too.

Nevertheless, we shall now try first of all at least to get acquainted with the rest of Schelling's reflection. For only then do we have sufficient knowledge of what the main reservation of anthropomorphism is directed against. We shall for the time being leave the suspicion of anthropomorphism in the treatise alone and attempt to comprehend the procedure in the first section as a whole.

d.) The Jointure of Being in God.

So far we have kept to Schelling's own external form of presentation: the elucidation of the structure of Being in two aspects: God and things. But let us not forget that in truth we are concerned with showing the inner possibility of evil. That distinction is completely in the service of this task. What Schelling calls an "elucidation" of this distinction itself already shows the inner possibility of evil. Thus, the distinction is by no means merely an external conceptual tool with whose help that demonstration is then brought about. Rather, the inner possibility of evil is grounded in the jointure of Being. The demonstration of how evil is rendered possible according to its inner possibility therefore becomes the task of showing how the conditions of the possibility of evil are created precisely by the fact that this jointure of Being is present in the nature of beings. It is surely not a matter of chance that the external form, and the inner development of just this first fundamental main section, remained very imperfect for here the most difficult task of all must be mastered. What was treated up to now in the external form of a first elucidation of the jointure of Being is still relatively easy to fathom—at least as far as its construction goes. The real difficulties begin—quite apart from the reservations about anthropomorphism—with respect to the construction and course now.

In order to get on here, let us free ourselves from the form of external presentation and attempt to place ourselves within the inner course of reflection. This can succeed only if we have the goal in mind and survey from that point whatever is necessary to attain it. Let us, therefore, now try to lay bare the core content of the whole first section according to these viewpoints. Then we shall pursue the movement in detail.

The task is to show the conditions of the inner possibility of evil. This showing projects and constructs the essential structure of evil guided in a peculiar way. According to its general concept and the assertions about it, evil is for us a possible *gestalt* of man's freedom. When it truly is, evil is thus in man, more precisely, is as human being. Therefore, the question is: How is this possibility of human being possible? And behind this question lies: How is man possible as the one who he is? But man is supposed to be the culmination and resting place of creation (I, VIII, p. 368/9). Thus, behind the question of the possibility of man lies the question of the possibility of this creature and thus of a creature in general. But behind the question of the possibility of what is created lies the question of the possibility of creation, and that is at the same time the question of its necessity, which can only be a freedom. Creation is a self-revelation of the god. And it is important in this context to avoid the idea of production which all too easily obtrudes itself. According to what we said before, however, the self-revelation of God concerns the nature and Being of God as the existing one. This nature of God's can only be shown by way of the nature of Being in general by returning to the jointure of Being and the essential lawfulness according to which in that jointure of Being, a being is structured as a being. God is truly himself as the Existent, that is, as He who emerges from himself and reveals himself. In that God, as He himself is, is with himself and purely from himself, he is the pure will. He is Spirit, for the Spirit in Spirit is the will, and the will in will is understanding. But understanding is the faculty of rule, of law, of ruling, binding unity in the sense of the unification of what is different belonging together. This articulating unity shines through what is confused and obscure. Understanding is the faculty of clearing. The pure will of the pure understanding is what primordially wills itself, Spirit. God as Spirit is as the existing one who, as Spirit, emerges from itself.

Now every being, however, can only be revealed in its opposite (I, VII, p. 373). There must be an other for him which is not God as He is himself and which yet includes the possibility of revealing himself in it. Thus, there must be something which, although it originates from the inmost center of the God and is Spirit in its way, yet still remains separated from him in everything and is something individual. But this being is man. Man must be in order for the God to be revealed. What is a God without man? The absolute form of absolute monotony. What is a man without God? Pure madness in the form of the harmless. Man must be in order for the God to "exist." Fundamentally and generally expressed, this means that certain conditions commensurate with the nature of Being and the nature of God must be fulfilled to make God possible as the existing Spirit, that is, to make man possible. But then this means that the conditions of the possibility of the revelation of the existing God are at the same time the conditions of the possibility of the faculty for good and evil, that is, of that freedom in which and as which man has his being. To demonstrate the possibility of evil means to show how man must be, and what it means that man is. After all this it becomes clear that the ground of evil is nothing less than the ground of being human. But this ground must be in God's innermost center. The ground of evil is thus something positive in the highest sense. Thus, evil itself cannot be something negative. Still more, it will not be sufficient just to emphasize some positive element in evil, too, and to understand it, for example, as the finite in opposition to the infinite. Finitude by itself is not yet evil; at any rate, not if we comprehend finitude as mere limitedness, as a mere no-further and stopping somewhere, corresponding to the limitedness of a material thing taken by itself. The principle of evil must be sought in a higher realm, in the spiritual realm. For evil itself is spiritual, yes, "in a certain regard the most pure spiritual thing, for it wages the most violent war against all *Being*, yes, it would like to incorporate the ground of creation" (Stuttg. *Privatvorlesung* 1810; I, VII, p. 468).

In our judgment of evil, we are either too hasty and superficial or too comfortable in that each time we take it to be merely a lack, in any case, at best as what is merely desolate, confused, coarse, and ugly, as when we all too easily misinterpret and underestimate an error as a lack of truth. However, error is not a lack of intelligence, but twisted intelligence. Thus, error can be highly ingenious and still be an error. Schelling once said:

> Whoever is even somewhat familiar with the mysteries of evil (for one must ignore it with one's heart, but not with one's head) knows that the highest corruption is precisely the most intelligent, that in it everything natural and thus even sensuousness, even lust itself finally disappears, that lust turns into cruelty and that demonic-diabolical evil is much further removed from pleasure than is the good. If, therefore, error and malice are both spiritual and come from the Spirit, it is impossible that Spirit be the highest thing. (*Ibid.* I, VII, p. 468)

Only if we take such a high perspective of questioning and understand the nature of evil—malice—as Spirit, do we have sufficient scope for the task of following the inner possibility of evil to its innermost realm of conditions.

We showed that a quite definite echelon of questions lies in this question which *leads back* to the jointure of Being starting from the possibility of evil. The demonstration of what makes the possibility of evil possible must thus allow this possibility to originate, conversely, starting from the jointure of Being. We shall now pursue more closely Schelling's manner of sketching this origin in an essential project. From what has now been said in preparation, it becomes clear that at bottom we can no more speak at all about a mere "elucidation" of the distinction of ground and existence guided by a consideration of created things. On the contrary, it is a matter of the "elucidation" (*Erläuterung*), making clear and bright, of the origin of evil with the help of the jointure of Being by going back to its essential lawfulness.

But this is not enough. We know that evil is a possibility of human freedom. Thus, the nature of human freedom must emerge in the clarification of the origin of the inner possibility of evil. In relation to what we have discussed up to now, this means that it must become evident how the various concepts of freedom now come into play and are transformed. In the course of our interpretation of the introduction, we have named six different concepts of freedom, apart from the concept of freedom now dominant. These concepts are not simply removed by the one set forth now. Rather, what they capture, but think one-sidedly and exaggeratedly, is now put within its limits and in its place. Only from the perspective of the truly metaphysical concept of freedom will we gain a view into the inner connection of what those concepts mean individually when only enumerated. Then there will no longer be six different concepts, but they will become *one* single jointure of human freedom active within itself. We shall now follow the essential steps of the first section.

It is important to remain closer to the text again now without claiming to clarify everything in a final way. But because the success of a true understanding depends above all on our actualizing the *movement* of the project, let us now once again—in brief statements—place the task before us.

As the essential possibility of human freedom, evil is an essential manner of human freedom. As the spirit separated from God and thus idiosyncratic, man is that being in which God reveals himself as eternal Spirit. This self-revelation of God in man is in itself at the same time the creation of man. But self-revelation belongs to the nature of God as the existing one. Existence is the primordial and essential self-revelation of God in himself *before* the eternal act of creating things. But existence is intrinsically related to that in God from which he emerges as existent, to the ground in God. Thus existence, self-revelation in general and the creation of the world in particular and thus human beings and thus the possibility of evil have their essential beginning, their "principle," in the nature of the ground.

Therefore, the reflection on the origin must begin with an essential project of the nature of this ground in God—all of this, however, in anticipation of the becoming of creation. The entire reflection on the origin is, however, carried out in the light of a concept of Being which has abandoned that decisive orientation toward the mere bodily presence of material things.

A consideration which proceeds from things leads to the same distinction. First, the concept of immanence is to be set aside completely insofar as it is meant to express a dead conceptual inclusion of things in God. We recognize, rather, that the concept of becoming is the only one adequate to the nature of things. But the process of their becoming cannot be in God, viewed absolutely, since they are distinct from him *toto genere* or—more accurately—in eternity. To be separate from God they would have to carry on this becoming on a basis different from Him. But since there can be nothing outside God, the contradiction can only be solved by things having their basis in that within God which is not *God himself* (footnote: this is the only correct dualism, namely a dualism which at the same time admits a unity. We mentioned above a modified dualism according to which the principle of evil does not stand alongside goodness, but is subordinated to it. It is hardly to be feared that anyone will confuse the relationship established here with that dualism in which the subordinate is always an essentially evil principle and for this very reason remains incomprehensible with respect to its origin in God.), that is, in that which is the basis of His existence. If we wish to bring this Being nearer to us from a human standpoint, we may say it is the longing which the eternal One feels to give birth to itself. This is not the One itself, but is coeternal with it. This longing seeks to give birth to God, that is, the unfathomable unity, but to this extent it has not yet the unity in its own self. Therefore, regarded in itself, it is also will: but a will within which there is no understanding and thus not an independent and complete will, since understanding is actually the will in willing. Nevertheless, it is a will of the understanding, namely, the longing and desire thereof; not a conscious but a prescient will, whose prescience is understanding. We are speaking of the essence of longing regarded in and for itself, which we must view clearly, although it was long ago submerged by the higher principle which had risen from it, and although we cannot grasp it perceptively but only spiritually, that is, with our thoughts. (PP. 33-34)

Now a part follows that does not belong directly to the train of thought and in any case is considerably disturbing if what is essential has not already been grasped. We shall leave this part (p. 34), "Following the eternal act of self-revelation . . grow clear thoughts" (p. 35), aside for now and take up the end of the main train of thought with the following sentence: "We must imagine the primal longing in this way—turning towards the understanding, indeed, though not yet recognizing it, just as we longingly desire unknown, nameless excellence. This primal longing moves in anticipation like a surging, billowing sea, similar to the 'matter' of Plato, following some dark, uncertain law, incapable in itself of forming anything that can endure."

The task of this part is the characterization of the nature of the ground in God as "longing." We have already shown how in general positing of the jointure of Being in God takes His nature away from the misinterpretation of this being in the sense of some gigantic, objectively present thing. The nature of being God is a becoming. By going back to the ground of this becoming, Schelling means something which is *in* God as that which is determined both by ground and existence in an equally primordial way. Schelling's presentation gives the appearance that God exists first only *as ground*. But God is always that which is determined by ground and existence, the "primal being" which as such is its nature—*before* any ground and *before* any existence, thus before any duality at all. Schelling calls it (p. 87) the "primal ground or, rather, the *groundless*," "*absolute indifference*," about which no difference, not even the jointure of Being, can be really predicated adequately. The sole predicate of the Absolute is the "lack of predicates," which still does not turn the Absolute into nothing.

But as soon as we speak of the ground in God, we do not, however, mean a "piece" of God to which the existing God belongs as the producer and counterpart. Rather, God's being a ground is a way of the eternal becoming of God as a whole. And this becoming does not have its beginning in the ground, but just as primodially in existing, that is, it is a becoming without beginning. But because the nature of being God is this becoming, the being of things can only also be understood as becoming, since nothing which *is* can be thought as being absolutely outside of God.

The treatise begins by explicitly pointing out that the "nature" of things is to be understood as becoming. This anticipates that whose possibility is to be shown. But with this, the concept of thing changes, too. The thinghood of things consists in revealing the nature of God. To be a thing means to present God's Being, which is an eternal becoming, itself as a becoming. Things refer through themselves to primordial Being. And this referring-through-themselves is not an act which they perform on top of being things, but being a thing is this referring-through-itself, this transparency. The way a thinker sees "things" depends upon how primordially he comprehends the nature of Being. Conversely, it is true that how primordially he views the nature of Being also depends upon the fundamental experience of things guiding him. The understanding of the thinghood of things in the sense of the referring-through-itself of the primal being permits us now to call man *a thing*, too, without the danger of misinterpreting his nature from the very beginning.

This interpretation of thinghood, however, is also a presupposition for correctly understanding what Schelling is trying to say in the statement that the being of things is a becoming. He does not mean that platitude that all things are continuously changing. Nor does he mean that external ascertainment that there is nowhere at all in the world a state of rest and things really do not have *being*. Rather, the statement means that things, of course, *are*, but the nature of their being consists in actually presenting a stage and a way in which the Absolute is *anchored* and *presented*. Being is not dissolved into an external flowing away called becoming; becoming is rather understood as a way of Being. But Being is now understood primordially as will. Beings are in being according to the joining of the factors "ground and existence" belonging to the jointure of Being in a willing being.

To say that the being of things is a becoming means that existing things strive for a definite stage of willing. The indifferent uniformity of a purely static multiplicity does not exist in their realm. Becoming is a manner of preserving Being, serviceable to Being, not the simple opposite of Being as it might easily appear if Being and becoming are only distinguished in formal respects and Being is understood as objective presence. (Without really taking hold of the problem, Schelling comes near the true, metaphysical relations between Being and becoming here which have always easily withdrawn from the thinker's view because he gets lost in the formal conceptual relations of both ideas. Nietzsche, too, never got out of the network of formal dialectic at this point.) Now we have a definite perspective on the metaphysical connection of Being between God and things.

The Being of the existing God is becoming in the primordial simultaneity of absolute temporality, called eternity. The being of things is a becoming as a definite emergence of divine Being into the revealedness of opposites still concealing themselves. The thinghood of things is so little determined by an indifferent objective presence of material bodies that matter itself is conceived as Spirit. What "we" feel and see as matter is Spirit which has congealed into the extended gravity of inertia.

But Schelling grasps the metaphysical connection of Being between God and things themselves in the following two statements (pp. 33): "To be separate from God they would have to carry on this becoming on a basis different from him. But since there can be nothing outside God, this contradiction can only be solved by things having their basis in that within God which is not *God himself,* that is, in that which is the basis of his existence."

The being of things is a being separated from God as absolute becoming. The being of things is thus itself a becoming. This becoming must thus be grounded, on the one hand, in a ground which is different *from* God and at the same time a ground which is active *in* God. How is this ground to be understood which grounds the separation of things *from* God as their inwardness *in* God?

Starting with this question, a metaphysical perspective on the leading question of the inner possibility of evil is now easily attained. We can characterize it by the following three questions:

1. How can something which is separated *from* God still be divine?
2. How is evil possible in the realm of this being?
3. How can it as a being be *grounded in* God *without* being *caused* by God?

The investigation must start with the ground which is different from God Himself, but active in God. Obviously, we must grasp this ground in two respects—which belong together. On the one hand, with regard to how God's becoming from Himself to Himself occurs in that ground, and then how this becoming a self of God is the creation of things which is nothing other than the overcoming of divine egoism and as this overcoming, not the manufacturing of nature, but the temporal bending of her eternal essence.

This double and yet unified regard to the nature of the ground in God must guide us when we now follow the individual determinations. They always remain untrue as long as we understand them one-sidedly.

What Schelling hastily writes here in a few pages subsequently stimulated his reflection to make new attempts again and again for decades. He himself knows more clearly than others that it is only a "beginning" (compare I, VII, p. 169, Answer to Eschenmayer).

e. Longing as the Nature of the Ground in God (The Existence of God in Identity with His Ground.)

The nature of the ground in God is longing? Here the objection can hardly be held back any longer that a human state is transferred to God in this statement. Yes! But it could also be otherwise. Who has ever shown that longing is something merely human? Who has ever completely dismissed the possibility with adequate reasons that what we call "longing" and live within might ultimately be something other than we ouselves? Is there not contained in longing something which we have *no* reason to limit to man, something which rather gives us occasion to understand it as that in which we humans are freed *beyond* ourselves? Is not longing precisely the proof for the fact that man is something other than only a man? It is indeed a bad choice if we specifically choose longing in order to demonstrate an anthropomorphization of the god which creeps in with it. But here we do not yet want to discuss in depth the anthropomorphic objection; its seemingly unshakable forcefulness is only to be generally shattered.

Right now it is more important to understand what this determination means philosophically. It is not supposed to attribute a quality to God, but the being a ground of the ground is to receive a determination. Of course, we must put aside all sentimentality with this concept and pay sole attention to the *nature* of the *metaphysical movement prevalent* there.

"Addiction" (*Die "Sucht"*)—which has nothing to do with searching (*Suchen*) etymologically—primordially means sickness which strives to spread itself; sickly, disease. Addiction is a striving and desiring, indeed, the addiction of longing, of being concerned with oneself. A double, *contrary* movement is contained in longing: the striving away from itself to spread itself, and yet precisely back to itself. As the essential determination of the ground (of being a ground) in God, longing characterizes this Being as urging away from itself into the most indeterminate breadth of absolute essential fullness, and at the same time as the overpowering of joining itself to itself. In that the general nature of the will lies in desiring, longing is a will in which what is striving wills itself in the indeterminate, that is, wills to find itself in itself and wills to present itself in the expanded breadth of itself. But since the will in this willing is precisely *not* yet aware of itself and is not its own, is not yet really itself, the will remains an untrue will. The will in willing is the understanding, the understanding knowledge of the unifying unity of what wills and what is willed. As the will of the ground, longing is thus a will without understanding which, however, foresees precisely being a self in its striving. Eternal longing is a striving which itself, however, never admits of a stable formation because it always wants to remain longing. As a striving without understanding, it has nothing which has been understood and is to be brought to stand and stability, nothing which it could call something definite, unified. It is "nameless"; it does not know any name; it is unable to name what it is striving for. It is lacking the *possibility of words*.

But in these reflections we are still taking the ground for itself, and thus we go astray. For itself, in keeping with its innermost nature, the ground is, of course, ground *for* existence. This relation to emergence from self lies in it itself. And only in this orientation toward existence does the understanding of longing required here become complete. In the absolute beginning of the primal being, it is a matter of emergence-from-self which is yet a remaining-within-itself, so much so that this remaining-within-itself constitutes the first coming-to-itself. Longing is *stirring*, stretching away from itself and expanding. And just in this stirring lies and occurs the excitement of what stirs to itself. The propensity to present itself is the will to bring itself before itself, to re-present *itself*. Thus Schelling goes onto the next step after the first characterization of eternal longing (pp. 35-36): "But there is born in God Himself an inward, imaginative response, corresponding to this longing, which is the first stirring of divine Being in its still dark depths. Through this response, God sees Himself in His own image, since His imagination can have no other object than Himself. This image is the first in which God, viewed absolutely, is realized, though only in Himself; it is the beginning in God, and is the God-begotten God Himself. This image is at one and the same time, reason—the logic of that longing. . . ."

We interrupt here.

Three things are to be emphasized here: (1) God's representing turned back to Himself is co-original with the longing of the ground, (2) this representation is the *word* of that longing, and (3) representing as the true coming-to-oneself out of the original being-outside-of-itself of longing is the first existence, the first manner, of the absolute reality of the God Himself.

Regarding (1): God's self-representation has nothing other than the ground which God is. In His ground, God sees Himself. This seeing encompasses the whole infinite un-unfolded fullness of his nature. Un-unfolded, this fullness is an emptiness and the desert of God. But this seeing encompasses God's nature and thus throws light upon it and finds itself as the illuminated ground. In the ground God sees Himself, that is, in this longing as the first excited stirring—Himself as the one who sees, Himself as the one who represents Himself. For by bringing something *before* itself, what represents also places itself in the scope of what stands before it. This self-representing occurs by the ground's being re-presented. Thus, God sees "Himself" in the darkness of the ground, but in the counterimage of the ground. He sees his "likeness," but hidden in the un-unfolded ground.

Regarding (2): this self-re-presenting brings about the first illuminated separation in God in which, however, the eternal being does not fall apart; but, on the contrary, gathers Himself to Himself and establishes His own essential unity in this gathering. Gathering, establishing unity as such, is called *legein* in Greek, from this, *logos* which was later interpreted for definite reasons (compare Introduction to Metaphysics) as *speech* and *word*. Because of a creative affinity to this tradition of metaphysics, Schelling can say that that representing of the image is the "word." In what follows we shall meet this "word" in God's nature several times. To begin with, let us remember its metaphysical meaning: the word as the naming of what is gathered in itself, of *unity*, the first establishing of unity still remaining, however, in God Himself. But we know from the introduction that unity always means *identity* in the primordial sense, unification of what is in itself differentiated and separate. Thus, the differentiated is just as much contained in representation and the word as the unified, since the unified needs the difference for the fulfillment of its own nature. Therefore:

Regarding (3): The first existing occurs in God's first seeing of Himself in longing's hidden search for itself. But the first existing does not follow a time of longing afterwards, but belongs co-originally to longing in the eternity of becoming. Just as the ground is only a ground for existence, the emergence from itself to itself is only an emergence from the ground. But thus this existence does not repel the ground—on the contrary. Existing, the primal being places itself precisely and explicitly back in the ground. As existent, it has eternally taken over the ground and thus affirmed longing as eternal. Thus, it is and remains the continual consumption of itself which never devours itself, but precisely burns toward what is inextinguishable in order to maintain the light placed in it in its innermost darkness. The word in God, the eternal "yes" to itself is the eternal speech in which God *co-responds* and grants a place and emphasis to what the will of longing wills.

Thus, both determinations of essence, ground and existence, are clarified in God. But we saw that an essential reference leads from each to the other, and that means that they already presuppose a primordial unity in themselves. But only since the ground is active as ground and existing is active as existing is this unity itself established and placed within itself. If the presentation of the jointure of Being in God is understood correctly in this respect, then the train of thought must lead immediately to the presentation of this *unity* of the jointure of Being. This shows itself in the interpretation in the middle of the sentence which at the passage "The *word* of that longing" continues with "and the eternal Spirit which feels within it the *Logos* and everlasting longing. This Spirit, moved by that love which it itself is, utters the Word so that the understanding together with longing becomes creative and omnipotent Will and informs nature, at first unruly, as its own element or instrument."

With "and the eternal Spirit" a new subject enters the sentence grammatically. What that subject is and how it is present is portrayed in what was read. It is said of eternal Spirit:

1. He feels in Himself on the one hand the word and at the same time eternal longing. This at the same time points to the fact that Spirit is that through which God as the existing brings Himself before Himself. But the existing one as such is related to his ground. Spirit means the unity of the ground in God and his existence. A unity, however, not in the empty sense of a relation merely thought, but as a unifying unity in which, as the origin, what is to be unified is present without losing its differentiation, is present precisely with it. Spirit feels in itself the word and longing at the same time—again, this "at the same time" does not mean empty simultaneity, but means the inner relation which word and longing have to each other. What longing always already was, it will always have been. But it will *be* this in the word which will only be what it already was. Longing is the nameless, but this always seeks precisely the word. The word is the elevation into what is illuminated, but thus related precisely to the darkness of longing. Spirit finds this reciprocal relation and in it what is related and thus itself. If ground and existence constitute the essence of a being as something existent in

itself, then Spirit is the primordially unifying unity of essence. This concept of Spirit should be borne in mind in everything that follows. Of eternal Spirit it is said:

2. It is "moved by love." Here it is indicated that *Spirit, too, is not yet the highest reality,* not yet the innermost origin of self-movement in God and in primal Being in general. On the other hand, being moved by love also does not mean that love is only a motive for the working of Spirit, but it is the essence ruling in Spirit. Spirit is the primordially unifying unity which arises above the reciprocal relation as the reciprocal relation of ground and existence. As such a unity, Spirit is *pneuma.* This wafting is only the breath of what most primordially and truly unifies: *love.* We already referred to its metaphysical nature. It is primordial unity which as such joins what is different and can be for itself, holding them apart.

"For not even Spirit itself is supreme; it is but Spirit, or the breath of love. But love is supreme. It is that which was before there were the depths and before existence (as separate entities), but it was not there as love, rather—how shall we designate it" (p. 86).

Here words leave the thinker, too. Love moves Spirit. That means that its primordial unification of the being with itself wants what is different, what could be for itself, precisely to *be* different and move apart. For without this, love would not have what it unified, and without such unifying, it would not be itself. The will of love thus wills not some blind unification, in order to have some kind of unity, but it wills separation initially and really always, not so that things should just remain that way, but so that the ground might remain for ever higher unification. Now we must grasp the core of the statement:

3. Eternal Spirit moved by love "utters the word." The "utterance of the word"—until now the word, the opening of the unity of what is disparate, the gathering of the unruly to its inner law, until now the word still remained in God. Now Spirit, that is, love, utters the word because it wants to *be* the unity of what is separated. Spirit speaks the word of the understanding. This word co-responds to the ground in the ground. Ground and existence in their unity, the jointure of Being is uttered. Into what? Into the other, what God is not as he Himself is, into the ground, the un-ruly and what is yet ordered in a hidden way, what still is present without gathering, into that which needs gathering, into the mere, unruly stirring of the ground. The utterance of the word is the speaking of the word into the ground, into the unruly in order for it to elevate itself to unity. As the will of love, Spirit is the will to what is in opposition. This will wills the will of the ground and wills this will of the ground as the counterwill to the will of the understanding. As love, Spirit wills the opposing unity of those two wills. But what is the unity of such opposing wills? What happens when what always strives back to itself, and yet expands itself, enters the will of opening and gathering and unifying? What happens when the gathering will as such must be broken by the

resistance of what strives apart? Form and gestalt come about, and the will becomes a formative will.

4. Spirit uttering itself is formative will. And it is formative in that to which it utters itself, in the ground which as longing—by itself—can never bring about the definiteness of a lasting formation and a name. "Original nature," the ground active in itself, now comes to word. "Now" the will of the ground is an awakened, formative will. Original, unruly nature is now creating nature, not just urging will. "Now" creation occurs in the creating rule of Spirit. And only as this creating will does time come about, more exactly, is its becoming prepared. This "now" is an eternal now. Creation is not added to God's nature as a particular act sometime—there is, of course, no time. For as the existing one, God *is* what emerges from Himself. He emerges from Himself by speaking the word into original nature. (Regarding the text: "utter the word *that* . . . ," not "which," and the "that" means the "that" of consequence, "so that"; but this consequence not as an external consequence, but just the consequence following in the word is uttered.)[14]

Now we are able to look over the whole sentence and thus to grasp correctly the meaning of the "and" with which it begins. This "and" does not simply connect what follows to what precedes. Rather, it joins what was said about longing for itself and about the understanding for itself together in the living unity of the Spirit. But it does this in such a way that Spirit itself as the existing one shows itself also only in the utterance of the word. Eternal Spirit is the primordial unity of ground and existence in God. Ground and existence are each in their way the totality of the Absolute, and as such they belong together and are inseparable. What longing insisting upon itself wills is the same as what the word of the understanding wills and raises to the clearing of representing. Ground and existence in God are only various aspects of the one primordial unity. But in that eternal Spirit becomes present as ground, it becomes present as that which it is not as itself, what its eternal past striving back to itself is. Ground and existence are eternally separated in eternal Spirit in such a way that they are eternally indissoluble as the same.

f. Creation as the Movement of Becoming of the Absolute and of Created Beings. The Individuation of Created Beings.

"Eternal Spirit" is the determination in which the unity of the God unto Himself, the identity of the Absolute, develops. This coming to oneself, however, is in itself self-utterance as speaking oneself into the unruly nature (*Natur*) of the ground. This means that the "eternal deed" of creation already belongs to God's essence. What belongs to the essence of creation itself is already prefigured here. Now, however, it is expressly analyzed in the following section (pp. 36-37):

The first effect of the understanding in nature is the separation of forces, which is the only way in which the understanding can unfold and develop the unity which had necessarily but unconsciously existed within nature, as in a seed; just as in man in the dark longing to create something, light comes about in that thoughts separate out of the chaotic confusion of thinking in which all are connected but each prevents the other from coming forth—so the unity appears which contains all within it and which had lain hidden in the depths. Or it is as in the case of the plant which escapes the dark fetters of gravity only as it unfolds and spreads its powers, developing its hidden unity as its substance becomes differentiated. For since this Being (of primal nature) is nothing else than the eternal ground of God's existence, it must contain within itself, though locked away, God's essence, as a light of life shining in the dark depths.

But longing, roused by reason, now strives to preserve this light shining within it and returns unto itself so that a ground of being might ever remain. In this way there is first formed something comprehensible and individuated; since the understanding, in the light which has appeared in the beginning of nature, rouses longing (which is yearning to return into itself) to divide the forces (to surrender darkness) and in this very division brings out the unity enclosed in what was divided, the hidden light. And this (forming of something comprehensible) does not occur by external discovery, but through a genuine invention, since what arises in nature is conceived in it, or, still better, through revival, the understanding reviving the unity or idea concealed in the sundered depths. These forces which are divided but not completely separated in this division, are the material out of which the body will later be molded; while the soul is that living nexus which arises, as the center of these forces, in their division, from the depths of nature. Because primal reason elevates the soul as inner reality out of a ground which is independent of the understanding, the soul, on this account, remains independent of it, a separate and self-maintained being.

It can readily be seen that in the tension of longing necessary to bring things completely to birth, the innermost nexus of the forces can only be released in a graded evolution, and at every stage in the division of forces there is developed out of nature a new being whose soul must be all the more perfect the more differentiatedly it contains what was left undifferentiated in the others. It is the task of a complete philosophy of nature to show how each successive process more closely approaches the essence of nature, until in the highest division of forces the innermost center is disclosed.

In order to grasp correctly the inner intention and movement of this train of thought, we must remember our task: projecting the inner possibility of evil as something spiritual existing for itself, that is, the possibility of human being. But because he is different and separated from God, man is something created. Therefore, it is first necessary to sketch out created beings in their essence.

It was shown now that the origin of creation lies in the essence of eternal Spirit. But it can be seen from the essence of the creator what belongs to the essence of what is created, how it *is*. Creating is not the manufacturing of something which is not there, but the bending of the eternal will of longing into the will of the word, of gathering. *For this reason* created beings are themselves a willing and what becomes in willing. But in this becoming what becomes is always, as a being, what it is purposely capable of as a willing being, no more and no less.

However, Schelling does not plan to report on what went on during the creation of the world back then, but attempts to make concrete how the movement of the creation of nature is constructed in itself. Yet that contains at the same time a determination of how created nature "is" as such, in what sense its independence and its self-ruling can be conceived metaphysically. Previously—and still now—one took the answer to this question very lightly: either one thinks of the creation in the sense of the manipulation of a craftsman who manufactures things and puts them on their feet—this interpretation does not do a thing for a real questioning of the essence of things, on the contrary—or one grasps the being-in-itself of things solely in terms of the side that they are objects of theoretical observation for us and then says how as objects they are independent of this subject in such observation and in relation to the observing subject. The question of this independence is indeed very essential. It has not yet been truly asked even today, let alone answered, but this independence of things of our observation is only an essential consequence of their being self-contained. But the latter cannot be explained by the former, at best it can be indicated.

Thus, in following Schelling's project of the essence of the movement of creating-created nature we must keep the metaphysical question of Being in mind. We must not slip back into the attitude of a naive curiosity which would like at this opportunity to take a look behind the secret of the workshop. This "back then" does not exist at all, because the occurrence is eternal and that means also a nowmoment (*ein jetzt augenblickliches*).

We heard that the Being of things is a becoming. Being created thus does not mean being manufactured, but *standing in creation* as a becoming. Thus, everything depends on grasping the movement of this becoming. But since the creature (*das Wesen*), the being-in-itself always has its essence in the unity of ground and existence and since this "unity" is not an external, mechanistic piecing together of two pieces, but rather the reciprocal relation as a unified self-relating and "self-attraction and repulsion," we must look for the movement in the essence of creation in this reciprocal relation of ground and existence. But, moreover, since "creation" as occurrence is the emergence from self of the Absolute coming-to-itself, the movement in the essence of creation and thus of the becoming and Being of created nature must be understood in terms of the essence of the eternal ground and eternal understanding and their eternal unity as that of absolute Spirit.

We can facilitate the understanding of the section cited by emphasizing a question which is in the air, but does not get asked explicitly. That is the following:

However creation is understood, a fundamental determination of the creature is essential, that is, that it is always something definite, individual, a "this." The question of the becoming of the creature is thus the question of the becoming of the individual, that is, of the essence of individuation and thus of the ground of determination of the individual in its individuality. This question is familiar in the history of metaphysics as that of the *principium individuationis*. We can say that Schelling gives one of the most profound and fruitful presentations of this principle in the movement of becoming of creation itself. We shall try now to understand the section by analyzing the movement of becoming of the creature and creating in its individual aspects sketched there.

1. We must begin by remembering that eternal Spirit is the unity of existence grounding itself in the ground and of the ground emerging from itself in existence. The "first" primordial *stirring* is the illumination of the understanding, seeing itself. But since the ground in God is indeed not he Himself, yet not separated from Him, and since the ground as longing seeks precisely what the understanding sees, seeing itself "is" at the same time the illumination of brightness in the darkness of longing. God sees Himself in the brightness illuminating in the darkness of the ground.

2. But just this seeing itself in the other as *its* other becomes a speaking-itself-into this other in the word of Spirit uttering itself. That looks like a union, and it is one. But it is not only that, it is simultaneously the separation. For the light of the understanding separates itself from darkness as the other. Separation and distinction rule in the becoming of the ground as opened ground.

3. However, the other, the ground is not repulsed, but in that light is spoken into the ground, what longing seeks "namelessly" becomes brighter in the longing of the ground. The essential consequence of this is that longing now really wants to reach and maintain for itself—*in* itself—what illuminates. Light opens up darkness. But since darkness is longing willing itself, what is illuminated is now really aroused to strive back to itself and thus to strive toward the opening. This means that the separation as illumination in the ground brings it about that the ground strives more and more fundamentally toward the ground and as the ground individuating itself separates itself.

4. On the other hand, however, the longing of the ground is aroused by the understanding to give up the darkness and thus itself in the illumination of itself. But illumination giving up darkness means gaining power over the articulating and ruling unity, over the law and the universal, over what determines.

5. The ground's arousal to itself by the understanding means the arousal of what is sundering itself to separation, to a separation which at the same time elevates itself to the light, that is, to the rule, and becomes definiteness. But a separation which determines itself in sundering and takes on definiteness is individuation into an individual. In that the ground in its active unity with the understanding strives back to itself and yet at the same time elevates itself away from itself to the light, this active unity, the word of Spirit, is nothing other than letting the individual sunder itself. The becoming of creation is thus an *awakening* of the still unactivated unity in the ground of longing. The understanding does not

place something external before itself. Rather, as what opens the closed unity, it only in-forms itself in the searching and striving of the ground. Creation is *in-forming* of the light in the dark, awakening of darkness to itself as to light and thus at the same time away from itself—separation.

6. But an important characterization is still lacking for the complete understanding of the essence of the movement of becoming in creation. The double, antithetical arousal of the ground to sundering *and* determination, this double, antithetical willing of the ground in the light of awakening reason is itself *what creates*. But in that what sunders itself brings itself to definiteness, that is, unified unification, what was hidden in the ground is always just elevated to light. The unity, the band itself, becomes lighter and more definite. This unity elevates itself from the ground of the separation of forces; it does not come upon them in addition as an external noose. The more the ground wants to contract into separation and yet the more a more open unity is sought thereby, the more the primordial unity of ground and existence emerges. Creating unity is the *band*, the copula, that is, what binds ground and existence of the actual being. Schelling calls this band elevating itself to definiteness and yet remaining in the ground the *soul*, in contradistinction to the Spirit. Elevated from the ground sundering itself, the soul continues to belong to it and thus to be an individual sundering itself.

The soul is that unity of ground and existence which does take shape elevated from the ground, but as that band which still remains bound in the unified individual it does not emerge from the individual and explicitly confront it and utter itself as such. That is the realm of nature as yet without language, but developing itself in an articulated and attuned manifold of forms.

7. In the becoming of creation a continual strife is present of longing contracting itself against expansion into the open. But the more light and definite the forms of nature become, the more oppositional and self-willed the ground becomes.

But the more separated what is separating itself is, the richer the inner jointure of the individuated being becomes, and the band still entangled in the ground must release itself all the more. This release of the band, however, only means a clearer, more definite bond in the sense of the unifying development and containing of what is separated. The higher the separation of forces, the deeper the contraction of the ground toward its innermost ground. The more primordial the contraction, the more powerful the opening unity of the band must become. Thus, what creates brings an increase in itself in accordance with this oppositional movement. Therefore, it is comprehensible that creation itself can only come about in definite stages. These stages in nature's becoming lead to nature's ever coming closer to itself without, however, ever completely reaching itself as nature itself and without ever completely releasing the anchor of its band in itself.

8. We can pin down the factors of the movement of becoming of creation in a summarizing list. Creation is the emergence from itself of the Absolute which

thus wills toward itself from the ground—is itself a willing. The original way of willing is the stirring of longing. Co-primordially, the understanding brings this stirring of dark self-seeking to arousal and thus to craving. But the separation from what arouses occurs in this craving and since the latter yet remains in unity with the ground, the understanding itself as the clearing of the dark becomes the in-forming of unity in the un-ruly. As clearing, in-forming is at the same time elevation of what is unified to the clearer unity and thus formation of the band as anchored in unity. Elevation to an ever higher unity includes the staging of nature's becoming in individual stages and realms. All of these terms which we are using—stirring, arousal, separation and in-forming, elevation and staging—characterize a movement in their reciprocal relation which can never be grasped mechanically as manipulation in a mass of things at all.

Schelling understands the creation of nature as a becoming which now yet determines its Being, a becoming which is nothing other than the ground in God urging toward itself. As what is sought for, God sees himself in this ground as in eternal longing.

Thus what existing and becoming nature seeks in itself is the formation of the glimpse of life seen in its darkness into its own special form. But it also belongs to the essence of nature to remain longing and never to find this form for itself as nature. The moment it is found, what creates must leave nature and transcend it, thus standing above it. In nature's highest stage where *her* creating finds rest and is transformed, man comes into being.

What was said in the last lecture has remained incomprehensible. Since a lecture cannot have the task of mouthing what is incomprehensible, we have to make up for this if possible. We do get into a strange position in our task, that is, in every philosophical lecture—for there *is* something incomprehensible in what we have to discuss. And we would thus go against our task if we even tried to dissolve everything into a flat comprehensibility and thus get rid of the incomprehensible element.

In our special case, Schelling's text should become comprehensible in this way. It may very well have been true in the previous lecture that the text was much clearer than what was said about it afterwards. That is quite in order. For the text gives the primordial motion of the thought. However, the "interpretation"—if we can call it that—, extracted the essential factors for themselves which are in motion in this motion in eight separated points. What was said must be transformed back to that motion. The goal of a correct interpretation must be to reach the moment where it makes itself superfluous and the text comes into its undiminished right. But we are again far away from that. How would it be if the interpretation tried to follow the movement of the train of thought instead of splitting everything up into points? That would be possible. But if as an interpretation it is supposed to be more than a feeble imitation of the text, the presentation on the other hand necessarily becomes more differentiated and extended and thus again not as easy to survey and less transparent. For that is a difficulty in understanding: to see what is multifaceted and at the same time in motion. However, the real difficulty of comprehension has a more profound reason. What is at stake here? The presentation of the essential origin of the creature from the Absolute, and indeed with the intention of determining man's essence. The essential origin of the creature can only become visible in the light of the movement of creating, of its essence. In presenting all this, it is a matter of an essential project, not the literal depiction of something objectively present somewhere which can be directly shown. To think in a project means to place before oneself the inner potentiality of being of something in its necessity. This is completely different from explaining something lying in front of us, that is, only referring and postponing it to another thing that can be shown.

But this projectural procedure must, after all, put something in the project, thus it must yet have something previously given as a beginning and point of departure. Certainly, and here is the second main difficulty. In projecting the movement of becoming of creation the realm is posited: God, creating and the creature, things including man. And just what is to be moved into the essential project with regard to its context of becoming must now be understood from the outset differently from the way that common representing understands what was named, God not as an old papa with a white beard who manufactures things, but as the becoming God to whose essence the ground belongs, uncreated nature which is not He Himself.

Created nature is not to be understood as nature as it is now, as we see it, but as becoming, creating nature, as something creating which is itself created, the *natura naturans* as *natura naturata* of Scotus Eriugena.

Man is not to be understood as that familiar living being gifted with reason who hangs around on a planet and can be dissected into his components, but as that being who is in himself the "deepest abyss" of Being *and at the same time* "the highest heaven."

God, nature, and man are understood from the very beginning in a different way and as such they must only now and at the same time move into the essential project of their becoming. This becoming is the essence of Being. Thus Being also cannot be understood as the brute existence of something manufactured, but must be understood as the jointure of ground and existence. The jointure is not a rigid jungle gym of determinations but—itself presencing in itself in the reciprocal relation—presences as will.

It was important now to follow this original becoming of the Absolute, how as this becoming it becomes something which has become, how the Absolute creating itself descends and enters the creature, in creating and as a creating. But this descending and entering is not a decline into something lowly, but in accordance with the inner reciprocal relation of the jointure of Being is in itself a fetching forth of what is always already hidden in the ground into the light and into individuation. Creation is eternal and "is," understood dialectically, *the* existence of the Absolute itself.

By constantly distancing the idea of creating as a manipulation, we see that in this creating a creator does not remain for himself and set up something manufactured merely as something other, but that the creator himself in creating transforms himself into a created being and thus himself still remains in the created being.

Forgoing an emphasis on the individual factors in themselves, let us once more go through the eight points.

The God in becoming emerges in his becoming to something which has become and *is* the one who he is *in* this becoming *as* it. The inner-divine becoming is originally the self-seeing of the God himself in his ground so that this look remains in the ground. Just as when one person looks at the other in a distant correspondence and, looking into him, kindles something in him by this look in order that it may become clearer in him, longing becomes clearer in the self-seeing of the God in his ground, but that means precisely all the more aroused and craving. The ground thus wants to be more and more ground, and at the same time it can only will this by willing what is clearer and thus striving *against itself* as what is dark.

Thus it strives for the opposite of itself and produces a separation in itself. The more groundly (striving into the ground) and at the same time the more clearly (striving for unification) the separation becomes, the further apart what is separated, ground and existence become; but what unifies comes all the more profoundly from the ground and the unification strives all the further into the light, the band becomes all the more relaxed, the manifold of what is bound together becomes all the more rich.

When ground and existence, what contracts and what determines strive further and further away from each other and thus precisely toward each other in the clearing unity, the creator himself changes into the individuation of what is created. For only where something separating itself and contracting itself in opposition is forced at the same time into the definiteness of the rule, of the universal, does an individual come about, a this which as a this is at the same time the particular and the universal, a this and, as a this, a such. The more oppositional the unity of what becomes, the more creating the creator, and all the more does it lose the indeterminacy of urging without measure or rule. The more selfish becoming is, the clearer and higher at the same time is what has become of it. But selfishness grows precisely when the ground clears. Thus, in this becoming oppositional in itself, there is a continual self-transcendence and a striving outward and upward to ever higher stages. Ground and existence separate further and further, but in such a way that they are ever in unison in the form of an ever higher being. Becoming creates stages in itself. The movement of creating-created nature is thus an urge to life which revolves in itself and, revolving, overflows itself and, overflowing itself, individuates itself and, individuating itself, elevates itself to a higher stage. Speaking formally, the identity of the jointure of Being, oppositional in itself, transfers the being commensurate with it, that is, what is becoming to ever higher potencies.

What Schelling attempts to grasp here in essence is just the *movement of any living being in general*, the essential construction of the movement of life, which is from the outset not to be grasped with the usual ideas about movement. We could and would have to appeal to Schelling's own philosophy of nature for clarification. But on the one hand, it takes on another orientation here and then it cannot be "reported on" briefly. Movement is what is essential in it, and thus the correct perspective is decisive for comprehension. It is not the content of the philosophy of nature and its unspoken presuppositions that hinder us from getting this perspective. What hinders us most is the common idea of nature and its reality, of what we admit as reality. Therefore, it is important for an assimilation of the philosophy of nature to know and recognize for what it is the common views of nature in their commonness.

g. The Questionability of Today's Interpretation of Nature. Reality and Objective Presence (*Vorhandenheit*)

With general consent, one will say that in order to get some correct idea about nature one must stick to real nature. Without this footing everything becomes a wild dream. But what does one mean here by "reality" of nature?

It is highly dubious whether what an investigator of nature today ascertains as really objectively present, is what is real. It can indeed be something which is ascertainable as something objectively present, but what has been ascertained as objectively present is not yet what is real. Admittedly, one would like to answer, but we can only find what is real if we stick to what is objectively present and go back from it. Counterquestion: go back to what? Who will show the way? The danger in this procedure is that we might just find something objectively present as something unreal. The reality of nature is a problem all its own. Nature "as we see it now" shows a stabilized order, rule, and form. What could be more obvious than to want to know this rule better by searching for the regularity of what is ordered and to bring the rules to more universal determinations, to higher rules. The intention of scientific questioning leads to what it already includes at its incipience as a prejudice. Everything is regular and according to rule, therefore everything must be explicable in principle. If the further prejudice is included in this prejudice that explanation is really thoroughgoing calculability, then the demand surfaces of explaining life phenomena in a completely mechanical way.

But if the possible one-sidedness and limits of mechanism are pointed out, then one explains that mechanism is only a "principle of investigation." One should not deny that there is something inexplicable in living beings, but one should only want at first to penetrate so far and so long until one comes to a boundary with this mechanical kind of explanation. This procedure alone is exact and objective. Behind this widespread opinion, which is strangely enough even fortified by atomic physics today, lies a series of fundamental errors.

1. The *opinion* that when one one day meets up with something which can no longer be explained mechanistically that this something inexplicable is really ascertained and recognized. In this way it is only misinterpreted by being locked within the scope of possible explicability which in this case becomes impossible.

2. The *deception* that one would ever come to such a boundary with mechanism. It is precisely the essence of mechanism that—as long as anything palpable is there at all, and that is always the case—it won't give up, it thinks up new ways and such ways can always be found in principle.

3. The *fundamental error* that a principle of investigation is already justified by one's getting somewhere with its aid. One always gets somewhere of necessity with the principle of mechanism, therefore it can not be demonstrated specifically in its truth in this way. The truth of a principle can in general never be demonstrated by success. For the *interpretation* of a success *as* a success is, after all, accomplished with the help of the presupposed but unfounded principle.

4. The *failure to recognize* that every true beginning of principles of investigation must be grounded in a project, grounded in the essence of truth itself, of the essential constitution of the realm in question. Thus, in relation to living nature what is decisive (and never yet seriously undertaken) is the essential project of life movement *as movement*.

Of course, when we look at nature in front of us in a way seemingly purely objective with our everyday eyes and in the direction of the everyday paths of experience; we see regularities and in the face of them look for the rules just as if they belonged to nature from the very beginning, just as if nothing different had ever happened. But perhaps this regularity is only what has become rigidified of a past stirring of that becoming viewed metaphysically, a rest behind which lies the original unruliness of the ground; just as if it could erupt again, unruliness not just being the lack and indeterminacy of the rule. However one might interpret this, it is certain that the "natural" everyday attitude to nature is finally very unnatural. The fact that nature permits itself to be reckoned with and calculated rather speaks for the fact that she deceives us thereby and keeps us at a distance rather than allowing us to attain a true knowledge.

h. Self-Will and Universal Will. The Separability of the Principles in Man as the Condition of the Possibility of Evil.

The project of the movement of becoming of creation should make clear how the creator does not have intrinsically just an individual as a result, but is intrinsically in-forming individuation. The essence of the ground is the heightening contraction together with the clearer emergence of articulated unities. But this occurs in such a way that both join themselves as unified in the unity of the actual life forms of an actual stage of being of nature. The deepening of the ground is the expansion of existence. Both together are the intensification of separation as the heightening of unity. All of this together is the stages of the individuation and withdrawal from each other of the principles (ground and existence) in the bond of individuation.

Schelling ends the essential project of the creation of nature with an explicit characterization of the principles which are active in every being in accordance with the movement of creation (pp. 37-38).

> Every being which has arisen in nature in the way indicated contains a double principle which, however, is at bottom one and the same regarded from the two possible aspects. The first principle is the one by which they are separated from God or wherein they exist in the mere ground. But as a primordial unity occurs between that which is in the ground and what is prefigured in the understanding, the process of creation consists only in an inner transmutation or transfiguration to light of the original dark principle (since the understanding or the light which occurs in nature is really only searching in the ground for that light which is akin to it and is turned inward). The second principle, which by its own nature is dark, is at the same time the very one which is transfigured in light, and the two are one in every natural being, though only to a certain extent. The dark principle since it arises from the depths and is dark is the self-will of creatures, but since it has not yet risen to complete unity with light, as the principle of the understanding self-will cannot grasp it, is mere craving or desire, that is, blind will. This self-will of creatures stands in opposition to the understanding universal will, and the latter makes use of the former and subordinates it to itself as a mere tool.

Of course, according to the fundamental principle these must be the factors of the jointure of Being, but now more definite in accordance with the being in becoming.

With regard to the ground, created things are separated from God. But what the ground's craving seeks is the same as what is prefigured in the understanding as something cleared. Thus creation is nothing else but the transfiguration of the dark, urging back to the ground, to light. The self-will of the ground striving back to itself is thus in what is created. But this self-craving stands against the will of the understanding which strives for rule and unity, and therein for the bond of everything everywhere to the one. Its will is the universal will. The particular will of the ground is subserviently subordinated to this universal will. Where craving for separation remains guided by the will for the universal, what craves itself determined by this universal will, becomes something particular, separate for itself. The latter does not relinquish self-will—every animal is evidence of this—but it is bound to the universal of the species, again, every animal is evidence of this.

The animal is an individual this. It could not be this if the craving for individuation were not in it. But the animal never comes to itself, in spite of this craving. It rather merely serves, again, the species in spite of this craving. And it could not perform this service if a universal will did not strive within it with the particular will at the same time.

We know that the project of the movement of becoming of creating creatures is oriented to the ongoing task of explicating the metaphysical possibility of man. This possibility in its turn is to show in what the conditions of the inner possibility of evil consist. Now everything is prepared for determining man's possibility of becoming and thus his essential origin and his position in beings as a whole.

But this will becomes one whole with the primal will or reason when, in the progressive transformation and division of all forces, there is totally revealed in light the inmost and deepest point of original darkness, in One Being. The will of this One Being, to the extent to which it is individual, is also a particular will, though in itself or as the center of all other particular wills it is one with the primal will or understanding. This elevation of the most abysmal center into light occurs in no creatures visible to us except in man. In man there exists the whole power of the principle of darkness and, in him, too, the whole force of light. In him there are both centers—the deepest pit and the highest heaven. Man's will is the seed—concealed in eternal longing—of God, present as yet only in the depths—the divine light of life locked in the depths which God divined when he determined to will nature. Only in him (in man) did God love the world—and it was this very image of God which was grasped in its center by longing when it opposed itself to light. By reason of the fact that man takes his rise from the depths (that he is a creature) he contains a principle relatively independent of God. But just because this very principle is transfigured in light—without therefore ceasing to be basically dark—something higher, *Spirit*, arises in man. For the eternal Spirit pronounces unity, or the Word, in nature. But the (real) Word, pronounced, exists only in the unity of light and darkness (vowel and consonant). Now these two principles do indeed exist in all things, but without complete consonance because of the inadequacy of that which has been raised from the depths. Only in man, then, is the Word completely articulate, which in all other creatures was held back and left unfinished. But in the articulate word Spirit reveals itself, that is God as existing, in act. Now inasmuch as the soul is the living identity of both principles, it is Spirit; and Spirit is in God. If, now, the identity of both principles were just as indissoluble in man as in God, then there would be no difference—that is, God as Spirit would not be revealed. Therefore, that unity which is indissoluble in God must be dissoluble in man—and this constitutes the possibility of good and evil. (Pp. 38-39)

In general and in anticipation we should say in man, nature's becoming comes to rest in such a way that at the same time nature is abandoned in man. But in order that we may retain a sufficiently broad scope for the understanding of man's metaphysical becoming, we must remember something said earlier. Eternal becoming in God has as its eternal beginning this, that God sees his image in what eternal longing seeks in the ground itself. But becoming in the cleared ground is in one respect a continual longing, striving back to itself, and the brighter the clearing, the more self-willed the craving in the creature to reach the deepest ground, in the center of itself. The heightened particular will in nature's beings is a return, eternally craving but never attainable by nature itself, to the deepest ground—a searching of the God.

As particular will, the becoming of creatures thus strives more and more to the innermost center of the ground where this divine life-look shines. But it does this in such a way that this self-craving is elevated to the universal will and remains bound in the band, the soul of the actual life unity of the actual stage of life. But when the particular will of the created-creating one reaches into the ground's deepest center and grasps this will, it grasps the center and the ground of all particular wills.

But in the becoming of creatures in unity with self-craving, the elevation to the pure light of the understanding corresponds to this striving back to the center of the deepest ground, the deepest self-craving of the longing of the ground, so that the universal will and the center of all particular wills now fold into each other and become the same. Thus the very deepest ground—containing itself—is at the same time elevated to the broadest clearing of the pure understanding. We find such a becoming in creatures only in man, better yet: as man.

The will of man "is" thus in itself nothing other than the restrained thrust of the God who now only dwells in the ground; longing hidden in itself *wills* in man, that is, the ground independent of God which is not God himself. But just this will of the ground in man is raised in him to the light of the understanding. In man the word is completely uttered. Man utters himself and becomes present in language. Thus man elevates himself *above* the light of the understanding. He does not just move within what is cleared like the animal, but utters this light and thus raises himself above it. In this standing above it he "is" another unity of the kind of that unity which we are already familiar with, that unification which itself rules the light and the dark in their reciprocal relationship—Spirit—and is Spirit. In man—and as far as we know in man alone—are both principles, the deepest of the ground, the self-will to be a self, and the highest of the word, the will to the cleared Being of the unity of the whole, a unity of its own. "The deepest abyss and the highest heaven" are in man.

Because self-will, the striving back to itself, is elevated in man to the understanding and the word, selfhood as such is Spirit in man. Man "is" a selflike, special being separated from God which in its separateness wills precisely the most hidden will of the ground and as Spirit sees itself at the same time in the unity of its separated particularity. In this self-seeing the self-will is elevated to Spirit, and thusly not perhaps weakened and diverted, but now truly placed in higher possibilities of its powerfulness. In this self-seeing, man is beyond all of nature and creatures in the previous sense.

In that selfhood is Spirit, it is free of both principles. How so? The principle of the ground, nature as self-willed, no longer simply serves an equally impotent species revolving within itself like the animal. Rather, being spiritual, self-will can be directed one way or the other. As self-will, it is freely flexible with regard to the universal will. The latter, being itself Spirit, is something for which man can decide one way or another. The spiritual universal will does not simply mean the preservation of a self-contained species, but *is* history and thus work and unwork, victory and defeat, form maintaining itself and decline. In the selfhood of man as spiritual, both principles are indeed thus together, but the unity of the principle is separable here, yes, it must be separable. For in order that God can exist as Spirit; that is, can emerge from *himself as such a one* and present *himself*, in order that he can become revealed *as* the unity of both principles, this unity which is inseparable in the eternal Spirit must now itself diverge and present itself in a separability. The band of the principles, of the particular will and the universal will, is in man a free band, not a necessary one as in God. Man's particular will is *as* spiritual a will elevated above nature, no longer merely a tool serving the universal will.

This separability of the two principles belonging to man's essential being is, however, nothing other than the condition of the possibility of evil. How so? Because self-will here is a selflike spiritual will, in the unity of human willing it can put itself in the place of the universal will. Being spiritual, self-will can strive to be that which it is merely by remaining in the divine ground also as creature. As separated selfhood it can will to be the ground of the whole. Self-will can elevate itself above everything and only will to determine the unity of the principles in terms of itself. This ability is the faculty of evil.

The inner possibility of evil is the question of the inner possibility of being

human. Man is a created being, not an absolute one, and indeed an extrao
stage and place within creatures creating themselves. We must define th
and place.

With this intention, the movement of becoming of nature creating itself had to
be followed in its essence. The result was: nature comes to a boundary which
consists in the fact that it never comes to itself.

Although nature emerges to the manifold of the stages of formation and
sequences of becoming within itself, the band which unified these formations
always remains itself bound to what is bound. The species does not emerge as a
law for itself in order as this emergence to ground a higher being in existence. Are
there other beings which are not nature? The sole being of this kind that we know
of is man.

Thus in him the principles are different. They are indeed the same principles,
but their way of being a principle is different.

But why is self-willed elevation itself evil? In what does the malice of evil
consist? According to the given new determination of freedom, freedom is the
faculty of good and evil. Accordingly, evil proclaims itself as a position of will of its
own, indeed as a way of being free in the sense of being a self in terms of its own
essential law. By elevating itself above the universal will, the individual will wants
precisely to be that will. Through this elevation a way of unification of its own
takes place, thus a way of its own of being Spirit. But the unification is a reversal of
the original will, and that means a reversal of the unity of the divine world in
which the universal will stands in harmony with the will of the ground. In this
reversal of the wills the becoming of a reversed god, of the counterspirit, takes
place, and thus the upheaval against the primal being, the revolt of the adversary
element against the essence of Being, the reversal of the jointure of Being into the
disjointure in which the ground elevates itself to existence and puts itself in the
place of existence. But reversal and upheaval are nothing merely negative and
nugatory, but negation placing itself in dominance. Negation now transposes all
forces in such a way that they turn against nature and creatures. The consequence of this is the ruin of beings.

By way of clarifying malice Schelling mentions disease. Disease makes itself felt
to "feeling" as something very real, not just as a mere absence of something.
When a man is sick, we do say that he "is not quite all right" (*dass ihm etwas
"fehle"*) and thus express the sickness merely negatively as a lack. But this: "Why
is he not quite right?" (*"Wo fehlt es?"*) really means "What is the matter with him,
something which has, so to speak, gotten loose from the harmony of being healthy
and, being on the loose, wants to take over all of existence and dominate it?" In
the case of sickness, there is not just something lacking, but something wrong.
"Wrong" not in the sense of something only incorrect, but in the genuine sense of
falsification, distortion, and reversal. This falsification is at the same time false in

the sense of what is sly. We speak of malignant disease. Disease is not only a disruption, but a reversal of the whole existence which takes over the total condition and dominates it.

The true essence of negation which revolts as reversal in evil can only be understood if we comprehend the concept of affirmation of the positive and position primordially enough. Affirmation is not just a simple yes as the affirmation of something objectively present, but is the affirmation of the harmony of what is in tune with itself, in the order of being. Thus in the "positive" lies the affirmation of the essential unity of a being as a whole. Correspondingly, negation is not just rejection of what is objectively present, but no-saying places itself in the position of the yes. What replaces the place of harmony and attunement is disharmony, the wrong tone which enters the whole. Primordially conceived, affirmation is not just the recognition coming afterward from without of something already existing, but affirmation as the yes harmonizing everything, penetrating it and putting it in tune with itself; similarly the no. We usually put yes and no with yes- and no-saying, correctly so. But in doing this we understand saying first of all and decisively as speaking a simple sentence about a thingly situation, "logically"; this, however, wrongly. Saying is not only and not primarily speaking. Saying and language have a primordial essence in human existence and, correspondingly, so do affirmation and negation.

Negation as reversal is thus only and truly possible when what is in itself ordered in relation to each other—ground and existence—becomes mutually free to move and thus offers the possibility of a reversed unity. For example, in the animal as in every other natural being the dark principle of the ground is just as active as that of the light and of representing. But here, as everywhere in nature, these principles are unified only in a fixed way and determined once and for all. In terms of the animal itself, they can never be altered in their relation to each other, and an animal can thus never be "evil" even if we sometimes talk this way. The animal never gets out of the unity of its determined stage of nature. Even where an animal is "cunning," this cunning remains limited to a quite definite path, within quite definite situations and comes of necessity into play there.

But man is that being who can turn his own essential constituency around, turn the jointure of Being of his existence into dis-jointure. He stands in the jointure of his Being in such a way that he disposes over this jointure and its joining in a quite definite way. Thus, the dubious advantage is reserved for man of sinking beneath the animal, whereas the animal is not capable of reversing the principles. And it is not able to do this since the striving of the ground never attains the illumination of self-knowledge because in the animal the ground never reaches either the innermost depth of longing or the highest scope of spirit.

Thus the ground of evil lies in the primal will of the first ground which has become revealed. Evil has its ground in the ground independent of God and is nothing other than this ground, this ground as the selflike primal will which has emerged to the separate selfhood of created spirit and stepped into the place of the universal will. Not only does something positive lie in evil in general, but the most positive element of nature itself, the ground's willing to come to itself, "is" the negative here, "is" as negation in the form of evil. It is not finitude as such that constitutes evil, but finitude elevated to the dominance of self-will. This elevation, however, is possible only as spiritual elevation and for this reason evil belongs in the realm of domination of Spirit and history.

Schelling gives his presentation of the essential origin of evil a yet sharper emphasis by adding a discussion with "other explanations" of evil, especially that of Leibniz. We shall omit them here because what is essential about this criticism becomes understandable in terms of the positive element presented and because a more precise treatment of the discussion with Leibniz would require us to talk of Leibniz's philosophy in terms of its fundamental metaphysical position, not possible within the framework of this interpretation.

With regard to the whole first section, and also with respect to all that follows a note is, of course, still necessary.

Schelling calls disease "the true counterpart of evil or sin" (p. 41). Accordingly, he equates evil with sin. But "sin" can be defined theologically only within Christian dogmatic philosophy. "Sin" has meaning and truth only in the realm of Christian faith and its grace. Thus that equation of sin with evil can mean either that Schelling secularizes the dogmatic theological concept of sin to a philosophical one or else that he, conversely, orients the whole question of evil fundamentally to Christian dogmatics. Neither of these two interpretations alone could get at the true situation because both are actually intermingled for Schelling, a secularization of the theological concept of sin and a Christianization of the metaphysical concept of evil.

This direction of thinking, however, characterizes not only Schelling's treatise on freedom, but his whole philosophy, and not only his, but that of all of German Idealism, especially that of Hegel. The historical situation ruling Western philosophy since the beginning of the modern period is to rule it until the end of this age and still further. Here it is not a matter of some "theological" inclinations of individual thinkers, nor a matter of Schelling and Hegel first being theologians, of Europe's history being and remaining determined by Christianity, even when it might have lost its power. And for this reason a post-Christian age is something essentially different from a pre-Christian one. And if one wants to call what is non-Christian pagan, then paganism and paganism are fundamentally different—if one wants to speak of paganism at all. For paganism is a Christian concept just like sin.

In philosophy we can no more go back to Greek philosophy by means of a leap than we can eliminate the advent of Christianity into Western history and thus into philosophy by means of a command. The only possibility is to transform history, that is, truly to bring about the hidden necessity of history into which neither knowledge nor deed reach, and transformation truly brought about is the essence of the creative. For the great beginning of Western philosophy, too, did not come out of nothing. Rather, it became great because it had to overcome its greatest opposite, the mythical in general and the Asiatic in particular, that is, it had to bring it to the jointure of a truth of Being, and was able to do this.

Thus it is evidence of a lack of understanding of the question, and above all a quite unproductive reaction, if one discards Schelling's treatise on freedom by saying that Schelling fell into a false theologizing here. It is certain that after the treatise on freedom, Schelling brings the positivity of Christianity more and more to bear, but this does not yet decide anything about the essence and the meaning of his metaphysical thinking because it is not yet at all grasped in this way, but remains incomprehensible.

With regard to Schelling's equation of evil with sin we must say that sin is evil interpreted in a Christian way, so much so that in this interpretation the essence of evil comes more plainly to light in a quite definite direction. But evil is not only sin and only comprehensible as sin. Since our interpretation is intent upon the true fundamental metaphysical question of Being, we shall not queston evil in the form of sin, but discuss it with regard to the essence and the truth of Being. Thus it is also indicated indirectly that the scope of ethics is not sufficient to comprehend evil. Rather, ethics and morality concern only a legislation with respect to behavior toward evil in the sense of its overcoming and a rejection or its trivialization.

This remark is important in order to estimate correctly in what regard our interpretation is one-sided, consciously one-sided in the direction of the main side of philosophy, the question of Being.

With the presentation of the essential origin of evil nothing has as yet been said about its reality in the form of man's freedom. And nothing can as yet be said directly about it until it is understood how evil could erupt from creation as an unmistakably universal principle everywhere in conflict with the good. Reflections on this will be given in what we demarcate as the second main section.

II. The Universal Reality of Evil as the Possibility of Individuals

The condition of the possibility of evil is the separability of principles in a being, the separability of ground and existence. Separability means (1) the movability of the principles with regard to each other so that one can take the place of the other and (2) not mere detachability of the one from the other, but the reversal of their actual unity since they must always be in a unity of reciprocal relation. Such separability is, however, only present when a being freely stands above both principles, that is, in relation to both principles, where beings are spirit. But a spirit in which the will of the ground can separate itself in a selflike way from the will of the understanding is a created spirit.

Thus evil is possible only in creatures and it is only possible as spirit. The realm of created spirit is determined as history. There is history only when there is man existing. Only man is capable of evil. But this capability is not one of his qualities. Rather, capable of being in such a way constitutes the essence of human being.

In that he is the faculty of evil, man, the faculty for the one, is at the same time a faculty for the other. For otherwise he would not be a faculty at all. In the essence and meaning of inner possibility considered by itself, man "is" thus neither good nor evil, but he is in essence that being which can be the one as well as the other, too, in such a way that when he is the one he is also the other. But inasmuch as man is real, he must necessarily be the one or the other in the sense of the actual dominance of one over the other. As possibility he is in essence an undecided being. But essentially he cannot remain in indecisiveness, insofar as he *is*. But he must be if the Absolute is to exist, that is, to emerge from itself into revelation. But something can be revealed only in its opposite. The opposition of the principles must come to light, that is, the one must decide against the other one way or the other. Herein is contained the fact that the good can only be in creatures if evil is, and the other way around.

Thus, if after the characterization of the inner possibility of evil the question of its reality now arises, the latter can be understood only in its essential counter-relation to the good, in such a way that evil and good are understood as actual realities of a faculty, which is the faculty of good and evil. But this is the essence of human freedom. If this question appeared to recede into the background in the previous section, it now emerges in full relief. For evil is nothing by itself, but is always only as something historical, spiritual, as human decisiveness. This decisiveness as such must always at the same time be decision for and against. What a decision goes against is not removed by that decision, but precisely posited.

But decision is what it is only as emergence from indecisiveness. Inasmuch as he is really man, man cannot persevere in indecisiveness, he must get out of it. But on the other hand, how is he to emerge from indecisiveness since he is this indecisiveness in his nature?

As this kind of created being, how is he particularly to emerge from essential indecisiveness to the decisiveness of evil and be real as something evil?

How does evil, whose possibility was shown, become real? How does the elevation of the self-will of self-seeking above the universal will come about? How does it come about that man wants to be the Absolute itself? How is this transition from the possible to the real to be thought? Our question is now the nature of this transition, *what* it is, not yet why it is.

What belongs to this transition from the possible to the real? We can see right away that as long as we ask the question in such a general way, it is underdefined and not a correct question. Possibility and reality have long since been understood as ways in which a being can be, as modalities of Being. But its being possible and being real differ according to the fundamental character of the being and the stage of Being in which it stands. The animal's possibilities correspond to its reality and vice-versa. What is possible for the animal (and how it is possible in the animal) has a different character of possibility from the corresponding factor in man, since man and animal constitute different stages of the creature's Being. Thus in order to bring the unattached question of the nature of realization of evil to its proper metaphysical realm, we would have to go far beyond the framework of Schelling's treatise and systematically present the essential transformations of possibility and reality in the various regions of Being, all of this on the foundation of an adequate concept of Being in general. Then the fundamental question would arise whether what is familiar and treated as the modalities of Being corresponds to a sufficient interpretation of Being at all. We must renounce all of these considerations here.

Instead, let us consider in retrospect on what preceded only the following: Evil is spirit and thus only real as spirit. But spirit is the self-knowing unity of ground and existence. The possibility of evil is a possibility of spirit, thus the possibility of such a self-knowing unity. The possibility of a unification, the possibility of unifying in one way or another, is the possibility of behaving.* But behaving is a kind of being in which beings as themselves relate to something else in such a way that this other in its turn is revealed as a being. We shall call the possibility of behaving the faculty of something.

We can say that a piece of wood "has" the possibility of burning up. But how does it "have" this possibility? In any case not in the manner of a faculty. The wood itself can neither strive towards burning up nor can it bring the burning about. Burning can only be caused in the wood by something else. Wood has the quality of consumability, but it does not have the faculty of consumption.

In contrast, a faculty is a being able to relate itself to a possibility of itself. This possibility stands in a definite relation to behavior. Possibility is something which a faculty has at its disposal, not only generally, but as something in which the faculty finds itself when it brings itself about. The possibilities of faculty are not arbitrary for it, but they are also nothing compulsive. In order to be itself, however, a faculty must cling to its possibilities. Oriented in its attraction to these possibilities it must incline toward them. An inclination to its possibilities always belongs to a faculty. Inclination is a certain anticipatory aptitude for striving for what can be done.

The inclination, that is, various directions of being inclined, are the presup-

---

* Behaving, behavior, *Verhalten*. If the prevalent connotation of behavior*ism* is avoided, behavior with its root *have* is close enough to the German *halten* (hold) to be usable. The English prefix *be-*, like the German *ver-*, is an intensification of the root verb— TRANS.

positions for the possibility of the decision of a faculty. If it could not and ⌐⌐⌐
have to decide for one inclination or the other, that is, for what it has a propensity
to, decision would not be decision, but a mere explosion of an act out of emptiness
into emptiness, pure chance, but never self-determination, that is, freedom.

Thus according to its nature, freedom must be a faculty. But to a faculty there
belongs inclination. Human freedom is the faculty of good and evil. Where does
the inclination to evil in man come from, man who originates from the Absolute as
creature?

This question must be answered to make the transition comprehensible from
the possibility of evil to its reality. The inclination to evil must precede the
decision. The decision as such is always that of an individual man. This evil to
which inclination is inclined in general can thus be neither evil which is already
real nor the evil of an individual man.

It must be evil in general, in general, but not yet real, still also not nothing, but
that which can be evil in general, fundamentally can and wants to become it and
yet is not real. What is that?

In any case we already understand better why a section is inserted between
Section I, The Possibility of Evil; and Section III, Reality and the Realization
of Evil. This section must treat the general reality of evil as the possibility, that is,
the making possible of individual and truly real evil.

At the same time we also see more clearly that "general reality" means here
evil's ubiquitous wanting to become real urging everywhere in creatures. Evil is
only just about to become real, it is only just somehow effecting, effective, but it is
not yet truly real as itself, it shows itself in another. If this other did not exist, no
inclination toward it would be possible, and if there were no inclination there
would be no faculty and if there were no faculty of . . . , there would be no
freedom.

After this clarification of the question, the direction of an answer is now to be
followed. As the reversal of human spirit, evil is the individual will gaining
mastery over the universal will. Thus, what is ground and should always remain
ground is, so to speak, made into an existent. As longing, the ground is a striving-
for-itself which becomes the craving for separation in the creature. The will of the
ground is everywhere what arouses self-will and drives it beyond itself. Wherever
it shows itself, it is indeed not an evil itself which appears, but a prefiguration of
evil. We find such prefigurations in nature: the strange and chance element of
organic formations and deformations, what incites horror, the fact that everything
alive is approaching dissolution. Here something appears which has been driven
out into selfish exaggeration and is at the same time impotent and repulsive. But
since it is not yet something spiritual, it can only be a prefiguration of evil as
something selflike dominant in nature.

But in the realm of spirit, too, of history, evil does not emerge automatically.
However, here it does not just offer a prefiguration as in nature, but announces

itself as the spirit of discord. It does this in a quite definite sequence of stages. Correspondingly as in nature the original unruly element develops into the separate and ever richer and higher manifold of forms.

"The same stages of creation which exist in the latter (the realm of nature) are also in the former (the realm of history); and the one is the symbol and explanation of the other" (pp. 54–55).

What follows from this for Schelling's procedure can easily be seen. Accordingly, the aim is to construct the stages of history, that is, the different ages of the world beginning with the primeval age when good and evil had not yet appeared as such, past the golden age of the world of which only the sagas still preserve a memory. From there the construction goes further past the Eastern to the Greek world, from there to the Roman and from there to the Christian age of the world (pp. 56–57). Since this historical construction is the common property of German Idealism, there is all the less reason to go into detail here. Already in the *System of Transcendental Idealism,* Schelling had begun with it, then especially in his *Vorlesungen über das akademische Studium.*

Because it is so rich and self-contained, the construction of the history of spirit in Hegel's first and greatest work, the *Phenomenology of Spirit,* is the most lofty. It presents and accomplishes nothing other than the appearance, that is, the emergence from itself to itself of the Absolute in the essential sequence of its essential forms. What corresponds to the essential historical meaning of evil in Schelling, but is not merely identical with it, is in Hegel what he calls the diremption of unhappy consciousness.

For us today these sketches of world history have something strange about them so that we do not find our way immediately with regard to their true intention and easily fall prey to misinterpretations. (At this opportunity let us give only one directive for the discussion of these constructions of history of German Idealism. So far, we have not yet gained the right fundamental relation to them because we measure them immediately and exclusively with the criteria of the positive and positivistic sciences of history. Their merits have their own place; their work is indispensable for present and future knowledge. But in those constructions it is not a matter of a supposedly arbitrary and inaccurate adjustment of so-called facts, but of the opening of essential, that is, possible, historical regions and their extension. To what extent the latter are occupied with "facts" and are occupied in the way presented in the context of the construction is another question. What is decisive is the creative wealth of the prefiguration of historical regions and landscapes, and all of this with the intention of grasping the essential law of Spirit. The most exact historical investigation is nothing if it is lacking these regions. But they also cannot be added afterwards.)

What Schelling want to clarify in our case is the nature of the historical movement in which the spirit of evil makes itself known. The spirit of evil is provoked by the good in such a way that it drives itself against the good in its revolt. But the good does not impart itself to evil as if there were pieces of itself which could then be changed into evil. It is not a matter of mutual communication and respective self-relinquishment and mingling, but "distribution" of the forces which are always already intrinsically separated and remain so. "Distribution" really means to allow that to emerge in which each, good and evil, actually participates.

For the characterization of the announcement of evil, of its actuality in which it still is not yet itself truly real, Schelling uses the term "the attraction of the ground." As the tyranny of self-will over the whole, evil is generally grounded in the craving of the ground in that the ground strives within creatures to make itself the dominant principle instead of just remaining the ground. "Attraction" of the ground: the same thing is meant by this as when we say, at least still in dialect, the weather "takes a turn"; that is, it is getting cold, something is contracting in such a way that it comes to a head and in so doing delimits itself from other things and in this delimitation exposes itself and its opposite out of indecisiveness and thus allows itself to incline in definite directions. This "attraction of the ground" spreads dissension in preparation and since every being is determined by ground and existence, in man, however, their unity is a spiritual, capable one, the "attraction of the ground" in man becomes the preparation of an attraction of a faculty. The faculty contracts, stiffens, becomes tense, and the tension toward . . . still at rest is the inclination to evil.

But where does this attraction of the ground come from? In the attraction of the ground the ground is in a way left to itself in order to operate as ground. But this is only an essential consequence of the Absolute, for the ruling of love must let the will of the ground be, otherwise love would annihilate itself. Only by letting the ground operate does love have that in which and on which it reveals its omnipotence—in something in opposition. The inclination to evil as the general operation of evil thus "comes" from the Absolute.

We can easily clarify that in a simple sequence. Love is the primordial unification of that which could each be for itself, and yet is not and cannot be without the other. Thus, love lets the ground operate. But this operating is the attraction of the ground and thus the arousal of self-will in the creature and thus the awakening of the inclination to evil. Thus, love (God) is the cause of evil!

Yet that is a very premature conclusion, premature because—following a very stubborn habit of thought—it immediately loses sight of what is peculiar to these connections of Being prevalent here and proceeds with the statements as with counters. We must see the following:

The ground does not arouse evil itself. It also does not arouse to evil, it only arouses the possible principle to evil. The principle is the free mobility of ground and existence in opposition to each other, the possibility of their separation and therein the possibility of the revolt of self-will to dominate the universal will. The inclination to evil, that is, to the reversal of self-will, is grounded in the operation of the attracting ground. In contradistinction to all "nature," the ground becomes the more powerful in man, the flight to self-craving becomes the more urgent because this craving is that through which the will of the ground striving for darkness wants to remove itself from the luminosity of the divine look of light. But in this look God looked at man, and in looking, elevated his essence to the light. However, as the purest essence of all will, this look is a consuming fire for every particular will. The sundered self-will of man is threatened by this fire. It threatens to extinguish all self-will and every being-a-self. The dread for its self, the "life dread" present in the ground of Being drives it to emerge from the center, that is, to cling to separation and further it, and thus to pursue its inclination.

Life-dread is a metaphysical necessity and has nothing to do with the little needs of the individual's intimidation and hesitancy. Life-dread is the presupposition of human greatness. Since the latter is not absolute, it needs presuppositions. What would a hero be who was not capable of letting precisely the most profound life-dread arise in himself? Either only a pure comedian or a blind strong-man and a brute. Dread of existence is not evil itself, it is also not the herald of evil, but the testimony that man is subject to this reality of evil, essentially so.

However, the inclination to evil is not a compulsion, but has its own necessity. This necessity does not prevent, but precisely requires, that the real realization of evil, that is, the reversal, contained in the will, of the unity of principles, is always man's free deed—in the individuation of his actual decisiveness.

III. The Process of the Individuation of Real Evil.

We already noted in recounting the individual sections and their titles that these titles only indicate the content of the sections externally. They are unable to convey anything of the movement of thinking in which alone the "content" is truly contained and is a content.

The previous section shows with regard to the first one that the possibility of evil, its being possible, is not only a formal possibility in the sense of that kind of possibility which we only characterize negatively and vacuously by saying and meaning that something "is" possible. That is supposed to mean that it does not contain a contradiction, in general there is nothing in its way. A golden mountain is possible, but this kind of possibility has no real being-possible in the sense that it inclines forward to the making possible of the possible and thus is already on the way to realization. Where evil is possible, it is also already operative in the sense of a throroughgoing attraction of the ground in all beings. Accordingly, the true realization of evil is not the keeping of this reality away from a mere possibility of thought, but is a decision within an already present operation.

Freedom is the faculty of good and evil. Freedom in the sense of being truly free includes the fact that the faculty has become a liking, a liking in the sense that it likes only being good or only malice, it has decided for one in opposition to the other. (Liking as inclination; liking as having decided for . . . , letting nothing disturb that.)

It is in the nature of the matter that just where the true reality of evil, that is, the actual decidedness in willing the reversal, there appears not just "one side" of freedom, but freedom in its full essence. If we read the title of the third section aloud, "The process of the individuation of real evil," it appears that only evil is being spoken about. But if we understand it in context and in terms of the direction of the whole movement of thought, we see that now precisely the full essence of human freedom must come into view in its complete clarity. Notwithstanding the guiding orientation toward evil, our reflection must now move to a higher level. It concerns the decision for evil and good as a decision. But the investigation thus again turns to the discussion, not pursued earlier, of the formal concept of freedom in the sense of self-determination. To speak more exactly, that earlier reflection on the formal concept of freedom—and that means the whole position of Idealism with regard to freedom—now moves into the context of the question of man's real freedom. We must now get the correct feeling for the factuality of the fact of human freedom which was tentatively discussed at the beginning of the treatise.

Thus the transitional passage from what we left out as Section II to the III section becomes clear in its intention (p. 59): "But just how the decision for good and evil comes to pass in individual man, that is still wrapped in total darkness and seems to require a special investigation. Up to the present we have, in any case, attended less closely to the formal side of freedom, although an insight into it seems to be connected with no less difficulty than the explanation of the concept of its reality."

We can get to understand what is essential in the III section in two ways:

1. By a more primordial version of the previous Idealistic concept of freedom on the foundation of what was now gained from the treatise.

2. By characterizing the determining ground for emerging from undecidedness to decision and decidedness.

But both ways coincide. For according to the Idealist concept, freedom is self-determination in terms of one's own law of being. But man's essence is to be created spirit; that is, that which God saw when he grasped the will to nature, and that means saw himself in the ground. Man "is" this look of light, in such a way that, according to his origin from creating-creature, selfish ground and existence are separable in man. Their unity must thus be in every real man as such in the decidedness of a definite union, in that union which constitutes the essence of just that man. But in accordance with man's essential origin from the look of life of the divine ground, this essence must be determined by eternity, and since it is the essence of man as an actual individual, determined in the eternal determination of itself to itself. Every man's own essence is each time his own eternal deed. Thence comes that uncanny and at the same time friendly feeling that we have always been what we are, that we are nothing but the unveiling of things long since decided.

The consideration of the question which determining ground breaks undecidedness as an undecidedness of a faculty leads to the same result. Of course, if one takes undecidedness in a purely negative sense, according to which no possibilities at all are prefigured and oriented in the inclination of a path, and if one understands self-determination also only in a negative sense—according to which there is no determining ground at all, but pure arbitrariness—the essence of freedom dissolves into empty chance. The will remains without direction and origin; it is no longer a will at all. On the other hand, if one understands the determining ground for the decision as a cause which itself must again be the effect of a preceding cause, the decision is forced into a purely mechanical causal context and loses the character of decision. Pure arbitrariness does not give a determining ground for decision. Mechanical force does not give a determining ground for what it is supposed to, for decision.

The decision must be determined, thus necessary. But it cannot be necessary in the sense of a compulsorily linked series of continuing relations of cause and effect.

What kind of necessity is determinative in the decision of freedom, then? An essential insight already lies in this question to which we are now led: The insight that necessity belongs in any case to freedom itself, that freedom itself *is* necessity. But what kind of necessity?

Along with possibility and reality, necessity counts as one of the modalities of Being. We saw that the kind of modality, in this case the kind of necessity, is determined by the actual fundamental kind and stage of the being in question. Now it is a matter of man and the way of his being in his freedom. But freedom is the faculty of good and evil. A directedness to the realm of prefigured directions of inclination belongs to a faculty. But freedom is not one faculty among others; it is rather the faculty of all possible faculties. It essentially contains what characterizes every faculty. That is the fact that the faculty of . . . reaches beyond itself, projects itself into what it is actually capable of. As the faculty of faculties, freedom is capable only when it positions its decision beforehand as decidedness in order for all enactment to become necessary in terms of it. True freedom in the sense of the most primordial self-determination is found only where a choice is no longer possible and no longer necessary. Whoever must first choose and wants to choose does not yet really know what he wants. He does not yet will primordially. Whoever is decided already knows it. The decision for decidedness and self-knowledge in the clarity of one's own knowledge are one and the same. This decidedness which no longer needs a choice because it is grounded in essential knowledge is far removed from all formalism, in fact it is its direct opposite. For formalism is sentimentality locked in prefabricated goals.

The necessity by which or as which freedom is determined is that of its own essence. But the determination of one's own essence, that is, the most primordial free element in freedom, is that self-overreaching as self-grasping which originates in the original essence of human being. The most futural element of all decidedness of human being in its individuality is what is most past. If man is free and if freedom as the faculty of good and evil constitutes the essence of human being, the individual man can only be free when he has himself decided originally for the necessity of his essence. This decision was not made at some time, at a point of time in the series of time, but falls as a decision to temporality. Thus where temporality truly presences, in the Moment, where past and future come together in the present, where man's complete essence flashes before him as this his own, man experiences the fact that he must always already have been who he is, as he who has determined himself for this. If one's own existence is really experienced in the sense of human being and not misunderstood as objective presence, there is nothing compulsory in this fundamental experience of one's own being, simply because a compulsion cannot be there, but rather necessity is freedom here and freedom is necessity.

Only a few, and they rarely, attain the deepest point of the highest expanse of self-knowledge in the decidedness of one's own being. And when they do, only as "often" as this moment of the innermost essential look is a moment, that is, most intensified historicity. That means that decidedness does not contract one's own being to an empty point of mere staring at one's ego, but decidedness of one's own being is only what it is as resoluteness. By this we mean standing within the openness of the truth of history, the perdurance (*Inständigkeit*) which carries out what it must carry out, unattainable and prior to all calculation and reckoning.

These moments alone are possible criteria for the determination of man's essence, but never an idea of an average man, compiled from somewhere, in which everybody recognizes himself complacently without further ado—this "without further ado" to be taken quite exactly and literally. But in the Moment of the decisive fundamental experience of human being we are, as in no other experience of self, protected from the vanity of self-overestimation and the self-righteousness of self-depreciation. For in the decidedness of our own being, we experience the fact that no one attains the height of what is his best as little as he attains the abyss of what is his evil, but that he is placed in this Between in order to wrest his truth from it which is in itself necessary, but, precisely for this reason, historical. It stands beyond the distinction of a truth for everyone and a truth for "special individuals." Only a wrested truth is truth. For it wrestles beings out into the open, and orders that open so that the bond of beings may come into play.

What is determinative for man's freedom is the necessity of his own actual being. This necessity itself is the freedom of his own deed. Freedom is necessity; necessity is freedom. These two sentences, correctly understood, do not stand in the formal mutual relation of an empty reversal. Rather, a process is contained there which goes back to itself, but in doing so never comes back to the same thing, but takes the point of departure back to a deeper understanding.

And only now that the reality of human freedom and real freedom have been characterized can we more or less formulate the essential delimitation already given. We said that human freedom is the faculty of good *and* evil. Perhaps we have not yet adequately noted that Schelling says the faculty of good and of evil, or we have at best only noted it to the extent that we are at bottom offended by this version as being imprecise. For it would really have to read of good *or* evil. No, as long as we think this we have not yet grasped the given essential interpretation of human freedom. For freedom as a real faculty, that is, a decided liking of the good, is in itself the positing of evil at the same time. What would something good be which had not posited evil and taken it upon itself in order to overcome and restrain it? What would something evil be which did not develop in itself the whole trenchancy of an adversary of the good?

Human freedom is not the decidedness for good or evil, but the decidedness for good and evil, or the decidedness for evil and good. This freedom alone brings man to the ground of his existence in such a way that lets him emerge at the same time in the unity of the will to essence and deformation of essence aroused in him. This aroused will is spirit, and as such spirit history.

Only now in terms of such an understanding of the "definition" do we have the correct point of departure to grasp the factuality of the fact of freedom, and that means at the same time to appropriate correctly what the next section presents.

IV. The Form of Evil Appearing in Man.

After all that we have said, two things must become clear: First, the form of evil is in itself the form of evil and good, and vice-versa. The apparently one-sided orientation toward the characterization of evil finds itself automatically placed in the essential relation of evil to good. Accordingly, the presentation of appearing evil becomes at the same time the presentation of appearing good. Second, the unity of both, the "and" does not mean an ethical, moral unity as if each time the other were only what should and should not be. Rather, appearing, emerging into beings as beings, evil in human being is at the same time an appearance of the good and vice-versa.

These two main points in the fourth section are to be further explained briefly.

Regarding the first point, as something real, evil is a decidedness of freedom, the decidedness for the unity of ground and existence in which the selflike ground, self-craving puts itself in the place of the universal will. The decidedness for the dominance of such a reversal, however, must—like all will to dominate—continually transcend itself in order to maintain itself in dominance. Thus, in evil lies the hunger of self-craving which dissolves all bonds more and more in its greed to be everything and dissolves into nothingness. Such a dominance of evil is nothing negative, not an incapability and a mere error. For this reason, it also not only arouses the mood of mere displeasure and regret, but also fills us with terror by virtue of its greatness which is, of course, reversed. Only what is spiritual is terrible. But what is reversed still rests in this longing as a reversal: longing, insofar as it has remained in harmony with existence. It is there in a remote memory, and thus the Absolute itself in its primordial unity, the good as itself. And even in the terror of evil an essential revelation occurs. For in its craving for self-consumption, the self-craving of malice mirrors that original ground in God, before all existence as it is for itself completely striving back into itself, and this is the terrible in God.

Correspondingly, the form of the good as a way of decidedness shows at the same time the appearance of evil, most of all just where the decidedness for the good reaches out so far in its decision that it decides from the Absolute itself for the Absolute as such. These highest forms of decision are enthusiasm, heroism, and faith. Their forms are manifold and cannot be presented here. But in every form of true decision the knowledge underlying it and radiating through it is always essential. For example, for heroism the following is characteristic: the clearest knowledge of the uniqueness of the existence taken upon oneself, the longest resolution to being the path of existence over its apex, the certainty which remains insensitive to its own greatness, and, lastly and firstly, the ability to be silent, never to say what the will truly knows and wants.

But all of this not as an easygoing urge just developing and fulfilling itself, but in the keenness of the knowledge of opposing forces, discord, and self-craving, of what tears down and turns everything around, from the knowledge of the essential presence of malice. The greater the forms of good and evil, the closer and more oppressive the counterform of evil and good.

From this brief reference to the co-presence of evil in good and good in evil, we can now see more clearly the truth of the dialectical sentence discussed in the introduction: The good "is" evil. It can also be turned around: Evil "is" the good; it helps to constitute the goodness of decidedness.

Regarding the second point, from this reciprocal relation between good and evil we take at the same time a reference as to how the "and" between both, their unity, and the reality of this unity, is to be conceived. In any case not as "morality," for here the good is what ought to be and the bad is what ought not to be. Here good and evil are the aims of striving and repugnance. They are held apart by the directions of this striving, and only this being apart and away from each other remains in view. Thus precisely in the moral interpretation we forget that good and evil could not strive apart from each other if they were not intrinsically striving against each other and that they could never strive against each other if they did mutually thrust into each other and were not together in the ground as they are.

Good and evil are what is separated in unity by virtue of the unity of the highest decidedness in which there is no mere-striving and no only-choosing. It is that knowledge which is certain of its own essential necessity and acts as such. This certainty is the conscientiousness, to be understood metaphysically, not morally, which acts from the presence of the God, but at the same time does not behave at all as if deviltry, the countergod of malice, did not exist.

Conversely, the reversed unity as malice, too, is the self-consuming decidedness of a knowledge, not a mere lack of conscience. Lack of conscience is simply base, but not evil. Malice is reversed conscientiousness which acts from the unique presence of the self-craving ground in which all compassion and forbearance has been burnt out; we speak of hard-boiled malice. It is so knowing that it would especially never dream of taking the God merely as a nursery tale. Rather, it knows inside that every attack is incessantly directed at him.

With this fourth section, the direct essential presentation of the possibility and reality of evil is concluded. It becomes more and more evident that it is not a special treatment of evil as a quality separable for itself. Rather, the question of evil is the essential presentation, aiming at the very center, of human freedom itself. And finally still another decisive insight was gained. In each of its fundamental forms freedom is essentially a knowing, that knowing which is what truly wills in the will.

But the question of human freedom is, as we heard in the preface, the question of the system, of the jointure of beings as a whole. Thus the course of the treatise must take the direction of the question of the system now that the essence of freedom has been clarified in its essential respects.

What we isolated as the subsequent three sections points in this direction. It is true that in accordance with the treatise's basic intention to show human freedom as a center of the system, the system itself and the question of the system are only delineated in the broadest and roughest outlines. And that occurs at first by way of a continuation of the train of thought just completed. Only sections VI and VII treat the system explicitly. Section V constitutes the transition.

V. The Justification of God's Divinity in the Face of Evil

The title already indicates that evil will now be considered in relation to the Absolute and that the perspective now aims at the whole. But didn't this already happen in the previous sections? Was it not their essential intention to show how the ground in God, originally creating nature, grounded that operation of evil which thoroughly rules the whole realm of beings, created nature and the realm of history, and finally determined the principle for evil? Indeed. And only because the possibility and reality of evil as a decidedness of human freedom extend metaphysically to the Absolute and claim the whole of beings for themselves can human freedom raise a founded claim to the basic character of a center of the system at all. It also follows from what has been said that as far as what concerns the question of freedom no essential enrichments are to be expected in the next sections, on the other hand that the content of these sections is more easily accessible mainly as essential conclusions from what preceded. It is not just due to the growing familiarity with the treatise that the following sections seem less strange to us. They are also stylistically more loosely constructed and move in their musical key back to the introduction. Of course, it would be a deception if we were to think that the questions treated with regard to the system had fewer presuppositions than those concerned with freedom. Still, we must ascertain that Schelling's beginning impetus and keenness of metaphysical questioning diminish toward the end.

The content of the fifth section concerns the question how God as the Absolute is to be justified in the face of evil. How is it possible that he can remain and be God if He is the ground of evil? This question is the true and sole metaphysical question in relation to evil in the history of thinking. This question is, so to speak, the usual package in which the "problem of evil" is passed around. For Schelling it is only an interlude, because on the one hand evil is not simply just a fact by itself, but belongs to the good and because on the other hand the Absolute neither operates determinatively in the manner of a mechanical cause, nor is it mere understanding and intelligent will in its essence.

The answer to the question of the justification of the Absolute in the face of evil has already been given in what preceded. We only have to repeat what was said. The question is really no longer a question because the point of departure of the traditional question has been relinquished, and everything is based upon a more primordial interpretation of Being.

Creation and all creatures are God's free act. Thus God is the originator of evil. If not, why did He not then keep creatures from being evil? If the Absolute is free and thus obviously free in the absolute sense, it must after all have infinite possibilities of choice, including that of not letting evil be at all. Schelling rejects this traditional and common consideration in two respects. He shows that (1) God does not have infinite possibilities of choice and cannot have them and (2) God cannot let evil not be.

Regarding (1): only a finite being which does not simultaneously dominate beings as a whole immediately and in every respect, only for this being does the possible exist, and the possible is therefore always relative, projecting in terms of a definite reality and for that reality. Here Schelling touches upon an essential question of metaphysics. We can clarify it as the question of the inner essential relation between possibility and finitude. The realm of the possible and the real exist only in what is finite, and if the distinguishability of possibility and reality belongs to the essence of Being, then Being in general is finite in essence. To choose means to relate oneself to possibilities and in doing so to prefer one to the others. Thus, to be able to choose means to have to be finite. Such a determination is incompatible with the Absolute. On the contrary, the perfection of the Absolute consists in only being able to will one thing, and this one thing is the necessity of its own essence. And this essence is love. Thus the second sentence is already founded, too.

Regarding (2): God cannot let evil not be, He must admit evil. This admission is not immediate, but rather a mediate one so that the originator of evil only comes about in this mediation. God lets the oppositional will of the ground operate in order that that might be which love unifies and subordinates itself to for the glorification of the Absolute. The will of love stands above the will of the ground and this predominance, this eternal decidedness, the love for itself as the essence of Being in general, this decidedness is the innermost core of absolute freedom. On the basis of this absolute freedom, evil is metaphysically necessary. Thus evil could only not exist under one metaphysical condition, namely, if the Absolute itself did not have to be. But it must be if beings are at all. With this we enter the essential idea of the sixth section.

VI. Evil in the System as a Whole

If beings are at all, there must be creation. Creation is self-presentation emerging from itself in the ground. Creation presupposes the will to self-revelation (existence) and at the same time that in which it presents itself as in another. This other is the ground, the basis. Letting the ground operate is necessary in order that a creator be able to be a creature. Of course, the Absolute makes the ground independent of its self its own. The creature, on the other hand, never gains complete control over the ground. It shatters itself upon it and remains excluded from it and thus burdened by its gravity. Thus, the "veil of sadness which is spread over all nature, the deep, unappeasable melancholy of all life" (p. 79). Thence all creators, creative people, the poets, thinkers, and founders of the state, are "melancholy spirits" according to Aristotle. What comes from the mere ground does not come from God. But evil is the insurrection of the ground's craving, as the ground not to be one condition, but the sole condition. Because evil comes from the ground, the ground, however, belongs to the essence of beings, evil is posited in principle with the Being of beings. Where beings as a whole are projected in the jointure of Being, where system is thought, evil is included and implicated.

But what does system mean here? We said that system was the self-knowing unity of the jointure of Being. Thus the jointure of Being must become determinant for the whole of system. How is the distinction of ground and existence of beings related to the system? This question echoes in this section and the last one, but it is not seized upon and above all not yet penetrated at all in its inner difficulty.

At the passage of the transition to the VI section there is the sentence: "In the divine understanding there is a system; God himself, however, is not a system but a life . . ." (pp. 78, 399). Here system is attributed to only one factor of the jointure of Being, to existence. At the same time, a higher unity is posited and designated as "life." We are familiar with the metaphysical significance of this term. It never means for Schelling merely "biological," plant-animal life. Schelling's language is "polemical" here. In contrast to the Idealist version of the Absolute as intelligence, he means that the will of the understanding exists in opposition to the will of the ground. But when the system is only in the understanding, the ground and the whole opposition of ground and understanding are excluded from system as its other and system is no longer system with regard to beings as a whole.

That is the difficulty which emerges more and more clearly in Schelling's later efforts with the whole of philosophy, the difficulty which proves to be an *impasse* (*Scheitern*). And this *impasse* is evident since the factors of the jointure of Being, ground and existence and their unity not only become less and less compatible, but are even driven so far apart that Schelling falls back into the rigidified tradition of Western thought without creatively transforming it. But what makes this failure so significant is that Schelling thus only brings out difficulties which were already posited in the beginning of Western philosophy, and because of the direction which this beginning took were posited by it as insurmountable. For us that means that a second beginning becomes necessary through the first, but is possible only in the complete transformation of the first beginning, never by just letting it stand.

At this stage of the treatise on freedom it is not yet clearly evident to Schelling that precisely positing the jointure of Being as the unity of ground and existence makes a jointure of Being as system impossible. Rather, Schelling believes that the question of the system, that is, the unity of beings as a whole, would be saved if only the unity of what truly unifies, that of the Absolute, were correctly formulated. That is the task of the last section.

VII. The Highest Unity of Beings as a Whole and Human Freedom

The highest unity is that of the Absolute. But since the latter exists as eternal becoming, the Being of this becoming must be understood in such a way that the primordial unity is present as that which lets everything originate. Thus, this unity also lies still before the duality of ground and existence. In such a unity, no duality can be discernible yet. Thus, this unity is also no longer the unity of what belongs together (identity), but what belongs together is itself supposed to arise from this primordial unity. This unity is "absolute indifference." The only predicate which can be attributed to it is lack of predicates. Absolute indifference is nothingness in the sense that every statement about Being is nothing with regard to it, but not in the sense that the Absolute is nugatory and merely of no use. Here, too, Schelling does not see the necessity of an essential step. If Being in truth cannot be predicated of the Absolute, that means that the essence of all Being is finitude and only what exists finitely has the privilege and the pain of standing in Being as such and experiencing what is true as beings.

However, just this last section is important for the basic sections 1-IV. It warns us in retrosopect never to think becoming in the essential project of the movement of becoming of the Absolute in such a way that initially there is only a ground and then existence accrues to it from somewhere. Rather, both are in their own way the whole, but they are not simply simultaneous in the Absolute. Their duality erupts directly from the neither-nor of absolute indifference. This primordial duality becomes an opposition only when the will of love enters the decidedness of being absolutely superior and lets the ground be ground. If opposition is not at all primordially "there" by itself in the Absolute, then the opposition of good and evil is certainly not there which first comes about when the creator drives himself out into the selfhood of created spirit, and human freedom is realized.

But according to Schelling's formulation of the concept of freedom, human freedom is the center of philosophy because from it as the center the whole movement of creatures' becoming as the creator's becoming and as eternal becoming of the Absolute becomes visible in a unified way in its opposition, its strife. According to the ancient saying of Heraclitus, strife is the basic law and basic power of Being. But the greatest strife is love because it arouses the deepest discord in order to be itself in conquering it.

The true weight of Schelling's treatise in its content and form lies in the introduction and the first four sections. The introduction develops the question of system; the four sections work out a basic position of philosophy. But however far Schelling travels on a new path into the essence of human freedom, Kant's basic position in the question of freedom is not undermined, but only confirmed. Kant says that the fact of freedom is incomprehensible. The only thing that we comprehend is its incomprehensibility. And freedom's incomprehensibility consists in the fact that it resists com-prehension since it is because freedom transposes us into the occurrence of Being, not in the mere representation of it. But the occurrence is not a blind unfolding of a process, but is knowing perdurance in beings as a whole, which are to be endured. This knowledge of freedom is certain of its highest necessity because it alone makes that position of receptivity possible in which man stands, and is able as a historical being to encounter a destiny, to take it upon himself and to transcend it.

The treatise on the essence of human freedom only speaks explicitly of man in a few passages. We do not find a self-contained analysis of human being at all. Rather the subject matter is the Absolute, creation, nature, the essential factors of Being, pantheism, and Idealism. And yet all of this speaks only of man, and the highest determinations are gained from an analogy to man. For this reason we were constantly pursued by that reservation which can be called "anthropomorphic." The objection that this treatise determines the Absolute, creating, nature, even Being in general, in terms of the form of man is so apt and convincing that one subsequently lets this treatise alone as a genial game of thought which, however, is unproductive for "objective" cognition, and is only seductive.

What about this reservation? We cannot take it seriously enough since it more or less concerns all such investigations in a veiled way. To be sure, we can only give a few references here at the end which might serve as a stimulus for independent reflection.

The most important thing in any position with regard to the "anthropomorphic" objection is to concede from the outset what it generally marshals, that everything is gauged according to the form of man.

But after this confession the questions just begin. The "anthropomorphic" objection immediately exposes itself to the most pointed counterobjections by being content with this ascertainment. Behind it stands the conviction which it doesn't explain further that everyone, of course, generally knows what man is.

But what is insidious about anthropomorphism is not that it gauges according to the form of man, but that it thinks this criterion is self-evident and believes its closer determination and formulation to be superfluous. However, the objection to anthropomorphism does this, too, with the sole difference that it rejects this criterion. But neither the proponents of regular anthropomorphism nor its opponents ask the decisive question of whether this criterion is not necessary and why it is so. If the consideration ever gets this far, then one sees that essential questions lie behind the argument, whether anthropomorphism or not, and they belong to a quite different level.

We shall name some of them.

1. Can human thinking and knowing ever proceed any other way at all than in a continual relation to human existence?

2. Does a humanizing of everything cognizable and knowable follow without further ado from the fact that man remains the "criterion" in this sense?

3. Does it not rather follow primarily that *before* everything the question must be asked who is man?

4. Does not every essential determination of man overreach him—as the question alone who he is already shows—as certainly as every knowledge of the Absolute falls short of it?

5. Does not one thing follow compellingly, that the perspective for the essential determination of man is neither man alone in the way that everybody is familiar with him nor the non-human either, but just as little the Absolute with whom one believes oneself in immediate agreement?

6. Does man not exist in such a way that the more primordially he is himself, he is precisely not only and not primarily himself?

7. If man, as the being who is not only itself, becomes the criterion, then what does humanizing mean? Does it not mean the precise opposite of what the objection takes it for?

But if this is true, we shall have to decide to read all great philosophy, and Schelling's treatise in particular, with different eyes.

Even if Schelling did not think through the "anthropomorphical" reservation in this fundamental way and did not see the realm of tasks behind it, one thing still becomes quite clear. The fact of human freedom has for him its own factuality. Man is not an object of observation placed before us which we then drape with little everyday feelings. Rather, man is experienced in the insight into the absysses and heights of Being, in regard to the terrible element of the godhead, the lifedread of all creatures, the sadness of all created creators, the malice of evil and the will of love.

God is not debased to the level of man, but on the contrary, man is experienced in what drives him beyond himself in terms of those necessities by which he is established as that other. The "normal man" of all ages will never recognize what it is to be that other because it means to him the absolute disruption of existence. Man—that other—he alone must be the one through whom the God can reveal himself at all, if he reveals himself.

There is throughout Schelling's treatise something of the fundamental mood of Hölderlin of whom we spoke at an earlier occasion (winter semester 1934/35 and summer semester 1935).

> "For because
> The most blessed feel nothing themselves,
> Another, if to say such a thing
> Is permitted, must, I suppose,
> In the gods' name, sympathetically feel,
> They need him."*

***Hölderlin: His Poems*, trans. Michael Hamburger (London: Harvill Press, 1952).

Appendix

This Appendix contains some excerpts from manuscripts, copied by Fritz Heidegger, in preparation for an advanced Schelling Seminar in the summer semester of 1941.

In addition, the Appendix contains an excerpt from seminar notes from 1941 until 1943.

Excerpts from the Manuscripts in Preparation for the Seminar on Schelling, Summer Semester 1941.

In keeping with the announcement, we shall discuss the metaphysics of German Idealism. We shall attempt that on the path of an interpretation of Schelling's *Treatise on Freedom*. Thus a single work of a unique thinker of this epoch is isolated. This procedure is all right if we limit ourselves to getting to know just this work of this thinker, and thus getting closer to a limited sphere of the thinking of German Idealism. However, this procedure becomes questionable as soon as the claim is made of thinking through "*the* Metaphysics of *the* German Idealists." To be sure, this claim guides us.

Therefore, the intentionally one-sided procedure does need a special justification. How else should that be accomplished than by a knowledge of what is thought in this single treatise of Schelling's? We already presuppose here that this single treatise attains the acme of the metaphysics of German Idealism. But we will be able to know this at best at the end of a completed interpretation, perhaps only after several interpretations.

When is this single and arbitrary way justified, and even necessary?

1. If Schelling's treatise is the acme of the metaphysics of German Idealism.

2. If all the essential determinations of this metaphysics are carried out in this treatise.

3. If the essential core of all of Western metaphysics can be delineated in complete clarity in terms of this treatise.

The procedure thus remains forced, at least in the beginning. Spoken more precisely, it always looks forced for common sense according to which often-cited "historical completeness" alone offers a guarantee for the knowledge of history.

But perhaps this common sense opinion is just an opinion, an assumption which is unfounded in terms of the essence of history. Perhaps that is so. In order to be certain of this supposition, and thus to justify our intention, we would, of course, need a reflection whose scope and difficulty would hardly lag behind an interpretation of the treatise chosen. For we would have to show that and how the historicity of the history of thinking is unique, that this history can indeed look like a historical reflection, but in truth has its own nature and also does not coincide with what one customarily otherwise opposes in this field to historical presentation, with "systematic" reflection.

These short references make it clear that our intention remains surrounded by a chaos of various doubts at its inception which all too easily mislead us into disentangling and clarifying all of this before the real work, but in the process to postpone the real work of the interpretation again and again. Evidently there is only one way out of this danger, to start blindly with the interpretation of Schelling's treatise and to rely upon some kind of use resulting from it.

This apparently "natural" lack of doubt could surely guide us if it were only a matter of bringing out what Schelling meant. It is true that the correct rendering of his thinking demands enough of our power of thought. Still, this re-thinking does not already guarantee that we, too, are thinkers ourselves in the sense of those thinkers whom we call thinkers. But we are not willing to renounce this. Why not? Because of some idiosyncrasy and will to think? That would be too little, much too little, to make us persevere in thinking.

But from where else can necessity come to us? If we could, so to speak, calculate it from our side, it would not be necessity which claimed us. Then are there mysterious experiences at play which determine us to persevere in thinking and to awaken a questioning thinking? This can be true least of all in the realm of thinking, here where only cold boldness has a say. But this, too, is again only an assertion which, moreover, believes that it has already been decided that we are really placed in a need to think. Thus we seem to race away anew on the path of doubts into endlessness, only in another direction. And is it not already clear now that doubts prevent us from thinking most of all?

Then it must be that the important thing is to "make" a beginning without doubts. But can we then get involved with "the historical" at all? If not, where should we begin? Viewed from here, how small are those doubts named at first with regard to the limitation to a single work of a single thinker compared with the objection that in our reflection on the metaphysics of German Idealism we are already running after something in the past and are "orienting ourselves historically." This kind of orientation contains after all the admission that philosophy is only the historical rehash *(Vergegenwärtigung)* of its past, which it has to be if it no longer has "either measure or rule" intrinsically. Schelling expresses himself clearly enough on this subject in the concluding paragraph of his treatise on freedom (p. 97).

If the dialectical principle (that is, the understanding, which divides but on this very account arranges and shapes things organically) as well as the archetype towards which it is directed, are withdrawn from philosophy at the same time, so that it no longer has either measure or rule in itself, then, to be sure, it has no other way than to strive to orientate itself historically and to take as its source and guiding principle the *tradition* . . . then it is time to seek for philosophy, too, a historical standard and foundation, just as it was intended to establish poetry among us through a study of the writings of all nations.

But Schelling objects to this time and says, "The time of merely historical faith is past, as soon as the possibility of immediate knowledge is given. We have an earlier revelation than any written one—nature" (ibid.).

But is this true straight away for our time, too? Or is this time, ours, different? For what law demands that thinking follow its time? Or is thinking untimely, always and necessarily? But what if the untimely were just the reversal of the timely, a still fiercer dependency on "time"? How is "an age" to be determined in order to be determinative for thinking? What if essential thinking first determines an age in what is most its own and does this without the age having or being able to have a public consciousness of its own historical essence? But then this decisive thinking must, after all, be so primordial that it cannot get lost in a past epoch and calculate in it what is necessary for the present and make it compatible with the present. That calculating is the essence of "historicism," this making compatible is the essence of "actualism." Both belong together. They are the enemies, sometimes openly, sometimes hiddenly, of decisive thinking.

But if we do not relinquish historical reflection on the metaphysics of German Idealism, as our intention hints, perhaps first introduce it and in doing so still act only from the one necessity of thinking in the sense of essential thinking, then that is a sign that our needs are different, different because the need has become different. Or perhaps it is even the same need, not the need of an age, not the need of a century, but the need of 2,000 years, the need that for this long a time thinking has been "metaphysics?" Perhaps this need has meanwhile become more urgent, which does not exclude the possibility that it has become still less visible. In fact, when our thinking attempts a historical reflection on German Idealism, it is not a historical orientation. But it is also not "immediate cognition" in the mode of the metaphysics of German Idealism. The thinking which has become necessary is *historical* thinking. What this means should be made clear by an actual attempt.

Therefore, we shall now put all doubts about our intention aside, noticing, however, how they dissolve and become clear at the proper time. Perhaps in the long run we cannot distinguish between historiographical *(historisch)* explanation and historical *(geschichtlich)* thinking, but we shall keep one thing in mind. The historical thinking attempted here cannot be subsumed either under philosophical-historical explanation nor under "systematic" reflection nor under a combination of both. It is sufficient if we can gather from what has been said, although only approximately, why we are not seizing upon Schelling's treatise arbitrarily and blindly in order to make it familiar for scholarly purposes.

In our reflection on the treatise on freedom we attain essential relations to that which "is." We experience that and how we "are" in such relations, we experience the abandonment of Being of beings and man's forgottenness of Being.

We are not interested in being edifying about something scholarly, even less so in snatching at something which is "practically" applicable, "close to life." But if a reflection is to be attempted on the essential relations in which "we" now stand, of what use is a treatise out of the past?

In spite of all the criticism, does not the danger of historicism or actualism remain? It does not. Historicism brings the past to the present and explains it in terms of what lies further back in the past. It flees to the past to find something to hold on to and counts on escapes from the present. It wants "restoration" or else "eschatology." Mere "relativizing" does not constitute the essence of historicism.

Actualism is the reverse side of historicism. Through it relativism is seemingly overcome. It calculates the present value of the past. The "future" is the pro-longed "present" whose plans are to be guaranteed by calculability.

The relation to the "future" changes nothing if it is only the prolongation of the present in a forward direction and is that present in its rigidification. The calculating game between origin and future turns out to be servitude to the uncomprehended present.

We are not concerned with the historical explanation of the past, relevant to the present, but with historically coming to grips with what has been *(Gewesenem)*, still presencing. The core section (pp. 31-39) as the "explanation of the distinction of ground and existence": the investigation "is grounded" on this distinction. But the investigation penetrates to the center of the system.

The distinction is "elucidated," various "reflections" of beings are supposed to lead to the same distinction, grounding them, namely: (1) God, (2) creation of the world, and (3) man. What does lead to mean here? Beings are introduced as being ruled by this distinction, that is, determined in their beingness. Is it only "examples" that are cited here? If not, what does this procedure mean?

The investigation aims at the *construction of the essence of man* in beings as a whole. This construction is supposed to present man as that being which is God in a very eminent sense. *Man "is" God.*

Man as the central being, the being which "is" in the center; the bond by which God takes creaturely nature *into himself,* "is" it.

The question of anthropomorphism must be explicated in terms of this concept of man who "is" God. Only thus does it lead straight to the question of the truth of Being.

"Being" is to be understood here decisively as existence of the ground: "subjectity." Man *existing in this way* as constructing: "philosophy." "Anthro-pomorphism," "circle."

For Schelling, and in a different way for Nietzsche, anthropomorphism is explicitly affirmed and required. Why?

How the insight into the relation of Being to man is possible and necessary for metaphysics and at the same time essentially limited. Thus it becomes one-sided and makes itself known as explicit anthropomorphism.

Man exists, that is, man is that creature in which what is elevated from the ground is completely awakened, is the understanding *as Spirit.*

Man is the Word completely uttered, in him Spirit reveals itself as Spirit, "that is, *God* existing as *actu.*" (And *for* this "being" the Absolute is thus also the "first" in every respect.)

In man the Word is completely uttered. Here Spirit is together with itself as Spirit, as uttered, as speaking.

System and subjectity: how *systasis* is determined in its essential jointure from the representation to oneself of representing and its representation in the element of being represented in general.

Representation to oneself and placing-together.

The together as unity in the sense of the "unity" "of" Being (the *unity* of persencing belonging to Being itself). Unity of the re-presentedness of representation re-presenting to itself. Subjectity.

It is not sufficient to develop "system" formally in terms of the dominance of *mathesis.* For *mathesis* is already the essential consequence of *certitudo,* and this belongs together with subjectity as Being.

Setting apart *(Aus-einander-setzung)* is the experience of the truth of beings as a mode of presence of the truth of Being.

It is the experience of how the history of Being penetrates us and thus bears us to unattained regions of dwelling in which a decision to ground the truth of Being must be made.

Setting apart is the transposition to this realm of decision.

Perhaps Schelling's characterization of beings as "ground" also has its origin in the modern interpretation of beingness as subjectivity. Still, that is not yet transparent. And it cannot be transparent because so far we have still taken Schelling's distinction in an external fashion, so to speak, according to the isolated, separated "pieces," existence and ground. But Schelling himself says for ground more precisely: merely ground of existence, and thus we must also say existence of ground and on the ground.

Schelling's distinction specifically aims at showing the belonging together of ground and existence in each "being," that is, in every thing that is. That means that the distinction formulates the jointure of every being.

Here the decisive question is raised: How is every being as such joined in this way? Where is the distinction of ground and existence rooted?

On what path do we meet the root of the distinction? By a simple reflection. If every being insofar as it is a being is determined by the distinction named, the distinction must be rooted in beings as such, that is, in their Being.

Thus, the next question which arises is the one: how does Schelling determine the essence of Being? Granted that we correctly acknowledge the treatise on freedom as the acme of the metaphysics of German Idealism, we may also suspect that Schelling speaks of the essence of the Being of all beings in this treatise and thus answers the Aristotelian question: *ti to on?*

We find in the introduction to the treatise a passage which in the manner of its formulation and delimitation unequivocally claims to be a statement on the essence of beings as such. After an important discussion, these sentences follow, explicitly set apart by a dash (p. 24): "In the final and highest instance there is no other Being than will. Will is primordial Being and all predicates apply to it alone—groundlessness, eternity, independence of time, self-affirmation. All philosophy strives only to find this highest expression." (Being as will.) Our task is (1.) to elucidate this essential determination of Being, (2.) to show how this distinction is rooted in Being thus determined.

Regarding (1): if we begin the elucidation of the passage with the last sentence, we immediately see that it is only the abbreviated and final version of Aristotle's statement: "kai de kai to palai te kai nun kai aei zetoumenon kai aei aporoumenon, ti to on, . . . (*Metaphysics* Z, 1028 b 2-4).

Ultimacy consists in the fact that the *aei aporoumenon* is lacking. It must be lacking, for the beginning of the passage declares the essence of beings as such to be found and determined in the highest degree. However, this is not a private conviction of Schelling's. Rather, the claim to this knowledge distinguishes German Idealism as the unconditioned Idealism of the Spirit.

"Will is primordial Being," that is, will corresponds to the primordial essence of Being. Why? Because the predicates which state the essence of Being are attributed to will in the eminent sense. It alone is completely sufficient for the predicates named. ("Being?" Beings conceived ab-solutely, at the same time *the* being as such.)

a.) What are the essential predicates of Being? Groundlessness, eternity, independence of time, self-affirmation.

"Groundlessness." We stop short. Did we not hear that to every being as such a "ground" belongs? Certainly. Thus the groundlike does belong to Being, to be sure. But that does not mean that Being means needing a ground. Being is intrinsically groundlike, what gives ground, presences as the ground, has the character of ground. Precisely because it is groundlike, groundgiving, it cannot need a ground. The groundlike is groundless, what grounds, what presences as basis does not need the ground; that is, it is without something to which it could go back as something outside of it, there is no longer any back, no behind itself, but pure presencing itself: the primordial. (The groundlike—that is, *subjectum.*). But Being and—time?

"Eternity": *aei; aeternitas* as *nunc stans?* Being means constancy in a unique presencing. (Not mere continuance into endlessness in every direction: *sempiternitas*. Endless duration is the longest persistence (*die längste Weile*). Limitless persistence. But "eternity"? One should compare the *Weltalter*, I, VIII, p. 260f. Not: *nunc stans*, but "overcoming of time," that is, inclusion!) (To what extent is it a matter here of traditional predicates, to what extent of Schelling's interpretation?)

"Independence of time." Does that not mean the same as "eternity"? And above all: is this not quite unequivocally a previous decision on the part of metaphysics itself against *Being and Time?*

"Independence of time" goes beyond an elucidation of eternity, it includes *sempiternitas* as well and means beings as such are not swept away in the flux of succession, but beings as such remain untouched by its change. Being means *constancy* (as movement) untouched by succession, presencing not affected by the change of disappearing and arriving. Thus it is Being in the traditional sense of metaphysics, Being which forms the basis for the original project of beings in *Being and Time.*

"Independence of time" cannot speak against *Being and Time*, because "time" in the case of "independence of time" is thought differently, and nowhere in *Being and Time* is an independence of beings, let alone of Being, from time understood in this way. (Being is "dependent" upon ecstatic time as an essential character of the "truth" of Being, but this "truth" belongs to the presencing of Being itself.)

The predicates groundlessness, eternity, and independence of time clarify the *hypokeimenon.*

"Self-affirmation." This last predicate points to the modern interpretation of Being in the sense of Leibniz's *exigentia essentiae* which includes the following: beings are in that they present themselves to themselves in their essence, and in this presentation represent, and representing, strive for themselves (*Ge-stell*).

b.) In terms of what are these predicates delineating the essence of Being taken and justified as the decisive ones?

Schelling says nothing about this, he lists them as self-evident determinations. And rightly so. For it belongs to the essence of metaphysics that these predicates of Being, Being in such a way of predication, are understood as a self-evident. The understanding takes its point of departure here, and stops here. The predication of the Being of beings raises and knows no other claim, especially since only beings in their beingness are considered everywhere, and Being is thought to be decided in its essence.

Meanwhile, however, this self-evident character has been shattered by *Being and Time* and has become what is truly worthy of question for thoughtful questioning. But since our next task is to understand Schelling's distinction in its root and necessity, and thus to create the only basis for a correct discussion, let us remain for the time being within Schelling's thinking. In relation to the passage cited we must ask:

c.) How does precisely the interpretation of Being as will suffice for the claim of Being which is required by the predicates? More precisely, how are "groundlessness, eternity, independence of time, and self- affirmation" contained in "will"?

What does Schelling understand by "willing" and "will"? In the tradition of metaphysical thinking the essence of will is determined in manifold ways, and the word is also used for many things. We always think of *orexis, desiderium, appetitus sensibilis,* striving for . . ., craving, longing (*nisus!*).

For what? Why is this mostly undetermined? *Appetitus* (*universum*) for Leibniz, on the contrary, means to strive for "oneself" in realization and reality as such. *Boulesis*.

In striving for . . . a certain sensibility of self is contained, finding oneself in something; striving to become oneself, to produce oneself. Longing.

Schelling says (p. 34), "the understanding is actually the will in willing" (compare also p. 96). That sounds strange at first, especially for our ears today. But what does the understanding mean?

Re-presenting of "unity," *logos,* gathering, original synthesis; re-presenting of the universal as such, rule, order, law. Aristotle says in *De Anima* (III, 9, 432b): "*en te to logistiko gar he boulesis ginetai.*" The understanding places striving in and toward the universal. The understanding is "*logos*" ("the word," says Schelling, p. 36) and thus raises the will above the stage of the merely "prescient will" (p. 34). The understanding is the "universal will" (p. 38). This reminds us of Kant for whom will means operating in accordance with concepts, operating in terms of representing something in general (aim); compare *Critique of Judgment,* §10. For Leibniz *appetitus* is *perceptio* and *apperceptio.*

Will is the will *of* the understanding, whether as longing or as Spirit. The understanding is what truly wills, strives for itself in realization and posits this (Idea). In contrast, we refer to the metaphysical reversal of this essence in Nietzsche: will to power, willing oneself as legislation and its accomplishment, will as the command of striving for being able to strive, of the empowering of power.

How does the "will" thus understood suffice for the decisive predicates of Being?

Schelling did not explicitly show that. However, he does say something else: Being is "becoming," "life," and thus he distinguishes "mere" Being from Being "in itself." "Only the eternal exists in itself, as self-secured, will, . . ." (p. 20) purely in terms of itself and through itself and intrinsically oppositional.

Groundlessness: the being which does not need another ground outside of itself, presencing from itself and constant.

Eternity: the being which is in advance of everything—already.

Independence of time: not succession, but "simultaneously," precisely as becoming, independent of "succession" and sequence. In what sense "becoming"? To bring oneself to oneself and thus precisely to "be."

Self-affirmation: to will oneself (to be in being, the "existentielle"; compare *The Weltalter*). How in this interpretation of Being as will does "Being" become important "in the highest and last instance"? Where does the responsibility for what beings are come from in general? From Being! But how? From what is most of all in being? And where does this come from?

Why do we speak of the "highest" and "last" instance here? We speak of the highest instance because now in every respect presencing and constancy (all "instances" of beings, subject-object) are not just things as object, but "subject," egoity. Beings in *and for* themselves. The being that neither is nor is not, is above being. It is the last instance because nothing beyond it can be, the unconditioned (*das Un-bedingte*)* and at the same time the im-mediate, the Ab-solute ("certainty"), the primordial in all things. (There still remains only what Nietzsche then brings: the reversal).

Regarding (2): how does Being determined in the highest way as will form the root of the distinction?

"Root" means that the distinction originates from the will, and what is distinguished has the character of "will." The highest being, what really exists is Spirit, but Spirit is the Spirit *of love*. "But love is supreme. It is that which was before there were the depths and before existence (as separate entities), but it was not there as *love*" (p. 86). For this reason the distinction must be developed with regard to the "will," for this reason Schelling also speaks of the "will of the ground" and the "will of the understanding."

The will is ground because as striving (longing) it goes back to itself and contracts itself, thus is a basis for . . . , because its flight precisely calls forth the other, "arrests," "attracts."

Will is the understanding because it moves toward reality, unity (*universum*), presence, the presence of what the ground is, selfhood.

The will is *subiectum*: (1) as *hypokeimenon*, but willfully, striving (*ex ou*), "basis," and (2) as egoity, consciousness, spirit, (*eis ho*) "Word," *logos*.

In Being as will the *subjectum*-character of beings was developed in every respect. If beingness is *subiectum* in all metaphysics (Greek and modern), and if primordial Being is will, then will must be the true *subiectum*, in the unconditional manner of willing oneself. Thus: denying oneself, contracting and bringing oneself to oneself.

---

*Emphasizing the unconditioned as beyond all possible things (*Ding*)—TRANS.

True will, true being, is love. The distinction originates here because it is essentially placed here.

But is the distinction then necessary, and in what sense is this necessity to be understood? The distinction is "a very real one," not "merely logical" and "introduced merely as a makeshift" (p. 88), says Schelling. It is not just as if it had to be thought by us, as if "we" could not get along without it in thinking and in the system, but Being itself as will needs it. Beings, as such, separate, distinguish themselves. Strife and opposition are willed and produced by Being itself.

Beings become sensitive to "themselves" in "becoming." "Becoming" comes from the opposition of ground and existence. What presupposes is what is presupposed and modern.

Will really means to take oneself together, to come to oneself, to will oneself, to be a self, spirit, *love*. As coming to oneself, revealing oneself, it is thus distinguishing.

Love is love only as letting the ground operate, in opposition to which it can be itself and must be itself in order that a unifying one and unity and it itself might be. Unity *as* unity is unification. (Compare Schelling's *Stuttgarter Privatvorlesung*, "Der Grundsatz des Gegensatzes." Compare Hegel's negativity.)

The center is "the purest essence of all will." *Ens entium, ens summum, causa realis:* Leibniz.

The different versions of the distinction:

a) "mere ground of existence"	: "Existence" (in the sense of existing)
b) "basis"	: "what exists"
c) "ground of existence"	: "the existing"
d) will of the ground	: will of love
e) Existence	: what exists ⎫ in the works
f) Being	: beings ⎬ after the treatise
"object"	"subject" ⎭ on freedom

The reciprocal relation of two equally essentially distinguished elements out of something which cannot be distinguished, but which in itself separates out of itself for the sake of the primordial unity. There is no figuration of the unity of the groundless, of what is "beyond being."

Versions e) and f) seem strange at first, and yet they are the truly adequate ones. Being as the being which has not yet emerged from itself, but contracts in itself. "Being" is selfness, beinghood (*Seinheit*), is separation. Love, however, is the not of selfness, it doesn't search for what is its own, therefore it can also not be of its own (*Weltalter*, I, VIII, p. 210).

Being as going back to itself, not "expanding," not "giving itself," the dark principle, the no, contracting, attracting.

"Beings": what takes upon itself to be beings. To be a being: "the existentielle" (*Weltalter,* I, VIII, p. 212).

Here the following becomes most clear:

1. How everything is thought in terms of what is in being and most in being, of the *summum ens, theion, akrotaton on.*

2. That everywhere only beings are thought as what is in being and Being as what is truly accomplished by what is most in being and accordingly thought by all beings.

3. That Schelling does not lead us away from the position of the *on* as *hypokeimenon* (compare the later doctrine of potencies). Schelling thinks metaphysically, onto-theologically, but in the highest completion.

The "core part" (Pp. 31–39) "elucidates" in its way the distinction now clarified so that it leads from beings to this distinction. And indeed:

(1) from God as the highest being, (2) from creation—as process of transfiguration, (3) from man.

God, world, man: *Metaphysica specialis.*

But here "beings" are already interpreted in the sense of distinction. Thus only that has been found which was already put in, thus a "circle"! Yes, but what kind of circle? What does "put in" mean here? Is that an express view of Mr. Schelling? Or? And in what sense "put in"? The system as the essential jointure of beings as such. Thus we must grasp its unity? How can it be grasped? By "intuition" and construction. With regard to the essence of "construction" the following is essential: (1) the pre-sentation (*Vor-gabe*) of the Unconditional, (2) that the "distinction" of beingness and beings is at the foundation, also *in* Schelling's distinction itself, and (3) how from here the essence of all metaphysics becomes visible.

On akrotaton (theion), on koinotaton, on analogon. How the essence of metaphysics is connected with this! (Compare our essay on Nietzsche).[15]

"Real" Idealism and "Idealism." "Idea" and "Life," "becoming," "Being." The negative as real counter-power.

The inner connection between the "core piece" and the "introduction" of the treatise on freedom. Our goal is the knowledge of the metaphysics of German Idealism gained by a discussion with Schelling's treatise on freedom. Metaphysics asks:

What are "beings as beings"?
What are beings in their Being?
What is the Being of beings?

(Compare Aristotle's statement, *Metaphysics* VIII, 1028b2 sqq.) To speak briefly and indefinitely, the question of "Being" is asked. Sometimes metaphysics means beings in their Being; sometimes it means the Being of beings.

Our path of interpreting the treatise on freedom might look at first like a detour in that the "foreword" prepares the interpretation of the "core piece." This piece treats the distinction between "ground" and "existence." The distinction concerns every "being", that is, every being as such. It aims at the Being of beings and thus concerns what is asked about in metaphysics. It shows how Schelling's metaphysics asks about the Being of beings and determines it. Thus the piece which treats the core of metaphysics is the core piece. It belongs to the treatise on freedom.

The treatise on freedom speaks of freedom as the center of the system. System is the essence of beings as such as a whole, thus it determines Being. How is Being "systematic"?

System is "the system of freedom." But freedom is human freedom, and the question of the system is how human freedom belongs to beings as a whole and that means to their "ground." (System arises from the essence of truth in the sense of certainty and from the essence of Being, preparing itself, in the sense of the will to will.) This ground of beings as a whole is called, and is, God,—*theos*, in Western metaphysics.

Schelling understands freedom not just as independence of nature, but more essentially as independence of God, but *of* God, that is, in relation to God and that means "*in*" God. For everything "is," insofar as it "is," godlike and thus, in a certain way, God.

System is determined in its unity by this statement. It names the Being of beings as a whole. Hence the introduction to the fundamental question of the system of freedom must explain this basic law of the system. Thus the introduction and the whole treatise discusses "pantheism," this term as the name for a, yes, for the metaphysical fundamental question hidden in it. How so? "Everything is God" requires the determination of the whole, the determination of God; above all, however, the determination of the "is," thus the determination how God "is" everything and everything "is" God. But the "is" names Being. The "is" is taken as a connective (copula) in propositions. The proposition *logos*, as the basic form of thinking. Thinking, *noein*, is the fundamental relation to Being (*ousia*, *idea*).

To ask about pantheism, to raise the fundamental question of system means to ask about the "is," that is, about the Being of beings as a whole (the "is" must not be understood in the manner of formal logic, but must be grasped "logically" in Hegel's sense, metaphysically and that means theologically). That is the question which is interpreted and answered in the core piece. Thus the inner connection between the "distinction of ground and existence" and the real perspective of the question of pantheism is clarified. However, the fact that "evil" becomes the leading theme in the treatise on freedom points to the fact that evil as Schelling conceives it constitutes the most extreme discord and repulsion against beings as a whole and within beings as a whole. This is the harshest rift endangering a "system," that is, the *systasis* of beings. And it is just this rift which must be metaphysically developed as such and conceived as the jointure of the system. It is not a matter of weakening this discord.

Evil attains its true essential reality only in Spirit, in the Spirit of the creature which as selfhood can place itself furthest away from God and against God and can claim the whole of beings for itself. Evil is only real together with freedom, that is, freedom is only itself with relation to evil. But evil is not a mere opposite separated from the good. It belongs to the good and to the distinction of good and evil. *The good "is" the evil.*

Thus if freedom is determined as the faculty for good *and* evil (not "or"), Schelling does not mean freedom of choice, but freedom as the metaphysical jointure and bond in the discord itself, as the strife and the endurance of the strife. Only when these connections are thought through does the illusion vanish that the treatise on freedom lands on the path of a one-sided treatment of the question of freedom with an interpretation of evil. But understood as the fundamental question of the system, the question of freedom is also not to be thought in the sense of a theodicy, but as a "systemadicee," as the justification of absolute metaphysics as the truth of beings as such as a whole.

Why does Schelling's *Philosophical Inquiries into the Nature of Human Freedom and Matters Connected Therewith* treat the problem of evil? Because system is to be thought? But why is this necessary? The system is innermost "Being," the standing together of beings as a whole where they are to *endure* the most extreme discord, not to smooth it over. Thus this most extreme discord must be developed and brought to its constancy and the ground of that constancy. This discord is evil in the sense of the independent revolt of creaturely spirit grasping the self-craving of the ground out of the intimacy with the primal ground.

But then why is the treatise on the system a treatise on freedom? Because evil is truly existent in human freedom and *as* human freedom. The most extreme discord in beings is truly existent in the freedom of *man*.

Understood in terms of the relation of freedom and necessity, freedom is the center of system. But system is in question because the beingness of beings as a whole is in question, the truth of beings. But truth means here certainty, that is, the guarantee of representing representedness, the ubiquitous availability of beings, beings in the unconditionality of their being with regard to all conditions, certain of themselves as a whole. But beingness is thought as "subjectivity."

For short we call Schelling's treatise the "treatise on freedom," and rightly so. But it really deals with the essence of evil, and only because it does this does it deal with human freedom. For evil *is* truly in man's essence as the most extreme opposition and revolt of the spirit against the Absolute (tearing oneself away from the universal will, being against it, the will replacing it in this "against"). Evil *"is"* as *freedom*, the most extreme freedom *against* the Absolute within the whole of beings. For freedom "is" the capacity for good and evil. The good "is" the evil and the evil "is" the good.

But why is evil spoken of at all? Because it produces the innermost and broadest discord in beings. But why discord? Evil is thought because in this most extreme and real discord as dis-jointure (*Un-fug*) the *unity* of the jointure of beings as a whole must appear most decidedly at the same time.

This is what is important, beings and their jointure, the basic jointure. Hence the question of pantheism is linked with the question of freedom in the introduction as the question of system. "System" is the name for the *essence* of beings as a whole as such, that is, for the beingness of beings. Being as *systasis;* the systematic element is the Being of beings because Being is now subjectivity. To think this is the essence and task of metaphysics.

However, metaphysics is not a discipline, but ever since Plato the basic understanding of the *truth* of beings as a whole. (Meanwhile truth has become certainty.) Our real intention concerns the metaphysics of German Idealism in which Western metaphysics completes itself in one respect. Hence the question anticipating everything in the interpretation of this treatise is that of the *beingness (Seiendheit)* of beings. Hence it was necessary to deal first with the "distinction of ground and existence."

The "distinction" as the character of Being itself. It presences as distinguishing, unifying in separating, and this "presencing" ("*Wesen*") has the character of the *idea*, of appearing: to reveal oneself, to emerge into multiplicity and thus only to let unity come to presence.

"Primordial Being is will." Where does this interpretation of Being come from? (Not a historical question!) Being is understood here as "*existentia*" in the literal sense, *existentia* as *actualitas*, as *actu esse*.

Since Descartes, the *actus* is of central importance, the *cogitare, ego cogito, repraesentare* (compare below), to represent oneself to oneself and thus to present oneself. Let us think of Leibniz: *exigentia essentiae, principium existentiae* is *perfectio, essentiae gradus, appetitus*, representing and striving, will.

Being (*existentia*, reality) as subjectivity (subjectity), that is, re-presenting. This contains the following:

(1.) "striving" beyond oneself ("negativity") (2.) distinguishing, "separating," "negativity," (3.) becoming (not as "succession" and "activity," but in essence; from—to, change, transition), and (4.) bringing to oneself, re-presenting, revealing.

Together with the *repraesentare* of unity (presencing of multiplicity in gatheredness), all four determinations delimit the essence of "willing." Hence "will" as the title of the modern interpretation of Being in the sense of *existentia*. Thus "phenomenology" belongs to the essence of Being, the history of self-revelation as the becoming of itself. The phenomenology "of" Spirit is to be understood in the same way as the "harmony of the spheres." "Phenomenology" is not the name of an additional "science."

Will as "will to power." The present age has not taken over Nietzsche's doctrine, but the other way around. Nietzsche prophesied and showed beforehand the truth into which modern history is moving because it already stems from there.

Every will is oppositional will in the sense of *a counterwill*, that is, *will against craving.* Will is in itself oppositional ("contradiction").

In the concluding remark of the treatise on freedom, Schelling says, "The time of merely historical faith is past, as soon as the possibility of immediate knowledge is given. We have an earlier revelation than any written one—nature" (p. 98). The rejection of "merely historical faith" comes from appealing to "the possibility of immediate knowledge" which is posited as given. Immediate knowledge is knowledge not mediated by propositions and cognitions which we then subsequently rely upon to attain further knowledge. Immediate knowledge is knowledge which grasps *straight away* what is to be known here, namely, what beings are as a whole. Immediate knowledge is not meant here in the sense of the individual perception of a single object. Rather, "knowledge" always means knowledge of the Absolute. In order for this to come about, the Absolute must show itself, open itself, reveal itself. "Earlier" than any written revelation (the Bible!) there is "nature." What does "nature" mean here? The Absolute itself. "Earlier" means prior in the sense that it must have first revealed itself (nature "in" God) in order for another revelation (God Himself) to be. This is a transformation, transposed to the unconditional, of the statement, *gratia supponit naturam.*

But Schelling speaks "only" of the "possibility of immediate knowledge" *if* it is given. It is given by the new fundamental position of German Idealism as opposed to Kant, prepared for especially by Kant. "Possibility" by no means signifies just that something is not excluded, but means in a positive sense that the faculty for it and the foundation are given, that is, the immediate relation to the Absolute.

The distinction between "historical faith" and "immediate knowledge" was at first rightly interpreted to mean that philosophy is not supposed to be "oriented historically" in order to found a new philosophy through knowledge of past ones.

However, the distinction has a larger scope and characterizes the fundamental position of the whole treatise and thus also that of the metaphysics of German Idealism. The reference to the "earlier revelation" takes a position with regard to biblical revelation. Knowledge based upon earlier revelation thus towers above the truth of Christian faith as "historical," too, in that it is based upon the "historical" fact, posited in accordance with faith, of God becoming man in Christ.

Thus System of philosophy, that is, science, is alone true in the sense of the absolute system; the *"system of religion becomes science."*

To this corresponds the demand that revealed truths should be developed into truths of reason. And this is in harmony with Hegel's fundamental position in his *Phenomenology of Spirit* where "religion" precedes and is subordinated to "absolute knowledge" as a form of reason. Absolute knowledge is philosophy.

Only in these terms does Schelling's final remark gain its full scope, but also the inner relation to what the whole treatise thinks through.

The unconditional priority of certainty (that is, beingness) *of the Absolute.* (Compare *Stuttgarter Privatvorlesungen*, I, VII, p. 423.)

If the Absolute is Spirit, the existing and unconditional subjectity, this priority of the Absolute, that is, its certainty, that is, truth, that is, its revealedness, that is, its existence, points to the priority of the *subiectum* as such.

We should remember how with the guarantee of the certainty of the *ego cogito (sum cogitans)* the *prior givenness of God* is entailed who Himself offers the last guarantee of certainty, of course, in the form of traditional theological metaphysics (Descartes. *Meditation* III). This connection of the guaranteeing of representing oneself is then grasped in decisive knowledge in terms of itself in its unconditionality. (In between lies the clarification brought about by Kant's transcendental philosophy.)

The Absolute is not only the *proton kath' auto*, but also *pros hemas*, the undemonstrable, that is, not needing a proof because all demonstration of beings is brought about in the ether of the Absolute. The most comprehensible thing of all is the fact that the Absolute is, for comprehending is thinking in the Absolute, thus its certainty.

Philosophy begins with the "confession" that it would not exist at all without the Absolute (compare I, VII, p. 423). Thus philosophy cannot already be philosophy "beforehand" and only then first of all want to prove the Absolute in its "existence." Philosophy is *absolute knowledge,* thus knowledge "of" the Absolute (genitivus objectivus and subjectivus).

It is true that philosophy is to be viewed as a human endeavor, certainly. But man is the "central being," the creaturely God. Philosophy is "spiritual presentation of the universe," of beings as such. The universe is God's manifestation. Thus philosophy is "the continual demonstration of God."

Philosophy is at the first step absolute knowledge, at the same time in the sense that it knows that it belongs to the Absolute (as unconditional subjectity). The priority of the Absolute must be understood in modern terms as the unconditional priority of subjectity: *The ether and the element of knowledge.* Schelling clearly states (p. 71) that God is the *spiritual light* itself "in us" in which everything else becomes clear. The clarification and its purity gain their clarity from this light. At first the claim of absolute construction seems arrogant and fantastic, and yet it is the confession "that everything already is." It renounces the curious will to explain everything by way of the idea of creation by a demiurge (*Deus faber*). The magic stroke: "In creation there is the greatest harmony, and nothing is so separate and sequent as we must represent it, but the subsequent cooperates in what precedes it and everything occurs at the same time in one magic stroke" (p. 65).

The divine magic: "From this it follows that, by contrast, the truly good can only be effected by a divine magic, that is, by the immediate presence of beings in consciousness and cognition" (p. 70).

The knowledge of what lies before all questionability is the relation to what one never even begins to ask about. *Quid "est" potius? Ens aut nihil?* What do *"est"* and *"esse"* mean? What is the area of decision of this question and what kind of questioning? And when beings rather are, must not the unconditional being be the most likely to be since it is present in every being (thought in terms of unconditional subjectity)? Then the Absolute is the first for us, too, is that which needs no demonstration and proof, that about which and in which we are in agreement. Most comprehensible of all is the fact that God "is." It is more comprehensible that the being (that is, the Absolute) is than that "nothing" is. But "nothing" is "in itself," after all, easier, for nothing at all is necessary for it. And yet the most difficult thing of all is that nothing should *be*, for Being (essence) is understood as *nisus*, as *exigentia essentiae*.

When does nothing appear as what is easier and more comprehensible? When beings are taken for what is more difficult, what requires more effort, in need of manufacturing if beingness is understood as being produced. But what if Being is intrinsically will as willing itself? Then nothing is what is more difficult. (Compare Nietzsche, "Man would rather will *nothing* than *not* will. . . ." (The *Genealogy of Morals,* end). If Being means will, what is most in being is most comprehensible. If Being means presence in the sense of objective presence which must first be produced and if its presencing is not "of itself" (spontaneous and essentially so), then beings are what need an explanation most of all (the proofs of God's existence).

THE CONCEPTUAL HISTORY OF THE ELUCIDATION OF THE ESSENCE OF GROUND.

It is guided by a double intention:

(1.) the aim is to show that and how the essence of ground goes together most inwardly with the metaphysical interpretation of beings (*idea, ousia, hypokeimenon, subiectum*); and (2.) in this way what is strange is removed beforehand from Schelling's distinction, but the insight into what is peculiar to it is also prepared.

The key term for what we call "ground" is the term *arche* in Greek metaphysics in the double meaning of beginning and dominance; in modern philosophy, on the other hand, the term *ratio* (*principium rationis sufficientis, grande illud principium,* Leibniz). How does *ratio* (*reor, rheo, rhesis,* saying, stating, opining) acquire the meaning of "ground" (*hypokeimenon, legomenon kath' auto, logos*)? This can only be understood if we grasp that key term in which *all* metaphysical determinations of the essence of "ground" are contained and which at the same time bears witness to an unequivocal reference to the leading project of beings.

Hypokeimenon: what lies present in advance of everything, what already presences and presences in advance. The concept is ambiguous, resulting from Aristotle's interpretation of *arche* and *aitia.* Enumerating we have as its content:

1. *ex ou*	: that *out of which*
2. *paradeigma*	: that *according to which*
3. *proaireton*	: that which is *anticipated* because it delimits in advance (*telos*) . . .
4. kath' ou legetai ti	: that *toward* which and *back* to which

Aitia: the relation to *physei onta.* The *arche kineseos* in the narrower sense, the later *causa efficiens* is remarkably unspecified. In Greek thought it is not the essential thing at all as it is later in Christian thought (creation) and in modern thought ("technology"). *Hypokeimenon* is called *sub-iectum* in the Latin translation. Every being as a being is *subiectum (SUB-stans).* This statement is valid for *all* metaphysics from Plato to Nietzsche. But only in terms of this statement can we understand how "subjectivity" becomes the fundamental metaphysical concept in modern metaphysics, where "subjectivity" and "selfhood" mean the representing relation back to oneself. Descartes takes the first step toward this determination on the basis of the transformation of the essence of truth (*veritas* as *certitudo cognitionis humanae*).

(Where does this transformation come from? From the history of Being.)

Leibniz takes the second step which is no less decisive. 1. How does the *ego* become the eminent *subiectum (mens- sive animus)*? 2. How does the essence of the *subiectum* thus become subjectivity in the sense of *selfhood?* (Compare Leibniz on the *Mentes,* Gerh VII, p. 291, also p. 307, *mentes* as *partes totales.*) His fundamental metaphysical position designates the real turning point from preceding metaphysics to that of German Idealism.

A brief reminder of certain of Leibniz's ideas is necessary for us, not to give a historical explanation for Schelling's distinction, but to comprehend it in its most hidden form. This is necessary even if we did not know that Schelling had already read a basic text of Leibniz, the *Monadologie,* when he was sixteen years old. (It was written in French, published in a German translation in 1720 after Leibniz's death, then in a Latin translation in 1721, and the *Urschrift* in 1840.)

How the change from *hypokeimenon* to subjectivity comes about. (Leibniz). We must consider that all of this supports the modern and thus the present and most proximate interpretation of beings. The scope of essential questions and decisions lies here. The reference to Leibniz is given with a view to his determination of "*existentia.*" Leibniz interpreted *essentia* and *existentia* in the sense of *potentia* and *actus,* possibility (lack of contradiction) and reality. Both of these "concepts" are transformed and formulated more primordially. In terms of the old distinction it looks as if *essentia* as *possibilitas* comes nearer to *existentia* and, on the other hand, *existentia* comes nearer to *essentia* so that they meet, so to speak, in the "Between." But in this way everything goes wrong.

ESSENTIA "is" possibilitas (not potentia); *possibilitas* is *nisus, conatus, praetensio ad existentiam.*

Liking (das Mögen) in the double sense: (1) it "might" be, that is, it "can" be (is possible), (2) he "likes" it, inclination toward . . . (love), being inclined and able to . . . (striving urge).

EXISTENTIA is *perfectio (gradus essentiae)*, or *essentiae exigentia* (compare Gerh. VII, p. 195 note). (*Exigentia* is here essentially ambiguous: *agere, actio, vis* and *exactum, actualitas* of the *exactus.*).

Existentia is to be understood as *wresting* out of the inclination to what is inclined toward . . . , that is, to itself, as *journeying out* to "essence," *perfectio*, but thus driving, too, *per-ficere* as placement. (Measuring, *"exactum," "exact."*) Now some of the key statements become clear: *"Et ut possibilitas est principium Essentiae, ita perfectio seu Essentiae gradus . . . principium existentiae." (De rerum orig.,* Gerhardt VII, p. 304) *("mathesis divina, "mechanismus metaphysicus").*

". . . *Ens necessarium* (that is, *id de cuius essentiae est existentia) est Existentificans"* (Gerhardt VII, p. 289), *"omne possibile Exstiturire"* (ibid) (*"exigit existere",* compare VII, p. 194).

ENS is *exigens; exigentia, exactum; appetitus—perceptio,* "will"—"drive."

SUBIECTUM: mens sive animus percipiens is the essence of the *ens* in the essential and universal sense. Hence the *mentes* have a special rank among the *entia.* The essence of "Being" can be seen in them. Here the twenty-four statements should be compared. (Gerhardt VII, p. 289–91*) Thesis 21: *"Et Mentium maxima habetur ratio, quia per ipsas quam maxima varietas in quam minimo spatio obtinetur."* Translated: "The *mentes* as *entia* are to be taken into account most of all because through them the greatest possible multiplicity is contained and held fast in constancy in the smallest space possible." The *highest presence* is here in the *mentes.* (The *spatium* of the "metaphysical points", that is, the *monas.*

But now, corresponding to the transformation of the *subiectum, praesentia (ousia)* has become *repraesentatio* (ambiguous), representing (striving) self-presentation. But the *perceptio* is *multorum in uno expressio.*

The *subiectum, existens, ens* is *monas,* one (unity). (Compare *hen*); (Compare "system.") The essence of the unity meant here is to be understood in terms of presencing and constancy, *gathering (logos:* Heraclitus, Parmenides) to presencing. This is what unifies, contains. *Existentia* is the driving of a being toward itself: "self-assertion" (will).

*Compare *The End of Philosophy,* trans. Joan Stambaugh (New York: Harper and Row, 1973), pp. 49–54.

Hegel and Schelling

The difference lies in what the agreement consists in.
1. Reality is the Absolute, the Spirit
2. The Absolute: the system
3. Reality—contradiction (negation)—distinction
4. Reality: becoming (will)
5. Reality as self-revelation
But:

	Hegel	Schelling
Spirit:	science	love
system:	"of science" (concepts-freedom) "Logic"	"of freedom"
separation:	negativity of the subject, "of thinking" as the self-think-ing of Spirit of knowing (rec-ognition)	the distinction in willing as the self-willing of love (letting the ground operate)
becoming:	The coming to itself of Spirit. World-Spirit.	creation—redemption—man.

And yet in spite of everything the same passion at bottom for the same thing, and therein precisely the separation of these two thinkers. Their strife is *the* evidence of their unity.

As what distinguishes and is distinguished, negativity is re-presentation repre-senting itself. Re-presentation and distinguishing (oneself). Re-presentation, consciousness, knowing, knowing knowing itself, pure negativity are the same. Still, how does precisely distinguishing (*dia*) gain priority in the essence of re-presentation (as self-presentation, appearance)?

Why is distinguishing understood as "negation"? Because the "no" has the character of a between and a transition in itself. The "yes" is simple remaining. "No" is *away from* as *toward*—the energy of motion, of becoming. But why the "no" in such a role? Where is everything brought to (in the sphere of unconditional representation)? Negativity and un-conditionality, the un- moves away from the conditioned, the activity of removing, bringing behind oneself and yet elevating (*Auf-heben*). "Work" within the absolutely guaranteed Ab-solute.

Hegel—Schelling—Nietzsche

| Hegel: | the will of knowledge (recognition)—(desire) |
| Schelling: | the will of love (the understanding—universal will) letting |

	the ground operate, no longer willing anything
Nietzsche:	the will to power (overpowering, abrogation of the distinction
	of the sensuous and the supra-sensuous) willing only will.

"Will" as willing oneself—being a self
Will and subjectity

Schelling—Nietzsche

Being is will *(perceptio, appetitio)*. The background of the tradition of theological metaphysics is the *"actus,"* *actus* as the Roman transcription of *energeia*. *Energeia, entelecheia, ousia* of the *kinoumena, kinounta* as the true *onta (physei onta) ousia—idea*.

All willing wills itself, but in different ways. In willing as willing oneself there are two basic possibilities of essential development:

1. Willing *oneself* as coming to oneself and thus revealing oneself and appearing before oneself ("absolute Idea"); unconditional subjectivity as "love" (no longer to will anything of one's own).

2. *Willing* oneself as transcending oneself, as overpowering and command, "will to power." (Command as the will in willing); "overpowering"; unconditional subjectivity as "power."

A. Why unconditional subjectivity each time? That can only be shown in terms of the essence of re-presentation. Re-presentation and negativity.

B. But in "love" and "power," dissension and strife, "struggle" "contradiction" are essential.

C. Schelling: to will nothing; released inwardness. Nietzsche: to will the same again and again; eternal recurrence.

D. The will of love: "letting the ground operate"; to will nothing, not anything one's own and not anything of love, not oneself either. The will to power: overpowering.

E. System as unity belongs to the will as Spirit and love. No system belongs to the "will to power." (Compare Kierkegaard, no system of "existence," but "organization," respectively "church.") (Nietzsche does not "want" a system because he knows that he stands in the system of all possible systems as modes of guaranteeing permanence in the unconditionality of the will to power. The *ability to control* the mode and insertion, the duration and retraction of these "systems," which are merely "conditions" of the will to power itself, is the systematic proper to the will to power. It also belongs to this systematic not to emerge, but to act as if it didn't exist.)

TOWARD A DISCUSSION WITH THE METAPHYSICS OF GERMAN IDEALISM AND METAPHYSICS IN GENERAL

The decisive discussion of Schelling's "system of freedom" occurs in the sphere which the interpretation of the "central part" reaches through the foreword. Here

Being itself is said in its essence as the beingness of beings. *Ousia* is understood in the sense of presencing (*idea*), in the modern and unconditional manner as subjectivity, as will. This essence of beingness is sufficient for all the "predicates" which are attributed to Being as if they were self-evident.

Here we must see that the interpretation of Being as will (the determination of primal Being, that is, of Being in its essential origin) is not an arbitrary "view" of Schelling's, but also not a historically conditioned computation of earlier views. Rather, Being itself reveals itself, but as beingness. Herein is contained the essence of every truth of beings (that is, every metaphysics). The first characteristic is that Being is *koinotaton* and *akrotaton* at the same time (*timiotaton, theion*), the most universal, the highest, the emptiest thing grasped by thinking. But this Being belongs at the same time to true being in its meaning, the *agathon*, the *epekeina tes ousias* which makes it possible and is able to do so. The *akrotaton* becomes the *primum ens*, the *absolutum* which is then interpreted in a "Christian" way and the Christian way then "metaphysically." As *akrotaton* (later *actus purus*), what is most in being takes over "Being" as pure "Idea" in the sense of being thought, re-presented, which is attributed to everything in that it is brought about and caused (created) as something effected and effecting (real) in accordance with this Idea. Thus the further quality belongs to the truth of beings that beings in the sense of a "correspondence" to Being develop in general in manifold stages.

The three perspectives of the truth of beings (of metaphysics) are thus: Being (beingness) in general, *koinotaton* (compare the transformation in modern metaphysics in the sense of the transcendental), the highest being which creates and receives everything (*akrotaton*), the multiplicity of beings correspondingly created (*analogon*). (For Kant's concept of analogy, compare *Prologomena, §58, Critique of Pure Reason*, A177.)

The origin and necessity of analogy lies in the unified project of beings to beingness as what is most universal (One) which at the same time demands causality from the highest One for all beings subsumed under the universal and their multiplicity. On the one hand, beings must suffice for the *koinotaton*, but at the same time they must be caused by the *akrotaton*, but in such a way that what is caused and is not the highest being cannot be in being in one and the same sense *(univoce)* with the first cause, and yet must be in being in the sense of the *koinotaton* insofar as it is at all.

The "analogy" of beings is then appealed to as an "explanation" of the multiplicity of beings and the solution to the problem of pan-theism (understood purely metaphysically). But it explains nothing and throws light on nothing. Rather, it only confirms and ensconces the obscurity enshrouding the distinction of *koinotaton* and *akrotaton* and their origin (Being as *idea*, as groundless *physis*) in such a way that Being itself aboriginally urges, so to speak, into the project of beings toward beingness.

The antithesis of consciousness and self-consciousness then joins the "analogizing" and interpretation of beings and their multiplicity ever since the interpretation of the *ens* as *certum* and *subiectum* (Self-consciousness as independence). This antithesis consistently (under the pressure of the truth of beings: *koinotaton, akrotaton*) leads to absolute self-consciousness (knowledge-will), and thus requires dialectic.

The architectonic of the school men (*metaphysica generalis* and *metaphysica specialis*, culminating in *theologia rationalis*) is only the doctrinaire reflection of the uncomprehended truth of beings which was absolutely founded by Plato as Idealism (understood metaphysically). In the first beginning of naming Being as *physis* and *aletheia*, this truth was prepared as that which exceeds metaphysics, too, so that the latter could never be able to know the first beginning essentially of itself, not even in terms of the whole of its history. Metaphysics can only misinterpret that beginning by relapsing. The last misinterpretation of the first beginning was brought about by Nietzsche.

By asking in terms of the first beginning (springing into the truth of Being), all questions of metaphysics arising from analogy and dialectic are especially overcome. Hence the discussion from beginning to beginning is starting now. The Saying of Being becomes completely different. In this discussion the distinction of Being and beings must first be recognized as such, questioned and taken back.

THE AMBIGUITY OF THE QUESTION OF BEING. METAPHYSICS AND *BEING AND TIME*

At first it appears as if *Being and Time* were at best an "epilogue" to metaphysics, so to speak, a kind of anthropological "epistemology" of "ontology." If *Being and Time* cannot be this, all that is left is that at best a more primordial metaphysical questioning is being attempted here, but still a metaphysical one.

But in truth there is no longer any metaphysics here either, but a quite different beginning. For this reason, however, there is really an original relation to the first beginning. Thus, the original recollection is necessary and also the sporadic naming and interpretation of this procedure as "metaphysics." (Compare *Kant and the Problem of Metaphysics* and "What is Metaphysics?") Being and essentiality of "essence." Indeed nowhere does *Being and Time* correspond to what is correctly expected of an "ontology" whose first step, if one may call it that, is exhausted by taking the essence of Being as decided and without question beforehand.

Being and Time has also among other things been equated with Fichte's basic position and interpreted by it, whereas if there is any possibility of comparison at all here, the most extreme opposition is dominant. But "opposition" is already false since the thinking in *Being and Time* is not just "realistic" in contrast to the unconditional "egoistic" Idealism of Fichte.

Schiller writes about Fichte to Goethe on October 28, 1794, thus at the time that the first *Wissenschaftslehre* was published. "According to Fichte's oral expression—for in his book there is not yet any mention of this—the *ego* is creative through its representations, too, and all reality is only in the ego. The world is for him only a ball which the ego has thrown and which it catches again in reflexion. Thus he would have truly declared his godhead as we were recently expecting." According to Fichte the ego throws forth the world, and according to *Being and Time* it is not the ego that first throws the world, but it is *Da-sein* (human being), presencing before all humanity, which is thrown.

TEMPORALITY AS ECSTATIC TEMPORALIZING

Presencing of the truth of Being—characterized by the Between, ground-lessly (in general, no "succession," lapsing, expiring and coursing).

Being and time both at the same time and in the same way inaccessible because of their immense nearness. (1) We immediately think right past it (hastiness), (2) we let ourselves be content with the indeterminate (superficiality), (3) because all such things are—apparently—without effect, incomprehensible and similar to nothing. (The turn to usefulness and accomplishment.)

Being is nothing. It "is" not a being in the way we know and think we know beings.

The difficulty to think the simple; the difficulty to leave habit behind as the sole criterion.

The concept of existence in *Being and Time* arises from the question named by this title. In the development of this question a reflection on the essence of "time" became necessary. That includes a historical discussion of the previous interpretation of the essence of time. We must distinguish:

1. Preconceptual calculating with time (time of day, time of year)

2. From here the possible conceptual formulation of the essence of time thus projected. Here a preconception of Being is decisive, since "time" somehow "exists."

(a) Greek *chronos*, corresponding to *topos*, calculated, counting time; *"datum,"* given, presencing time. Time as "dated." *touto gar estin ho chronos, arithmos kineseos kata to proteron kai hysteron.* (Aristotle, *Physics* IV, 219 b 1 f.).
To de proteron kai hysteron en topo proton estin (ibid, 219 a 14/5).

(b) modern: as the dimension and scheme of order for all events and human procedure. "Time" as "parameter," that is, that measured along which points and distances can be measured.

3. The question of time with regard to the "temporally" limited journey, experienced in a Christian way, of the individual human soul on earth. "Temporality"—"Eternity."

4. Time as a first name for the projective realm of the truth of Being. "Time" is the ecstatic Between (time-space), not the wherein of beings, but the opening of Being itself.

We must bring closer the mode of thinking within which the present discussion with Schelling moves. It is not important to emphasize a "perspective of one's own" nor to defend an "originality" which appears threatened. However, the difficulty remains that we must speak of what is our own. Self-deception is inevitable even when a temporal distance from what was said earlier is present. (I am not saying that *Being and Time* has become something past for me. I have still not "gotten any further" today because I know with ever increasing clarity that I must not get any "further," but perhaps I have gotten closer in some things to what was attempted in *Being and Time*.)

We take *Being and Time* as the name of a reflection whose necessity lies far beyond the deed of an individual who cannot "invent" this necessity, but also cannot master it. Thus we can distinguish the necessity designated by the name *Being and Time* from the "book" with this title. (*Being and Time* as the name for an Appropriation in Being itself. *Being and Time* as the formula for a reflection within the history of thinking. *Being and Time* as the title of a treatise which attempts to bring about this thinking.) That this book has its faults I believe I know myself. Here it is like climbing a never-climbed mountain. Because it is steep and at the same time unknown, whoever climbs here sometimes falls. The wanderer has suddenly gone wrong, sometimes he also falls without the reader noticing it, for the page numbers do go on. One can even fall several times here. But one should not talk too much about this nor make too much of it. These remarks already overstep the line, inevitably of course, because today we can hardly find our way to the necessities reigning within themselves without such aids. Nietzsche once said, with a different intention, however, "One only has the courage very late for that which one really knows." We might add that that, too, which one "knows" in the realm of thinking which attempts to think Being is, after all, each time only a light surmised which hovers over Something which far outreaches the thinker.

EXCERPTS FROM SEMINAR NOTES 1941–43

The tacit method in conversation: interpretation as dis-cussion (*Aus-einander-setzung*).* The latter as trans-position to the appropriate measure. Discussion between metaphysics and the thinking of the history of Being. Under-standing in the fundamental mood. Under-standing in standing-within. Ex-perience of *Da-sein*.

Mood—being attuned—to hear the attunement. To be able to hear: *calls* of the stillness of Being. What tunes attunes, but has no "effect."

*Like many of the hyphenated terms in this section, discussion should not be understood in a vague, general way, but as concretely as possible. The literal meaning of *discutere* is to strike apart, to separate. A further example would be *Er-fahrung*, ex-perience, to go through TRANS.

"Thinking" as thinking ahead to the beginning, not thinking about things objectively present, about past things, future things. In the prelude of a unique, simple experience that beings can never replace Being because the former transposes to the latter. This ex-perience cannot be forced.

No hospital perspective with regard to time. What is happening now and has been happening for centuries has long since been decided. But *for this reason*, because of this decision made, something else is imminent—provided that there is history of Being.

Toward the interpretation of Schelling:

The next intention purely in thought is the dis-cussion (in the literal sense) of the thinking of the history of Being with metaphysics in the form of the metaphysics of unconditional subjectivity. (This intention can hardly be made valid in the teaching element of the classroom situation. We can only get as far as the questionability of "metaphysics" and its essential determination in terms of that.) Everything historical is to be avoided. What is essential follows:

1. The metaphysics of unconditional subjectivity as *having been (gewesene)* and thus presencing back into the first beginning. How this outstrips all history of Being.

2. Hölderlin's poetry remains completely outside of the metaphysics of German Idealism, but at the same time ungrounded; premonition. ("Ripe are. . . .")

3. The *Saying of Being* and standing-within (*Inständigkeit*) in Da-*sein; leap.* (Beforehand: *abandonment of Being*, evidenced by the forgottenness of Being. Its signs are the "preponderance of experiences," historicism, "world view," "the business of ontology." Metaphysics and technology.)

Reflection and "analysis": reflection is the questioning of the *essence* of truth. Springing into the perdurance of this worthiness of question. Standing in history, "historical" reflection, reflection standing in history.

"Analysis" (not "Analytic of *Dasein*") as dissecting the "situation" is put to work for the further procedure of the calculating, planning arrangement of everything. The metaphysics of German Idealism and the thinking of the history of Being of Appropriation.

If comparison and contrast can ever offer a support and an occasion to elevate us to a different thinking (which can always be attempted only with essential reservations), then the reflection on the metaphysics of German Idealism is of special help because what cannot be compared emerges most sharply. It emerges more sharply than in a discussion with Nietzsche where this metaphysics is already engaged in the accomplishment of a reversal. This reversal introduces at the same time the beginning of the "world view" which, to be sure, is already faintly visible in the metaphysics of German Idealism ("view of the world").

The essence of the metaphysics of German Idealism as modern metaphysics is thought with complete decisiveness in Hegel's "System of Logic" in the *Phenomenology of Spirit*. Here the essence of transcendental reflection is unconditionally fulfilled which thinks the conditions of the appearance of nature and the essence of the *idea* itself.

But the metaphysics of unconditional re-presentation (that is, will) is thought from its whole essential depth in Schelling's treatise on freedom which is an answer to the *Phenomenology*.

The "matter itself" (which metaphysics is to think) is "the Absolute." Because the Absolute is thought as unconditional subjectivity (that is, subject-objectity), as the identity of identity and non-identity, and subjectivity essentially as will-full reason and thus as movement, it looks as if the Absolute and its motion coincided with what the thinking of the history of Being thinks as Appropriation. But Appropriation is neither the same as the Absolute nor is it even its contrary, for instance, finitude as opposed to infinity.

Rather, Being itself is experienced in Appropriation as Being, not as a being and not at all posited as the unconditional being and the highest being, although Being presences, after all, as that which alone "is." The Absolute, on the contrary, is what it is in terms of the *abandonment of Being* of beings like every "being," yes, even more essentially than every being, only that precisely in the *subjectivity* of the Absolute the abandonment of Being is most of all hidden and cannot appear.

The "Absolute" is beings as a whole in such a way that knowledge of beings as a whole, and as such knowledge which knows itself to be such, constitutes the "Being" of beings. Beings "are" there as this knowledge and "are" beings in the "element" of the (unconditional) concept.

What is essential is the concept and position of the "Absolute."

1. first cause   *aition*
  condition   *arche*
2. the divine   *theion*
3. what is unconditionally certain
    (of knowledge)
(*fundamentum absolutum inconcussum*)
4. the highest Ideal   *agathon*
  goal
5. the totality of beings *holon* "world"
6. subjectivity
7. the absoluteness of the Absolute
  (un-questioned Being)

The incomparability of metaphysics and the thinking of the history of Being are revealed where the illusion of their sameness is strongest and most immediate, in the metaphysics of *unconditional subjectivity* (Hegel, Schelling, Nietzsche). Why is this so? Because unconditional subjectivity dissolves everything in beingness and develops it as what is most in being and as movement and will, thus strengthening and rigidifying the illusion that Being is being questioned here, whereas precisely "Being," after all, has long since been decided upon as "Idea," *agathon, theion*. Hence the contrast with absolute metaphysics is essential for the discussion.

Freedom: metaphysically as the name for capacity by itself (spontaneity, cause). As soon as it moves metaphysically into the center (into true metaphysics) it intrinsically unifies the determinations of cause and selfhood (of the ground as what underlies and of the toward-itself, for-itself), that is, of *subjectivity*. Thus ultimately we have freedom as the resolve to the inevitable (affirmation of "time"!), as essential self-deception.

"Freedom" forfeited its role *originally in the history of Being*, for *Being* is more original than beingness and subjectivity. The Absolute: the Being of beings as a whole and at the same time the highest being. In Schelling's treatise, too, this ambiguity remains unsolved and is the source of all mutual misinterpretations.

Subjectivity and the Absolute.

How *subjectivity* intrinsically contains unconditionality and must develop as the Being of the unconditional being (the Absolute). How the possibility is thus given of transforming revelation into reason in Schelling's and Hegel's sense.

The absolute knowledge of the Absolute. This knowledge is not outside of the Absolute and cannot be so, but it is also not "inside" in an indeterminate way, but is the *occurrence of the essence of the Absolute itself.*

But how can that be man? Man is "*in*" God (p. 92). How are God and man and above all beings understood? Man and the relation to Being: Plato: *psyche, "ratio"* in later metaphysics. The two equally great *dangers* (dangers within absolute knowledge: external play which is always possible and seemingly always fruitful): the danger of "analogizing" and the danger of antithetic (the play of dialectic). Where do they come from and why do they exist? How is one to meet them, how is one to escape them at all?

The "analogy" of beings and the correspondence in their being ("Metaphysics"). Beings "co-respond," follow in what and how they are, obey the ruling cause as something caused, appearing in the light of capability (*agathon*).

Analogy belongs to metaphysics, in the double sense:

1. That beings themselves "co-respond" to the highest being.

2. That one thinks and explains with regard to correspondences, similarities, universals.

Where, on the other hand, one thinks in terms of Being itself, "analogy" no longer has any basis. And the danger of a pan-theism or a uni-versal "explanation" of beings also does not exist.

The concept of system (compare Schelling, p. 97)

1. The mathematical: *intuitus, deductio.*

2. *Certitudo:* the certainty of representation. "Knowledge" as calculation and figuring out what makes things possible.

3. *Subjectivity.*

4. *Ratio* and the producibility of all beings.

5. *The unconditionality of representation and knowledge* (here subjectivity is central).

Kant's will to system: Philosophy is *teleologia rationis humanae* (A 839). The attraction to system and the necessity of developing the absolute system are to be understood in terms of *subjectivity* as beingness.

What does Schelling mean with the question of *freedom,* with the emphasis on "human freedom"? His goal is *"a system of freedom,"* a system of beings as a whole with the fundamental fact of freedom as the ruling center.

Subjectivity as the selfhood of unconditionally willing knowledge—thus freedom. "System" in what sense?" "System of freedom" is another name for *subjectivity.* Of course, the anthropological interpretation of the "subject" in terms of consciousness intrudes itself here. Subjctivity as the true and single ground of the system. System of "freedom": seemingly, what is contradictory, but really what is alone essential to the *system.*

The difference between Hegel's and Schelling's systems lies in the determination of "Being." The difference is only possible where agreement in what is essential prevails in advance. Being is subjectivity, reason, Spirit. But how is Spirit to be understood? As absolute Spirit which unifies everything in itself. The unification occurs as mediation and binding. The inclusion of what is not spiritual, the sensuous, belongs to this.

And here, in the determination of "nature" and the sensuous, and thus in the relation of the understanding" (of reason) to the sensuous, lies the difference.

Hegel regards the sensuous as what is one-sided and abstract. He does not negate it, but his interpretation is a purely rational one, that is, an irrational one.

Schelling attempts to grasp the sensuous in terms of will and drive—which Hegel is also familiar with—but the *unity* as that of ground (basis) and existence is different.

Schelling's idea of identity and of the groundless as in-difference is more primordial within the absolute metaphysics of subjectivity, but only within it. A merely negative thought. (*Ab-sagen*).

Kant and German Idealism:

German Idealism goes *beyond* Kant to the *unconditional* knowledge of "the" Absolute. But this knowledge remains, *after all, only* in the realm of *transcendental subjectivity* opened up by Kant, but not completely entered.

If one takes Kant only as the critic of metaphysics (in the sense of the destroyer of all metaphysics) or even only as a theoretician of epistemology and consciousness, a psychologist, a neo-Kantian, then German Idealism appears as a decline from Kant and a retrogression. Then it looks as if what is essential in this thinking had been disregarded and every boundary which Kant had set up had been skipped over in irresponsible enthusiasm.

However, if one understands Kant in terms of what he must be understood from alone—in terms of the concept of the philosophy which he develops in his first main work at the end of the *Critique of Pure Reason*—then we see that German Idealism is the first and sole "attempt" to be serious about this concept of philosophy (and that means about the history of metaphysics).

German Idealism does not skip over Kant. But it begins where Kant brought philosophy to. It begins there immediately and in terms of the whole. And here the true and sole appreciation of Kant reveals itself. Why does the *Critique* become superfluous? Because absolute Idealism is not a retrogression to pre-Kantian rational metaphysics, but the unconditional development of transcendental philosophy to absolute metaphysics.

Construction in German Idealism is not to be understood as metaphysical cognition in Kant's sense, as "knowledge of reason through concepts," but in the sense in which Kant determined mathematical knowledge as knowledge of reason through the construction of concepts. Of course, pure intuition is necessary for this. But Kant himself proved and applied the possibility of pure intuition: (1) space and time as pure intuitions; (2) freedom as a suprasensuous fact.

Kant (Lecture course on metaphysics, 1792–93): "I construct my concepts when I present them *a priori* in intuition" (*Philosophische Hauptvorlesungen Kants*, ed. Kowalewski, 1924, p. 522).

Construction is the presentation of a concept in intuition, the presentation of the concept of beingness in terms of the pure intuition of Being. ("Intellectual intuition" is intuition purely reflected in itself.)

Thus it is true for German Idealism:

1. The *principle* of philosophical construction is the Absolute.

2. *What* is constructed is Ideas. Everything that is derived is *constructed* in its Idea.

Construction as knowledge and cognition. (Beings and Being: metaphysical!) Only what is possible is constructed, but not what is real (real as beings), but *reality* as Being is *unconditional*.

AUTHOR'S NOTES

1.) The treatise encompasses pp. 397–511 there. The only separate edition in Schelling's lifetime was published in 1834 by the Ensslinschen Buchhandlung in Reutlingen.

2.) F. H. Jacobi's work was published in 1785, the second enlarged edition came out in 1789.

3.) *Vorlesungen über die Methode des academischen Studium* was published by Schelling in 1803.

4.) The texts which Schröter newly ordered are an anastatic reprint based on the old edition prepared by Schelling's son.

5.) The collection of letters was supposed to serve as preliminary material for a comprehensive presentation of Schelling's life and work planned by the editor of the collected works. Plitt was entrusted with the edition after the editor of the works, Schelling's son, died before finishing Schelling's biography.

6.) The editors were I. H. Fichte and K. Fr. Schelling. This correspondence is also now available in the excellent edition: *J. G. Fichte, Briefwechsel*, edited by H. Schulz, 2 vols., 1930.

7.) On the situation of Schelling scholarship, compare H. J. Sandkühler's report, *Friedrich Wilhelm Joseph Schelling*, 1970 (Sammlung Metzler M87).

8.) The third enlarged edition came out in 1910.

9.) Compare Schelling's note on p. 31.

10.) Fichte's *Wissenschaftslehre* was published in 1794, Schelling's work *Über die Möglichkeit einer Form der Philosophie überhaupt* also in 1794, the next *Vom Ich als Prinzip der Philosophie oder über das Unbedingte im menschlichen Wissen* in 1795, Hegel's treatise on the *Differenz der Fichteschen und Schellingschen Systems der Philosophie* was published in 1801.

11.) Plato, *Politeia* 379 a. Among other things, *theologia* has the task of prefiguring the outlines for a truthful *mythologia*.

12.) Werke, I. Abteilung, Band I, p. 345–375.

13.) Compare Werke IV, 1. Abteilung Abt., p. 216 ff., 2. Abt. p. 127 ff.

14.) In the text of the "Philosophischen Bibliothek" of F. Meiner Verlag which serves as the basis for the lecture course there is a misprint, "das" instead of "dass." The original edition and Schelling's son's edition have correctly, "dass."

15.) The reference is presumably to Heidegger's essay (1940) "Nietzsche's Metaphysics" published 1961 in *Nietzsche,* vol. II by Günther Neske, Pfullingen. (ed.)